Language, Migration and In/Exclusion in the Workplace

LANGUAGE AT WORK

Series Editors: **Jo Angouri**, *University of Warwick, UK* and **Rebecca Piekkari**, *Aalto University Business School, Finland*

Language at Work is a new series designed to bring together scholars interested in workplace research. The modern workplace has changed significantly in recent years. The international nature of business activities and the increasing rate of mobility around the world create a new challenging environment for individuals and organisations alike. The advancements in technology have reshaped the ways employees collaborate at the interface of linguistic, national and professional borders. The complex linguistic landscape also results in new challenges for health care systems and legal settings. This and other phenomena around the world of work have attracted significant interest; it is still common however for relevant research to remain within clear disciplinary and methodological boundaries.

The series aims to create space for exchange of ideas and dialogue and seeks to explore issues related to power, leadership, politics, teamwork, culture, ideology, identity, decision making and motivation across a diverse range of contexts, including corporate, health care and institutional settings. *Language at Work* welcomes mixed methods research and it will be of interest to researchers in linguistics, international management, organisation studies, sociology, medical sociology and decision sciences.

All books in this series are externally peer-reviewed.

Full details of all the books in this series and of all our other publications can be found on http://www.multilingual-matters.com, or by writing to Multilingual Matters, St Nicholas House, 31–34 High Street, Bristol, BS1 2AW, UK.

LANGUAGE AT WORK: 10

Language, Migration and In/Exclusion in the Workplace

Edited by
Jo Angouri, Julie Kerekes and Minna Suni

MULTILINGUAL MATTERS
Bristol • Jackson

DOI https://doi.org/10.21832/ANGOUR6949
Names: Angouri, Jo, editor. | Kerekes, Julie, editor. | Minna, Suni, editor.
Title: Language, Migration and In/Exclusion in the Workplace/Edited by
   Jo Angouri, Julie Kerekes and Minna Suni.
Description: Bristol; Jackson: Multilingual Matters, [2023] | Series:
   Language at Work: 10 | Includes bibliographical references. | Summary:
   "This book focuses on the lived experiences of migrants who (try to)
   access the workplace and explores the barriers and support they
   encounter. The chapters look at the ways in which inclusion and
   exclusion from the workplace are done linguistically from historical,
   discourse analytical, narrative and language assessment perspectives"—
   Provided by publisher.
Identifiers: LCCN 2023010368 (print) | LCCN 2023010369 (ebook) | ISBN
   9781800416949 (hardback) | ISBN 9781800416932 (paperback) | ISBN
   9781800416956 (pdf) | ISBN 9781800416963 (epub)
Subjects: LCSH: Immigrants—Language—Case studies. | Language in the
   workplace—Case studies. | Communication in organizations—Case studies.
Classification: LCC P40.5.S57 L33 2023 (print) | LCC P40.5.S57 (ebook) |
   DDC 306.44086/912—dc23/eng/20230511
LC record available at https://lccn.loc.gov/2023010368
LC ebook record available at https://lccn.loc.gov/2023010369

Library of Congress Cataloging in Publication Data
A catalog record for this book is available from the Library of Congress.

British Library Cataloguing in Publication Data
A catalogue entry for this book is available from the British Library.

ISBN-13: 978-1-80041-694-9 (hbk)
ISBN-13: 978-1-80041-693-2 (pbk)

Multilingual Matters
UK: St Nicholas House, 31–34 High Street, Bristol, BS1 2AW, UK.
USA: Ingram, Jackson, TN, USA.

Website: www.multilingual-matters.com
Twitter: Multi_Ling_Mat
Facebook: https://www.facebook.com/multilingualmatters
Blog: www.channelviewpublications.wordpress.com

Copyright © 2023 Jo Angouri, Julie Kerekes, Minna Suni and the authors of individual chapters.

All rights reserved. No part of this work may be reproduced in any form or by any means without permission in writing from the publisher.

The policy of Multilingual Matters/Channel View Publications is to use papers that are natural, renewable and recyclable products, made from wood grown in sustainable forests. In the manufacturing process of our books, and to further support our policy, preference is given to printers that have FSC and PEFC Chain of Custody certification. The FSC and/or PEFC logos will appear on those books where full certification has been granted to the printer concerned.

Typeset by SAN Publishing Services.

Contents

	Contributors	vii
1	Migration and Language at Work: Current Trends and Future Opportunities for Multidisciplinary Research *Jo Angouri, Julie Kerekes and Minna Suni*	1
2	Contextualising Diversity, Work and Mobility Across Time: Cases from Norway's 'High North' *Florian Hiss*	13
3	'Doctor Johnny': The Discursive Construction of the Medical Doctor as an Immigrant *Nóra Schleicher*	32
4	Multilingual Professionals, Monolingual Contexts and Multicultural Mindsets: Towards an Intercultural Mindset *Fiona O'Neill*	52
5	'Getting the job done': Conventional Expressions as Shibboleths in Multilingual Job Interviews *Marta Kirilova*	74
6	Assessing and Analysing Health Care Finnish: Test Performance and Lived Experiences *Marja Seilonen and Minna Suni*	95
7	The Role of Soft Skills in Vocational ESL: Their Potential to (Dis)Empower Migrant Employment Seekers *Julie Kerekes and Jeanne Sinclair*	122
8	Impression Management Games: Language and Mobility among Southern European Migrants in a London Call Centre *Johanna Tovar*	149
9	Understanding the Immigrant Actor through a Multilingual Lens *Art Babayants*	172

10 '[They] thought I didn't know how to be a chef because I didn't speak Finnish': Gatekeeping and Professional Role Enactment in a Multilingual Kitchen Context   191
    Kristina Humonen and Jo Angouri

Index   216

Contributors

Jo Angouri is Professor and the Academic Director for education and internationalisation at the University of Warwick. She has published extensively on language and identity, teamwork and leadership in professional settings and migration, mobility and multilingualism. Jo is the author of *Culture, Discourse, and the Workplace* (Routledge) and has co-edited *The Routledge Handbook of Language, Gender, and Sexuality* and *Negotiating Boundaries at Work* (EUP). She is a National Teaching Fellow (UK) and Principal Fellow of the Higher Education Academy.

Art Babayants/Արտ Բաբայանց is a multilingual artist-scholar who lives and works in what is now called Canada. He holds a PhD in theatre and performance studies from the University of Toronto and publishes on the issues of stage multilingualism, diasporic/immigrant theatre, queer dramaturgy, applied theatre and contemporary musical theatre. Art has also co-edited *Theatre and Learning* (2015) and the special issue of *Theatre Research in Canada/Les recherches théâtrales au Canada* (Fall 2017) dedicated to multilingual theatre in Canada.

Florian Hiss is associate professor of Norwegian language at the Department of Education at UiT The Arctic University of Norway in Tromsø. His research is anchored in sociolinguistics and discourse studies and covers minoritised languages, historical and contemporary diversity and language practices in applied contexts such as workplaces and education. His contribution to the present volume builds on his postdoctoral project on 'Linguistic and Cultural Diversity at Work' in Northern Norway, funded by the Research Council of Norway.

Kristina Humonen is a lecturer in management at Newcastle University Business School, UK. Before lectureship, she completed a fully funded PhD in Intercultural Communication at the University of Warwick and then won further ESRC funding (grant ES/V011413/1) for her postdoctoral research project: 'Managing for Inclusion in the Multilingual Workplace'. Kristina is passionate about themes related to (linguistic) diversity management, language and power, and employee voice.

Julie Kerekes's research and teaching focus on language and power in intercultural institutional settings and on additional language learning and teaching in and beyond academia. Her current projects examine the acquisition of academic English skills by multilingual university students; the employment trajectories of internationally educated professionals; interlanguage pragmatics; and supporting English learners in Ontario through teacher education. A proponent of action research, she strives to apply her research findings to real-world problems related to intercultural communication and English language learning and teaching.

Marta Kirilova received a PhD in interactional sociolinguistics and is currently an associate professor at the Department of Nordic Studies and Linguistics at the University of Copenhagen, Denmark. Her research interests include sociolinguistics, job interviews, multilingualism at the workplace, and language ideology and practice. She has published in Nordic and international journals, edited books and handbooks. Currently, she is part of a large project on sociolinguistic perspectives to interpreter-mediated interaction in the Danish public sector.

Fiona O'Neill (PhD) is an applied linguist and Program Director of the Bachelor of Arts at the University of South Australia. A member of the Research Centre for Languages and Cultures and the AILA ReN, *Migrants in Working Life: Language and Im/mobilities*, Fiona's research focuses on ways that language, communication and interculturality matter in professions and organisations. Her collaborations with community and industry partners explore the significance of language in shaping understandings and experiences in people's social and professional lives.

Marja Seilonen, PhD, works as a university teacher of Finnish language and Finnish as a second language at the Open University of the University of Jyväskylä, Finland. She teaches courses on second language pedagogy, features of learner language and theories of second language development. Her research interests include second language learning and assessment, field-specific language use and second language constructions.

Nóra Schleicher is associate professor of sociology at Budapest Metropolitan University, Hungary where she teaches courses on sociology, media sociology, qualitative research methods, identity theories, among others. Her main research interest is focused on the relationship of language, power and identity. She has researched and published in the areas of qualitative methodology, bilingualism, gender and language use, migration and language use and the narrative construction of identity both offline and online.

Jeanne Sinclair researches and teaches in language and literacy assessment and learning. Her current interests are in integrating divergent paradigms of language learning and assessment – such as measurement-focused and sociocultural approaches – toward valid, meaningful outcomes for all stakeholders.

Minna Suni, PhD, is professor of Finnish language at the Department of Language and Communication Studies, University of Jyväskylä, Finland. She has led several research projects focusing on Finnish as a second language in educational and working life settings. She has also published on multilingualism, L2 literacy skills and language education policies in migration contexts.

Johanna Tovar, née Woydack, is assistant professor at WU (Vienna University of Economics and Business). She received her PhD in Sociolinguistics from King's College London. She is the author of *Linguistic Ethnography of a Multilingual Call Center* (2019) and co-editor of the *Research Companion to Language and Country Branding* (2021). She has published on ethnographic fieldwork in a variety of workplaces, including call centers in Europe and Asia, pertaining to issues such as standardisation, text trajectories, invisible work, resistance, Covid-19 as well as on place and nation branding.

1 Migration and Language at Work: Current Trends and Future Opportunities for Multidisciplinary Research

Jo Angouri, Julie Kerekes and Minna Suni

Introduction

The continuous increase in large population movements is documented in both academic research and policy documents (e.g. OECD, 2020). For migrants and refugees, as newcomers to a different socioeconomic environment, the quest for successful settlement depends on the ability to access work and economic security (Hellgren, 2014; Özdemir & Yücesan-Özdemir, 2004). The workplace occupies a central position in the process, as it is one of the core domains of activity where societal integration of migrant professionals is enacted in situ. Exclusion from the labour market has dire consequences, not just for migrating professionals whose economic, social, mental and physical wellbeing is at risk, but also for society more generally (European Commission, 2016). Accessing work, however, is subject to more than technical skills and securing the right to work. Having the necessary language capital (Bourdieu, 1986) is *sine qua non*. This is the focus of this volume, which zooms in on the lived experiences of migrants in different temporal, geographical and linguistic contexts, and discusses the barriers and enablers in the process. The volume is the product of the *Migrants in Working life: Language and Im/mobilities* International Association of Applied Linguistics (AILA) Research Network (ReN) and emerged through interactions in AILA/Applied Linguistics and Professional Practice (ALAPP) conferences which gave us the opportunity to bring together a multidisciplinary and multimethod approach to the study of the questions we are addressing. We were committed to bringing together early career academics and disseminating diverse voices. The collection is part of this process; it contributes to and expands work on language policy and gatekeeping as well as, more broadly, identity and multilingualism at work. Beyond its academic impact, the volume aims to problematise and contribute to language/linguistic education and curriculum transformation. Despite education being the natural locus of research activity, rarely do we turn our eye on the learning outcomes and overall (allegedly a/political) design of our own programmes on multilingualism and language education more broadly. The volume aims to raise the significance, and complexity, of pedagogical practice for enhancing the impact of research in the areas addressed in the volume. We return to this issue later in the closing of the chapter and while summarising the overall contribution of the collection.

Language policies surround and underpin all migration processes. In labour migration, so-called 'sufficient language and communication skills' are frequently portrayed as a condition and facilitator for accessing work. In recruitment, language education, and language assessment for professionals migrating or acquiring residence status (McNamara *et al.*, 2015), language policies have a direct impact on the lived experiences of those who seek to or already work in an additional language (Suni, 2017). Evidently, certain professions are more strictly regulated than others when it comes to language requirements. For instance, in health professions formal licensing is required, and criteria for language proficiency are clearly set. Teaching professions and public services also have official language requirements. These requirements draw on established values and societal priorities such as patient safety and, broadly, the public interest – which are, unquestionably, important. Having 'enough' language to serve the needs of the profession is essential. However, how adequate proficiency is framed, regulated and assessed is not straightforward.

In more detail, professional skills and professional language skills are tightly intertwined with each other (Härmälä, 2008). In addition, work on language policy and planning has shown the mismatch between 'top-down' and 'bottom-up' asymmetric relationships at national as well as institutional (particularly education) levels. In his influential work, Spolsky (e.g. 2009) has argued that language policy consists of three interrelated components: language practices, language beliefs and language management. His work, and that of others (Bonacina-Pugh, 2012; Shohamy, 2006), has shown that policy and practice need to be studied with reference to a particular context or institution and that policy is always political – despite the neutral façade of the genre. Terms such as 'covert/overt' and *de facto/de jure* policies (Angouri, 2013; Hultgren, 2014) indicate the attempt to capture the ideological, and often hidden, side of language policy. That is, policies exist and are visible in different contexts beyond what is formally written on policy documents. Language policies perpetuate 'native' ideologies which, in their turn, perpetuate and strengthen a 'locals-first' rhetoric. They also allow for enough ambiguity to become the ultimate regulator of who is 'in' and who stays 'out'. This has been well captured in sociolinguistic gatekeeping research (Kirilova & Angouri, 2017; Roberts & Campbell, 2006).

Research in linguistic gatekeeping has shown the process by which symbolic events, such as the iconic job interview, constitute focal points where professionals need to linguistically display competence in 'doing' 'being' one of 'us' in order to pass through the gate. While all languages are equal in serving the linguistic needs of speakers, they carry and perpetuate societal ideologies that separate those in (social) power from others; varieties associated with margins are stigmatised and, in turn, the stigma is projected onto the speakers. The 'language' gate, therefore, is a linguapolitical gate. From mundane interactions in different domains of activity to the representation of migrants in media and political debates, applied and sociolinguistic research has repeatedly shown the multi-layered relationship between language use and negotiating belonging and fitting in for newcomers to a socio-economic environment. The linguapolitical divide applies to varieties that have the status of 'national languages' and of 'dialects'. These are terms loaded with ideological meanings which indicate exactly what the issue is; language use is never neutral, some varieties are associated with 'us' and some with the 'other', and some varieties have an elevated status as languages of 'all people of a nation'. The latter brings clear reference to the 19th-century 'one people, one nation, one language' motto according to which people are grouped together on, allegedly, common characteristics. National language is supposed to be one, while other varieties, dialects, are perceived as smaller and often inferior to the standard (O'Mahony, 2018).

Languages and, therefore, language proficiency, are commodified and evaluated against an abstract, ideological market value. Framing the matter on a 'skills' base provides a neutral façade for a deeply political matter. Supposedly, the skills are either 'there or not'. This commodification process is in line with the broader commodification of human capital which has been and is being exhaustively studied by a range of disciplines, reducing human ability to a set of 'skills' that carry (or not) market value, depending on needs, preferences and politics. Bourdieu's (1977) work has provided a powerful conceptual framework for the study of language as capital and the complex relationship between communication and wealth in both tangible and intangible terms. Bourdieu has written on the linguistic marketplace, capturing, structure, agency and power associated with the position speakers claim/are denied in specific (institutional and everyday) fields. Bourdieu's concept of symbolic power is particularly useful for the study of multilingual organisational practice; chapters in this volume directly and indirectly expand Bourdieu's work in implications of non-conformity to dominant institutional discourses and ideals.

Overall, the multilingual reality of the modern workplace (Angouri, 2013) is deeply political, and it encapsulates and perpetuates societal power asymmetries. The scholarship of Heller and Duchêne (2016) and Piller (2016) has shown the impact of language hierarchies at work.

Despite the narrative of 'language as a resource' for the workplace – a narrative that neutralises the valorisation of language – research has shown repeatedly that all languages, including global languages, carry different values depending on the speaker's role and their agency in context. While in low-paid, stigmatised jobs employees' language capital is very limited (see e.g. Piller & Lising, 2014, on meat processing jobs, and chapters in this volume), in white collar jobs, access to a company's language can lead to access to decision-making centres and, thereby, capital in an organisation.

Using sociocultural knowledge effectively is necessary for aligning with expected behaviours and, by extension, with the norms of the host society. It is a critical factor distinguishing between those who are allowed 'in' and those who are kept 'out'. Dominant ways of doing, and hegemonic practices in different domains of activities, are established by those in power and perpetuated in mundane events. They can also be challenged and, sometimes, changed. Power in the workplace comes in different formats and guises; it is related to but not equated with senior positions and roles in organisations. Power is negotiated in situ in everyday events in professional domains. Through this negotiation process, inclusion and exclusion are perpetuated, resisted and challenged. This is *done* linguistically, despite the fact that language use is far from the spotlight of equality acts and policymakers.

In the workplace, accessing and retaining work requires social knowledge and awareness of norms, which is challenging for those doing so in their second or third language. The disproportionate number of migrant professionals 'crashing on the gate' has been well described by the *linguistic penalty* (Roberts, 2021; Roberts & Campbell, 2006) term, which linguists have embraced. The term refers to the penalty paid by those who sound and look different to the majority. It comes in different guises with not 'enough' language proficiency being common. Language proficiency is 'not a simple technical ability, but a statutory ability' (Bourdieu & Wacquant, 1992: 146). Classic sociolinguistic work has shown that using language in a way that is considered appropriate and can secure access to resources is related to sociopragmatic knowledge that goes beyond knowledge of language as a system of meaning-making signs (Gumperz, 1982; Hymes, 1972). Speakers whose linguistic habitus is marked by late acquisition often suffer the implications of inadvertently breaking the societal rules of expected behaviour. Studies drawing on both low- and high-skilled professionals have shown that those who 'succeed' are those who can successfully negotiate the reference points which are visible or shared by those in power (Roberts, 2021). The linguistic penalty also morphs into a wage penalty if and when the newcomers access work.

Summing up, the 'workplace' has gone from being of peripheral interest to sociolinguists to becoming central in current concerns, which is very much in line with the essential role of work in social, economic and personal wellbeing. While gatekeeping studies have shown power asymmetries in and through language at work, further research is needed to unpack more layers of the issues involved and potential impact of the linguistic evidence we have gathered over the decades. Language/multilingual education also has an opportunity to engage, creatively and through multiple angles in the issues involved to empower students to consider ways to make research relevant and useful to those who are most impacted by exclusion.

In this volume, we explore processes of transition into work for migrant professionals from historical, discourse analytical, narrative and language assessment angles. We also argue for a need to understand the experience of 'the migrant employee' from an intersectional angle. We turn to that next.

Language and a Holistic Study of Identity

The ideological use of 'language skills' as a blanket strategy to justify exclusionary practices and perpetuate the narrow representation of the 'migrant worker' as not being able to 'fit in' is now a given in the lines of scholarship discussed earlier. Moving forward, we argue that migrant identity, and the stigma that is often associated with migrant professionals outside the spectrum of elite jobs, needs to be studied holistically. Categories that are projected onto the individual, such as class, gender, ethnicity or L2 speaker/L1 migrant language, carry significant social meanings and moral value. Abstract characteristics associated with a category are projected onto an individual on the problematic assumption that members of the group are homogenous in their behaviour and attitudes. When category labels are mobilised, existing ideologies are also foregrounded; addressing a professional's ethnicity or L1 is not a neutral description. Consider a syntagma such as '[nationality], [race], engineer with three years of experience': depending on the labels in the brackets, different social meanings are alluded to.

This complexity is addressed by recent research taking an intersectional approach to the study of identity, following Crenshaw (1989). Crenshaw and others after her have convincingly shown that social categories never exist in isolation from one another (Angouri & Baxter, 2021). Class, gender, ethnicity, age and all other social categories intersect and are relevant to the ways in which power asymmetries are negotiated; societal privileges and/or penalties are accentuated or lessened in the process. The term 'language', in and of itself, is either too narrow or too vague to capture the complexity of the matter. Intersectionality has influenced identity studies in general and, directly or indirectly, most current work argues for a dynamic study of the relationship between identity, social categories and the social order. Intersectionality is, by definition, research on identity and plurality – areas directly related to all the chapters in this volume. We see identity as a multi-way process (Angouri, 2015), actively done by the individual but also projected onto the individual by others. This is in line with the constructionist paradigm according to which identity is not seen as fixed, but discursively constructed in different contexts. This is a process which perpetuates social structures not in the abstract but as perceived and enacted by individuals engaged in specific encounters in different domains of activity; individuals who have their own historicities and roles that come with expectations of performance. This approach to identity is associated with established traditions in sociolinguistic and applied linguistic research (see e.g. Scollon & Scollon's, 2004, approach to the historical body).

Current applied linguistic research also advocates for an intersectional approach to the study of language. Our volume aims to contribute to this agenda and argues for a multi-layered approach which is presented in Figure 1.1. This aims to show the need to identify and address the interfaces between established methods, categories and theories in our fields. By opening up and connecting across different traditions and schools of thought, new layers of meaning (Angouri, 2018; Angouri & Baxter, 2021; Holmes *et al.*, 2011) come to the fore.

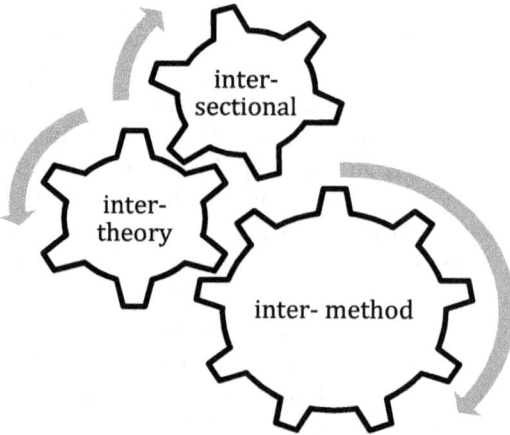

Figure 1.1 A multifaceted approach to the study of the linguistic construction of (professional) identity

The chapters in this volume address different parts of the figure, showing how power asymmetry and, more specifically, processes of inclusion and exclusion need to be approached beyond a narrow focus on the migrant and their language. We make a case for inclusion and exclusion to be understood as a process in which policy, ideologies and practices are intertwined and negotiated in the different contexts of human activity.

We argue that a similar, holistic approach would also benefit multilingualism programmes which typically privilege particular angles or disciplines, despite the interdisciplinary 'ideal' that has been prevalent in the higher education since the turn of the century.

We explore professionals' lived experiences in and through the lenses of the researcher, primarily through ethnographic, qualitative data from workplace interactions and interviews. This relationship is significant, as the researcher's readings have often been presented as a semi-neutral account of the participants' experience. The authors in this volume seek to cast a critical gaze on this relationship, through exploring the epistemological hegemonies that influence knowledge production. The core themes that will guide the reader concern the interface between social justice, employability and belonging as negotiated in different settings in and through language.

We present the organisation of the volume in more detail next.

Structure and Content

While several of the chapters in this book examine the construction of immigrants as 'other' and somehow deficient in the public imaginary, at the same time they also depict the complementary construction of national identities as superior, normative and monocultural. Taking an overall critical stance, they show how ideals of social justice and processes of belonging are embedded in historical relationships and the sociopolitical status quo, and re/enacted in the moment of an encounter.

This book begins with a historical perspective on multilingualism in workplaces (Chapter 2). Situating his study in Northern Norway of the last century, Hiss uses a historical lens through which to make sense of contemporary multilingualism in workplaces. He draws parallels between the multilingual and multicultural communicative patterns of the 19th century and contemporary multilingual workplace communication in Norway. Importantly, he points out that in contemporary workplaces, language diversity is disproportionately prevalent at the bottom of workplace hierarchies, while employers and others in high-status positions rarely possess proficiency in the dominant languages of their migrant employees.

Hiss's chapter is followed by Schleicher's (Chapter 3) discursive de- and re-construction of an immigrant medical doctor's professional identity as depicted in media representations on a popular Hungarian television channel. Through a multimodal analysis, Schleicher demonstrates how migrants are constructed as threats to national security. 'Doctor Johnny', the subject of the television program, is pejoratively described by the Hungarian government as an 'economic migrant', having immigrated to Hungary from his native Nigeria. Parallels are drawn between his identity and the severe poverty of the region of Hungary in which he works. The Hungarian government's anti-immigrant stance and attribution of poverty to Hungary's minority populations are intricately connected to the identity of the doctor – a Black immigrant who is 'not a bad doctor' (p. 42).

The next three chapters address different aspects of migrant workers' needs or pressure to fit into the perceived dominant culture in order to gain cultural capital in the workplace.

O'Neill's chapter (Chapter 4) investigates perceptions and treatment of multilingual migrant professionals in workplace interactions in Australia. She argues that, while monolingual mindsets are problematic, multilingual mindsets can serve to invisibilise languages and essentialise cultures. While acquiring and using formulaic speech is thought of as enabling language learners to emulate their monolingual/L1-speaking counterparts, these ways of thinking lead to practices that reproduce categories and stereotypes, and frame diversity as a problem, with consequences for how people live and work together. In response, these professionals develop intercultural mindsets, enabling them to disrupt attitudes that devalue multilingual practices and marginalise migrants in the workplace.

Adopting native speaker norms is addressed in Kirilova's chapter (Chapter 5), which argues that 'candidates who do not communicate according to native speaker norms (linguistic, cultural, professional) will be judged not only as "poor" language users but also as incompetent workers' (p. 77). Kirilova applies a language ideological framework to analyse job interviews with Danish L2 speakers, and uses the notion of shibboleth as an index for linguistic and cultural belonging to a particular group with a positive effect in gatekeeping encounters such as job interviews.

In Chapter 6, gatekeeping encounters with multilingual language learners are addressed by Seilonen and Suni, in the context of having created a custom instrument for assessing the work-related language proficiency of Finnish L2 speakers in the healthcare sector. Their test construct reflects the specific circumstances and needs of these language learners, who acquire many of their professional language skills on the job. The necessary skills include both linguistic and pragmatic competence, such as knowing how to establish a trusting relationship with their patients and achieving an appropriate level of indirectness when giving instructions and/or suggestions to patients.

Similar so-called 'soft skills' are addressed in Chapter 7, in which Kerekes and Sinclair analyse an eclectic set of collaborations and observations of ESL (English as a Second Language) pedagogy in a Canadian settlement organisation. They offer a critical perspective on instructional approaches which may indicate societal/cultural expectations that immigrant workers remain at the bottom of workplace hierarchies, reminiscent of claims made by Hiss in Chapter 2. Their work highlights the sometimes unrecognised association of migrant workers with low-wage workers by the very institutions and individuals who genuinely seek to facilitate their successful transitions to professional life in their new home country.

Chapter 8 examines the identity management of migrant call centre workers in London. In contrast to the potential limitations placed on immigrants in terms of dominant cultural attitudes towards them and their abilities described in the first seven chapters, Tovar argues that identity challenges for which researchers have often criticised call centre work actually provide helpful conditions which allow for learners to become full 'participants' (Pavlenko & Lantolf, 2000) and for successful linguistic and cultural adaptation. Drawing on long-term participant observation and interviews with agents and team leaders, Tovar examines the demands for impression management that agents face, and the tactics they use to create good impressions. The participants indicate that impression management at the call centre allows them to cope with stress, rudeness and xenophobia, and prepares them for interactions in other societal and professional settings.

In Chapter 9, Babayants examines the multilingual expression of emotions in the context of theatrical performance. Using a 'practice as research' (PaR) approach, he looks at two first-generation Canadian actors' experiences of performing in a variety of languages, and examines their so-called 'language-body-emotion disconnect' when performing in their L2(s). Together with Babayants (the author of this chapter and also the director of the theatrical piece his participants performed), his participants co-created *In Sundry Languages*, a theatrical piece centring on multilingualism. Participants reveal, in follow-up interviews, the sometimes-surprising freedoms and constraints they experience while performing in different languages, and the different masks these languages afford them to wear. Babayants suggests that a plurilingual stance enhances our understanding of the complex interplay between performers' emotions, their multiple languages, their perceptions and how they are received by their audiences.

Also addressing multilingualism at work, but in contrast to Babayants's descriptive study, Humonen and Angouri (Chapter 10) take a more critical stance in their discussion of the positions migrant employees are assigned or claim within the power structures of a multilingual workplace. In their study of workplace interactions in a Finnish restaurant, they illustrate how kitchen environments can become 'battlegrounds' between different international chefs and sites in which power (im)balances are reproduced.

To conclude, the chapters approach multilingualism as a conduit to the study of multi-layered manifestations of the social order and power asymmetries in professional relationships. While the chapters take different theoretical stances, they all show the negotiated and emergent nature of professional identities, and the tensions between individual agency and top-down societal constraints. This has direct implications for (language) policy at work and in training programmes for newcomers to a different linguapolitical context.

Moving Forward: Beyond Linear Asymmetries and Gatekeeping

As population movement is intensifying, accessing employment is central to settling in a new and different societal context. This is not a technical gap-filling exercise. It is a deeply political and ideological process, and a product of these political times. 'Work' and the way it is framed and understood are central to the interests of applied linguists and sociolinguists, well beyond the endeavours of workplace discourse analysts. Taking a critical stance to the 'so what' and 'where next' questions is paramount for the social relevance of our research and the impact potential of our scholarship.

Sociolinguists and applied linguists, with the notable exception of those who work under the critical discursive umbrella, often stay away from political and activist agendas in the areas we are researching. However, if we believe in the need for change, a more engaged political agenda (small p) is necessary. Language is mis/ab/used to conceal exclusion from work. With the addition of 'soft skills', which is a convenient shorthand to mark those who are not familiar with the norms of the local context as unable to 'fit in', 'language' becomes a backdoor to inequality under the radar of equality acts[1] and civil rights.

In closing, our field/s have come of age; we need to revisit the purposes and relevance of our research on language in the workplace, and to consider the ways in which we can reframe political action and activism so that they are appropriate for the 21st century. Evidently, this does not mean that everybody will or should get onboard with an activist stance. There are many ways to engage with policies and policymakers. There is a need, however, to address the fact that our research has not yet managed, with notable exceptions, to make a significant difference to policies and practices affecting newcomers in our societal contexts.

At the time of writing, COVID-19 has deepened inequalities between the haves and have nots. Unemployment, fatalities, mental illness and overall lack of wellbeing are disproportionally felt by the most vulnerable in society. Climate disasters and political movements most certainly will add to the migration flows towards the politicised and political 'west' and the centres of 'global power'. Through our research and education agendas, we need to provide our students and future researchers with the theoretical tools to explore multilingualism and diversity, and with a pedagogy that enables them to find their voices early in their studies. We hope this volume makes a contribution to sociolinguistics and applied linguistics research, and also, fundamentally, to the educational offerings in applied and sociolinguistic curricula. We sought to create a space for scholars from different career stages to come together and we believe this is a model that we need to develop and grow. As we argued, while, as academics, we analyse language education policies, we devote less time to analysing our own departmental policies and whether what we stand for is adequately present in our programmes of study. The post-COVID-19 academia can be more connected and even more oriented towards problem-based pedagogies; that is, enabling students from early stages to apply their knowledge to real world issues. We strongly supported this agenda through the ReN network (under AILA) which led to this volume[2], and we hope to continue creating connections of relevance for a better world.

Notes

(1) The Equality Act provides Britain with a discrimination law which protects individuals from unfair treatment and promotes a fair and more equal society. A new Equality Act came into force on 1 October 2010, bringing together over 116 separate pieces of legislation into one single Act. The full Equality Act 2010 is available here: https://www.legislation.gov.uk/ukpga/2010/15/contents.
(2) We are grateful to Pauliina Puranen, Rosariina Suhonen and Yiran Zhang for their efficient editorial assistance during the preparation of this book and to Polina Mesinioti for her support during the final stages of the volume.

References

Angouri, J. (2013) The multilingual reality of the multinational workplace: Language policy and language use. *Journal of Multilingual and Multicultural Development* 34 (6), 564–581.
Angouri, J. (2015) Studying identity. In Z. Hua (ed.) *Research Methods in Intercultural Communication* (pp. 37–52). Oxford: Blackwell.
Angouri, J. (2018) *Culture, Discourse, and the Workplace*. Abingdon: Routledge
Angouri, J. and Baxter, J. (eds) (2021) *The Routledge Handbook of Language, Gender and Sexuality*. New York: Routledge.
Bonacina-Pugh, F. (2012) Researching 'practiced language policies': Insights from conversation analysis. *Language Policy* 11, 213–234.
Bourdieu, P. (1977) *Outline of a Theory of Practice* (trans. R. Nice). Cambridge: Cambridge University Press.
Bourdieu, P. (1986) The forms of capital. In J. Richardson (ed.) *Handbook of Theory and Research for the Sociology of Education* (pp. 241–258). Westport, CT: Greenwood.
Bourdieu, P. and Wacquant, L.J. (1992) *An Invitation to Reflexive Sociology*. Chicago: University of Chicago press.
Crenshaw, K. (1989) Demarginalizing the intersection of race and sex: A black feminist critique of antidiscrimination doctrine, feminist theory and antiracist politics. *University of Chicago Legal Forum* 1 (8). https://scholarship.law.columbia.edu/faculty_scholarship/3007.
European Commission (EC) (2016) Communication from the commission to the European parliament, the council, the European Economic and Social Committee and the Committee of the Regions. Lives in dignity: From aid-dependence to self-reliance. https://ec.europa.eu/echo/files/policies/refugees-idp/Communication_Forced_Displacement_Development_2016.pdf.
Gumperz, J.J. (1982) *Language and Social Identity*. Cambridge: Cambridge University Press.
Härmälä, M. (2008) Is just a moment a sufficient demonstration of the language skills required in the qualification of business and administration? Language assessment in competency-based qualifications for adults. PhD thesis, University of Jyväskylä.
Heller, M. and Duchêne, A. (2016) Treating language as an economic resource: Discourse, data and debate. In N. Coupland (ed.) *Sociolinguistics: Theoretical Debates* (pp. 139–156). Cambridge: Cambridge University Press.
Hellgren, Z. (2014) Negotiating the boundaries of social membership. Undocumented migrant claims-making in Sweden and Spain. *Journal of Ethnic and Migration Studies* 40 (7–8), 1175–1191.
Holmes, J., Marra, M. and Vine, B. (2011) *Leadership, Discourse, and Ethnicity*. Oxford: Oxford University Press.
Hultgren, A.K. (2014). Whose parallellingualism? Overt and covert ideologies in Danish university language policies. *Multilingua* 33 (1–2), 61–87.

Hymes, D. (1972) On communicative competence. In J. Pride and J. Holmes (eds) *Sociolinguistics: Selected Readings* (pp. 269–293). Harmondsworth: Penguin.

Kirilova, M. and Angouri, J. (2017) Workplace communication practices and policies. In S. Canagarajah (ed.) *Routledge Handbook of Migration and Language* (pp. 540-557). Abingdon: Routledge.

McNamara T., Khan K. and Frost, K. (2015) Language tests for residency and citizenship and the conferring of individuality. In B. Spolsky, O. Inbar-Lourie and M. Tannenbaum (eds) *Challenges for Language Education and Policy: Making Space for People* (pp. 11–23). New York: Routledge.

OECD (2020) 2020 Annual international migration and displacement trends and policies report to the G20. https://www.oecd.org/migration/mig/FINAL-2020-OECD-ILO-UNHCR-IOM-G20-report.pdf.

O'Mahony, C. (2018) An analysis of dialects and how they are neither linguistically superior nor inferior to one another. *International Journal of Humanities, Arts and Social Sciences* 4 (5), 221–226.

Özdemir, A.M. and Yücesan-Özdemir, G. (2004) Living in endemic insecurity: An analysis of Turkey's labour market in the 2000s. *South East Europe Review* 7 (2), 33–42.

Pavlenko, A. and Lantolf, J. (2000) Second language learning as participation and the (re)construction of selves. In J.P. Lintolf (ed.) *Sociocultural Theory and Second Language Learning* (pp. 157–180). Oxford: Oxford University Press.

Piller, I. (2016) *Linguistic Diversity and Social Justice: An Introduction to Applied Sociolinguistics*. Oxford: Oxford University Press.

Piller, I. and Lising, L. (2014) Language, employment, and settlement: Temporary meat workers in Australia. *Multilingua* 33 (1–2), 35–59.

Roberts, C. (2021) *Linguistic Penalties and the Job Interview*. Sheffield: Equinox Publishing.

Roberts, C. and Campbell, S. (2006) Talk on trial. Job interviews, language and ethnicity, *DWP Report* 344.

Scollon, R. and Scollon. S. (2004) *Nexus Analysis: Discourse and the Emerging Internet*. London: Routledge.

Shohamy, E. (2006) *Language policy: Hidden Agendas and New Approaches*. London: Routledge.

Spolsky, B. (2009) *Language Management*. Cambridge: Cambridge University Press.

Suni, M. (2017) Working and learning in a new niche: Ecological interpretations of work-related migration. In J. Angouri, M. Marra and J. Holmes (eds) *Negotiating Boundaries at Work: Talking and Transitions* (pp. 197–215). Edinburgh: Edinburgh University Press.

2 Contextualising Diversity, Work and Mobility Across Time: Cases from Norway's 'High North'

Florian Hiss

Introduction

Research into language, work and migration has evolved rapidly during the past decade. The majority of studies focus on contemporary cases. However, work migration and linguistic diversity in the workplace are not phenomena solely of the early 21st century; many workplaces have been sites of multilingual encounters throughout history. While this has been acknowledged in contemporary studies (e.g. Duchêne & Heller, 2012), there exist only a few studies on language and diversity in historical workplaces (e.g. Boutet, 2001; Hewitt, 2012; Hiss, 2017). Considering the major effects of globalisation on communication and mobility, when we look at longer timescales, we see that history has shaped the current conditions. A consideration of the temporal dimensions of work and mobility as well as surrounding contexts and conditions can help make sense of present and future changes.

Connections between contemporary and historical working life can be established in at least three different but intertwining ways. First, past conditions and developments can tell something about the emergence of contemporary conditions over time. Second, when challenges are similar, experiences from earlier times can provide valuable knowledge applicable to contemporary challenges, e.g. the management of diversity in the workplace. Third, the past can be mobilised and explored discursively to make sense of the present or recontextualised as an added value within the contemporary context. The aim of this chapter is, therefore, to demonstrate that the relationship between a multilingual past and contemporary working life encompasses more than a chronological development. This study examines the interplay of these aspects as displayed in the case of multilingual Northern Norway.

Norway's High North – more precisely, its two northernmost counties, Troms and Finnmark[1] – hosts a growing economy as well as a multilingual history. The exploitation of natural resources, ranging from fish to natural gas and ore, as well as tourism, play a central role in the contemporary development of the area. This development has drawn national and global attention to the region (Jensen & Hønneland, 2011; Røvik et al., 2011); its economic growth has also increased the need for a broad and flexible workforce in both its urban centres and its rural periphery. While work migration makes many contemporary workplaces linguistically and culturally diverse, the diversity of Northern Norway is not a new phenomenon; it has been linguistically and culturally diverse for centuries. The country is the home of Sámi, Kven and Norwegians, and there are traditionally strong contacts with neighbours in Russia, Finland and Sweden. The coast, providing food, work and easy transportation, has continuously attracted people from abroad.

Sámi and Kven, both Finno-Ugric languages, have been in use in the region for centuries. Today, the Sámi are recognised as indigenous people of Norway, and the Kven as national minority. The majority language is Norwegian. Norwegian itself has a vast range of dialects, which are used actively in all social domains, marking local and regional identity, for individuals as well as corporations. Norwegian also has two official written varieties, Bokmål and Nynorsk. In the north, the majority uses the former. In brief, we encounter a linguistic diversity with actively used dialectal variation, two heritage minority languages, and a broad variety of new minority languages spoken by immigrants. As in many western countries, English functions as a lingua franca in many work settings.

Regional history encompasses many examples of workplaces as arenas of multilingual encounters and negotiation of language policies. Here, I present two cases from the 19th century in more detail: a copper mine run by British industrialists, which employed almost exclusively migrant workers, many of them Kven from Finland and Sweden; and the so-called Pomor Trade between the inhabitants of the Norwegian coast and Russian merchants, who came during the summer season to exchange flour, corn and other products in exchange for fish. I juxtapose these historical cases with instances of their contemporary contextualisation, arguing that communication and multicultural encounters are a continuous thread in Northern Norwegian history. Scrutinising such threads and investigating the interplay of different ways in which history becomes meaningful requires an understanding of how time affects the making of meaning in different and intertwining ways. I therefore begin with a theoretical overview of time and temporal diversity surrounding language use, followed by two brief sections on methodological implications and the data which inform this study. Then I present a broad overview of languages and diversity in Northern Norway, its contemporary situation and historical development. In the core part of the article, I present and compare historical cases and instances of contemporary contextualisation. Finally, I attempt to gather patterns emerging from the data and discuss the interplay of different ways of temporal sensemaking.

Time and Temporal Diversity

Language, mobility and work patterns are intertwined and time sensitive. However, scholars have repeatedly pointed out that time and temporality are too often neglected in the study of language and social life, criticising the detemporalisation of language in linguistic research (Auer *et al.*, 1999) and a preference for synchronicity (Blommaert, 2018). Historical sociolinguistics has highlighted the importance of studying 'layered simultaneity in diachrony' (Nevalainen, 2015), i.e. to include multiple levels of context and social relations in the study of historical language use and language change. Such a perspective is indispensable to a proper understanding of language use in historical contexts. Here, I want to go one step further. Temporal experience and the ways in which we understand, interpret and appropriate time are multi-layered and complex. They affect the ways in which we make sense of the past, present and future.

Time can be understood as a continuum measurable in seconds, hours, years, centuries etc. Any event can be placed on a timeline of chronological order. But chronological order tells little about social meaning (Blommaert, 2018: 65). Ideas of absolute, measurable clock- and calendar-time are radically different from the ways in which we experience the relations between past, present and future. In discursive practice, the past is continuously reconstituted with reference to the present and future. The experience of time is context-sensitive, relational and constructive: 'past and future change with each new present, and each present is defined with reference to a particular event, system, biography or person' (Adam, 2004: 69). In this sense, historical contextualisation contributes to the emergence of something new. Sherover (1991: 43) puts it this way:

> We cannot authentically escape the varied aspects of our heritage, but we are continually compelled to appropriate it selectively. By selecting some possibilities it offers rather than others, we are continually reshaping and remolding it into the legacy we will be passing on.

Simultaneously, any social action in the present (including its social and material contexts and the experiences of all participants) is affected by historical processes of becoming (Scollon & Scollon, 2004).

Every action or event of whatever duration, in the present, past or future, takes time and unfolds in time. This aspect of past events is easily erased in the retrospective: historical processes appear synchronic, e.g. when summarised in a single word such as *industrialisation*, *assimilation* or *migration*. But the time during which processes unfold in different historical settings gives meaning to the overall process, including some of the most central concerns of this article. The temporal aspect of mobility has changed radically over time. People have migrated throughout human history, but technologies such as airplanes and the internet allow us to move back and forth much faster and to communicate with other people anywhere in the world without losing time. Time is also central to the organisation and valuing of labour in industrial and capitalist economies. In Marx's (1867) view, time has become an abstract exchange value that enables the transformation of labour into capital in capitalist economies. This marks an essential difference between pre-industrial and capitalist, industrial economies.

Adam (2004) speaks of 'temporal diversity'. The same applies to the interplay of processes on radically different timescales (Lemke, 2000): developments on long, historical timescales can be equally relevant to the making of meaning in a here-and-now setting (e.g. interactional processes on much shorter timescales). The parallel and intertwining use of different timescales and radically different and seemingly contradictory perceptions of time in everyday social practice is enabled by the means of language – while language itself is deeply embedded in time. When comparing historical cases of multilingual work practices with instances of modern contextualisation, it is important to keep in mind the temporality of language and social life and methodological implications in the way in which realities are represented. As Fabian (1971) pointed out, language use was a central means of social organisation and articulation in historical settings; but it is also the channel through which researchers engage with historical conditions.

Methodological Implications

Methodological approaches to studying the dynamic interplay of such diverse understandings of time should encompass several different perspectives. It is useful, first, to integrate emic and etic perspectives on time and history, as both can be selective in different ways; and, second, to pursue a broad overview of relevant historical developments and temporal relations while, at the same time, acknowledging the importance of small fragments of history and single instances of communication, especially in discursive contextualisation. Third, it is necessary to map relevant contextual relations, roles and voices surrounding historical cases (e.g. Meeuwis, 2011; Nevalainen, 2015; Thomas, 1994) and the present contexts and discursive means of dealing with the past (e.g. Bamberg *et al.*, 2011; Scollon, 2008). Fourth, combining and juxtaposing these perspectives allow us to view the interplay of processes on different timescales and the emergence of meaning in time.

The challenge arising from the combination of such different perspectives is a potentially unlimited amount of information. Provided that we are compelled to appropriate the past selectively (Sherover, 1991), one is obliged to work with comparably small fragments of language use in time. Selectivity not only applies to language users producing discourse about the past in any temporal context, but also to us as researchers. The combination of different perspectives will help to develop a critical awareness concerning researcher positionality and the selections we make (cf. Hiss, 2022).

Data

I am interested in instances and processes on radically different timescales, which are difficult to capture within a homogeneous dataset. Accordingly, this study is informed by and synthesises research data and findings from previous research which were collected and produced at different times and through different methods. This study is built around three instances of contemporary communication and the ways in which they contextualise the region's multilingual history. I encountered these instances when working on my postdoctoral research project on *Linguistic and Cultural Diversity at Work* (2014–2018). In the project, I followed up on early findings in two ways: I decided to investigate some of the historical cases economic agents refer to today, and I included questions about the region's historical diversity in a telephone survey consisting of short interviews with 140 company representatives. Here, I expand on the findings from these studies.

Altogether, I draw on four sources of data and scientific knowledge surrounding contemporary and historical workplace multilingualism in Northern Norway. First, my main focus is on the cases of contemporary contextualisation. Second, I compare these with two cases from the 19th century: the Pomor Trade and its linguistic practice, *Russenorsk*, which have been studied extensively by several generations of linguists (e.g. Broch, 1927; Broch & Jahr, 1984); and the *Alten Copper Works*, which I studied based on the company's archived correspondence (Hiss, 2017). Third, for background information on diversity in contemporary working life, I draw on findings from the survey study (Hiss, 2019; Hiss & Loppacher, 2021). Fourth, I draw on previous research by sociolinguists and historians surrounding the sociolinguistic conditions of the region. In the following sections, I will first present a broad sketch of the contemporary situation and historical development, before I focus on contemporary contextualisation.

Languages and Diversity in Northern Norway

Work migration and the recruitment of workers from abroad are among those factors that make many contemporary workplaces linguistically diverse (see also Chapters 5, 6 and 8). Approximately 13% of the population of Troms and Finnmark (ca. 243,000 inhabitants in total) have an immigrant background[2] (Statistics Norway, 2022). The statistics count people from 147 different countries. The 10 largest groups (which account for over 50% of all people with immigrant background) come from Poland, Lithuania, Russia, Syria, Somalia, Finland, Sweden, Thailand, Eritrea and Germany, thus exhibiting highly heterogeneous linguistic, cultural and social backgrounds. Job opportunities have caused a strong increase in migration to the region during the last two decades (Aure, 2012). The increasing number of immigrants is a vital, stabilising force in small communities. De-industrialisation of rural communities and educational institutions in the cities have caused many young people to move to urban centres. As a consequence, 'to the extent that manufacturing industries survive, they are likely to be operated by immigrant labour rather than locals' (Aarsæther, 2015: 66).

Historically, most inhabitants in many parts of the region spoke Sámi or Kven, both Finno-Ugric languages. Today, Ethnologue (Simons & Fennig, 2017) estimates that there are 1500 speakers of Kven and 20,000 speakers of North Sámi in Norway (though the validity and reliability of such numbers can be questioned). Sámi languages are spoken in a large geographical area covering parts of Norway, Sweden, Finland and Russia. In Norway, the Sámi are recognised as an indigenous people who have their own political and educational institutions which also provide job opportunities for Sámi speakers (Rasmussen & Nolan, 2011). The Kven population has its geographical roots in northern Sweden and Finland. In several waves, they settled at the North Norwegian coast from the 16th century onwards (Niemi, 2003). The Kven are recognised as a national minority, with limited institutional support. The Kven language is largely mutually intelligible with Finnish. Today, it is mainly used in private homes among the elderly, and revitalisation attempts are ongoing (Lane & Räisänen, 2017). Beyond those who speak or understand Sámi and/or Kven, many have Sámi and/or Kven backgrounds without speaking their ethnic heritage languages; some show their ethnic belonging overtly, while others remain silent or even reject it (Johansen, 2013; Lane, 2015; Olsen, 2007).

I next turn to an overview of linguistic diversity in contemporary workplaces, examining how historical diversity entangles with contemporary working life as well as the role of labour and economy during three phases of historical development.

Linguistic and cultural diversity in contemporary working life

Hiss and Loppacher (2021) analyse telephone interviews with 140 company representatives to sketch the use, management and sociolinguistic contextualisation of linguistic diversity in contemporary working life in the region. A multitude of 'immigrant' languages are used among migrant workers not only in the fishing industry, which is important for the region, but also in other industries such as manufacturing and construction. This diversity is largest at the lower end of organisational hierarchies (on linguistic diversity and workplace hierarchy, see also Chapter 10 in this volume). While many workers have migrated to Northern Norway, most managers and administrators have a local or regional background. Practically none of them reports knowledge of the language(s) of their employees. Though they express a preference for workers competent in Norwegian, the job market does not allow companies to employ solely Norwegian-speaking workforces.

Many companies lack proper strategies for handling linguistically diverse workforces, or they let language ideological principles rule rather than practical considerations. For example, Norwegian is usually treated as an undisputed linguistic norm to which many workers are required to adapt, even if the majority of employees speak other languages. English is used whenever competences in Norwegian do not suffice. Some companies use language brokers (e.g. Lønnsmann & Kraft, 2018) – multilingual employees in key positions – to mediate between leaders and employees and between workers with different cultural and linguistic backgrounds.

Concerning the position of the region's historical minority languages (i.e. Kven and Sámi) in contemporary working life, the survey findings reveal two significant aspects. First, both minority languages are used in work contexts, albeit to a limited extent (Hiss & Loppacher, 2021). Aside from traditional professions such as reindeer herding and handicraft (for which Sámi terminology comprises expert knowledge), we encountered several examples, within limited geographical areas, where Sámi is used first and foremost orally among colleagues and in contact with customers. The cases where Kven is used in work contexts are typically found at the intersection between professional and private spheres, e.g. in elderly care or in situations where individual employees speak Kven with individual customers.

Second, based on the same dataset, I show in Hiss (2019) that many company representatives explicitly and implicitly position themselves vis-à-vis language ideologies and societal expectations when asked about the role of Kven and Sámi in their workplace. Such reactions can only be understood against the backdrop of the shifting social evaluation of linguistic diversity throughout history. It was a common ideology that using minority languages was connected with social and economic disadvantages. This view is challenged by the currently ongoing ethnic emancipation, as discussed below.

Three historical phases of diversity politics

Multilingual and multicultural development in northern Scandinavia has been described in three historical phases (Huss & Lindgren, 2010; Niemi, 2008): an era of varying multilingualism, lasting until the mid-19th century; a period of linguistic and cultural assimilation from the 1860s until after World War II; and a period of ethnic revival, which gained momentum in the 1980s. Despite this chronological segmentation, the political, cultural and sociolinguistic processes of each phase overlap.

The era of varying multilingualism was also an era of pre-industrial economy. Many families made their living through a combination of fishery and farming or reindeer herding (especially parts of the Sámi population) (e.g. Blom, 1830). Harbours and trading posts along the coast were meeting points for fishermen, merchants and sailors from the greater region, Southern Norway and other parts of Europe. The combined fishing and farming livelihood had an immediate impact on multilingual development and language choices. Friis (1871: 102–103) reports that many Sámi and Kven men were mobile along the coast, as fishermen, or selling and buying products. Many of these men showed a good command of Norwegian in work and trading contexts. Friis mentions also that many Norwegians could speak Sámi or Kven in these encounters. At the same time, very few Sámi or Kven women and children (running the farms) in their remote home villages spoke or understood Norwegian. Thus, many multilingual practices were connected to work and mobility. From the harbour town of Vadsø, Friis reports his impression of multilingual practices:

> Wherever one walks around in Vadsø itself, the Norwegian centre between the eastern and western Kven town, in the streets, wharfs and stores one hears more often Kven than Norwegian. Of course, virtually all merchants could speak Kven, just as well as many of them could speak Russian. Many could also speak Lappish [Sámi]. (Friis, 1871: 105, author's translation from Norwegian)

During his visit to Hammerfest, Janson (1874: 21–22) described his impression of being in another country because Kven, Sámi and Russian were spoken everywhere. Though he did not understand most of these languages, Janson reported that most of the talk he heard was connected to work activities. Friis's (1871) observations in particular suggest that communication did not rely on one common lingua franca but on the ability to make oneself understood in several languages and to accommodate to other interlocutors.

Both Friis and Janson mentioned the use of Russian. Throughout the 19th century, during the summer season, merchants from northwest Russia visited harbours and villages along the coast. The linguistic practice of the so-called Pomor Trade between the Russians and the local population was called *Russenorsk* ('Russian-Norwegian'), or *moja på tvoja* ('me to you/I (speak) like you'). It received great scientific and public attention and was subsequently described as a pidgin (Broch & Jahr, 1984). Friis described it as follows:

So, during this trading, a kind of lingua franca is spoken, which is called Russenorsk and which consists of a roughly equal mixture of both languages. The Russian believes, by the way, that he speaks pure Norwegian, and the Fisherman, for his part, is convinced that he speaks perfect Russian. But they do not come to an understanding, and after some shouting and gesticulation, they agree about the deal. It is quite amusing to see these people and listen to their strange gibberish. (Friis, 1891: 27, author's translation from Norwegian)

These linguistic practices remained for a long time, when most people earned their primary livelihood in traditional, pre-industrial and pre-capitalist economies. The use of Russenorsk ceased when the barter trade was replaced by a monetary economy (Broch & Jahr, 1984). Sámi and Kven came under pressure from the middle of the 19th century onwards, when the government launched assimilation (i.e. Norwegian-only) policies, aiming to strengthen the nation on its periphery and exclude outside influences (Huss & Lindgren, 2010; Pietikäinen *et al.*, 2010). These policies went hand-in-hand with the impact of modernisation on public and professional domains. Professional education was moved from the communities to the school system (Huss & Lindgren, 2010: 261). As a result, Kven and Sámi identity was stigmatised, and many speakers abandoned their heritage languages in favour of Norwegian.

Economic measures were used to implement assimilation policies. Speaking Norwegian became a necessary precondition to accessing all areas of economic life (Eriksen & Niemi, 1981; Huss & Lindgren, 2010; Lane, 2010). Eriksen and Niemi (1981) report several cases in which construction workers and miners were recruited from among ethnic Norwegians rather than local Kven and Sámi. In this way, more ethnic Norwegians could be brought to the North, and the state could exert assimilation pressure on the Sámi and Kven: the language of modern economy and working-life was Norwegian. The decision of many Kven and Sámi to abandon their mother tongues and shift to Norwegian was connected to a wish for an economically better life (Huss & Lindgren, 2010). Sámi was so stigmatised by the 1960s, for example, that Sámi men travelling on coastal boats would switch to Norwegian whenever others could hear them talking (Eidheim, 1969).

Today, the workplace is considered an important domain for preserving and revitalising minority languages (Fishman, 1991; Rasmussen & Nolan, 2011; on the workplace as a politicised site, see also Chapter 10 in this volume). Numerous revitalisation activities have been undertaken during the last decades. Some Sámi communities have succeeded relatively well in maintaining and reclaiming language and identity. The Kven are no longer considered foreigners in Norway, but a part of Norway's cultural heritage.

Contemporary Contextualisation and Historical Cases Compared

The historical overview has revealed multiple connections between the development of linguistic diversity and labour, mobility and economic development in the region throughout the last 300 years. I will now turn to instances of contemporary recontextualisation of this multilingual history and, in light of the interplay of temporal understandings outlined above, I will compare these with two historical cases.

Instances of contemporary contextualisation

Example 1 is an extract from the 2013 annual report of High North Petroleum,[3] a company specialising in the search for offshore resources of natural oil and gas. In addition to the statutory annual account, annual reports usually contain statistics or descriptive information on the company's activities and, quite often, statements about social and environmental responsibility. Annual reports are publicly accessible and provide information to anyone interested in the company's activities. High North Petroleum presented the following account of its corporate social responsibility:

Example 1
High North Petroleum is a multicultural workplace with nine nationalities represented among the company's employees. High North Petroleum's identity will always be shaped by the region we come from. Communication and multicultural encounters run like a red thread through Northern Norwegian history. The trading connections between Northwest Russia and Northern Norway relate back to the Viking age. The Pomor Trade in the 19th century took place during summer along major parts of the coastal and fjord areas in Northern Norway, between the local population and Russians from the White Sea region. During the union with Denmark, the official class and the bourgeoisie were recruited to the north from Denmark and Northern Germany. From Finland, the ancestors of today's Kven population immigrated over the border to Finnmark. High North Petroleum as a multicultural workplace represents a continuation of this tradition. (author's translation from Norwegian)

The text is accompanied by a picture of three employees in front of a poster about the arctic wilderness. The people in the picture have different skin- and hair-colours, a prototypical symbol of cultural diversity. Sámi culture is also discussed in the report.

Example 1 establishes links between the company as a contemporary, multicultural workplace and historical cases of multilingual and multicultural encounters in the region. By explicitly embedding itself in the described historical context, the company constructs a regional identity.

Accounting for corporate social responsibility, the text uses the means of narrative (e.g. Bamberg *et al.*, 2011) to merge historical past with present conditions and to shape an impression of responsible future actions. In addition, the accompanying picture suggests a relationship between cultural and natural diversity. It is a known fact that activities of the oil and gas industry can affect the vulnerable natural environment. Corporate social responsibility is simultaneously about 'doing good' for society and 'doing well' economically (Aguinis, 2011). Thus, one aim of the account is to present the company in a good light vis-á-vis social and environmental interests. The presentation of historical examples is highly selective; a critical view of the text reveals a number of contrasts hidden behind the construction of historical continuity. Can we really compare the company's employees (highly educated experts in geology and engineering) with the fishermen, farmers, tradesmen, miners and officials from earlier times?

High North Petroleum is not the only contemporary actor using the region's history for communications. Similar elements of the linguistic and cultural diversity and historical processes are foregrounded in Example 2, a blogpost about a new international cooperation posted by the rector of UiT The Arctic University of Norway on the university's news blog (Husebekk, 2016). The blog text opens with the following:

Example 2
Collaboration has shaped the history of people who have lived and made a living in Arctic areas. The Sámi culture does not know any national borders in the north. The Kven population moved across the borders, and the Pomor trade is an example of borderless collaboration.

The text concludes:

Challenges and opportunities in the Arctic do not know any borders. Therefore, we intensify our collaboration in important areas such as research, education and innovation across the national borders, through the Joint Arctic Agenda. (author's translation from Norwegian)

While Example 1 uses the past to underscore the company's regional embeddedness, Example 2 highlights the context of international collaboration. In both examples, the authors present diversity and historical examples as special and unique to the High North and as a strength of their own activities.

Example 3 (Figure 2.1) is a historical photograph from 1902, showing workers bringing fish ashore at a fish reception facility on Sørøya island in Finnmark. The large photograph (ca. six square meters) is installed in a restaurant in *Kystens hus* (the 'House of the Coast'), a futuristic building by the harbour of Tromsø, the location of various facilities in the seafood and fishery sector, as well as restaurants and shops. The picture shows one of the historical, multilingual meeting points (e.g. Friis, 1871,

Figure 2.1 Example 3: Photograph titled 'Bringing fish ashore on Sørøya, Finnmark (1902)', inside the 'House of the Coast' (picture taken by the author)

see section on the three historical phases of diversity politics). Neither the historical diversity nor the fact that most contemporary fish reception facilities are operated by migrant labour are made explicit in the contemporary presentation. However, the photograph explicitly addresses a linguistically diverse audience: tourists and international customers. In the upper left corner, it includes a description in Norwegian, English, German and Japanese. A box contains leaflets in the same languages, linking traditional fish production to present products. The focus is, thus, on the products and not on the workers or their communication. The website of *Kystens hus* (www.kystenshus.no) advertises a future-oriented focus on the coast as well as a 'manifestation of the new centrality of the coast and an active driving force for increased value creation' (author's translation from Norwegian). The leaflet and photograph transmit a sense of regional and historical rootedness of this future-orientation. Thus, the creation of something new ('the new centrality of the coast' and the advertisement of current products) is linked to the past – but in a highly selective manner.

The Pomor Trade

The Pomor Trade is mentioned explicitly in Examples 1 and 2 to establish a sense of historical continuity in 'communication and multicultural encounters' (Example 1) and in 'borderless collaboration' (Example 2).

Historically, the trade developed between the local population and merchants from White Sea Russia, who brought timber, corn, flour and other goods in exchange for fish. For the local population, this trade was much more advantageous than buying the same products from Southern Norway. A common code of communication was essential for both parties to negotiate a fair deal. This linguistic practice was called Russenorsk. Most likely, it emerged in the late 18th century and was used until the early 20th century when the barter trade was replaced by a monetary economy (Broch & Jahr, 1984). Interestingly, witnesses have recounted some of the oral practices such as what we see in Example 4.

Example 4: Dialogue excerpt in Russenorsk
Fisherman: kaptein! moja har fisska selle.
Captain! I have fish for sale.
Russian: kak sort fisska på tvoja båt?
What kind of fish do you have on your boat?
Fisherman: paltuska, tresska, sika, piksja
Halibut, cod, coley, haddock.
Russian: kak pris på tvoja fisk? moja lita penga.
What is the price for your fish? I don't have much money.
(Broch, 1930: 119, author's translation)

Russenorsk had a simple grammar and a limited lexicon specific to trading, and consisting of elements from Norwegian and Russian, but also Sámi and international sailors' languages such as English and Dutch.

The case of the Pomor Trade is an interesting historical example of how a multilingual practice emerged and finally ceased because of mobility and economic conditions. But it is also a story of attention and contextualisation. Some contemporary witnesses documented examples in Russenorsk because it was extraordinary and exotic to them. Later, the reported materials were valued as important artefacts for research on language contact and pidgin languages (Broch & Jahr, 1984). In the process of passing on knowledge over time, Russenorsk and the Pomor Trade have been recontextualised and reinterpreted several times (Hiss, 2022). Examples 1 and 2 show how the historical Pomor Trade is used to add meaning to 21st-century working life and economy. Though the temporal contexts are radically different, the red threads constructed at different points in time build on the same aspects: diversity, work and regional peculiarities.

Kven migration and industrialisation

The ancestors of today's Kven population lived and travelled in northern Scandinavia for centuries. One reason they settled at the coast was to have better chances of survival through access to fish when the harvest from agriculture was poor. Through their labour to cultivate the land, the

Kven established themselves as industrious and persistent workers. The immigration of the Kven is mentioned in Examples 1 and 2, likely because of obvious parallels with contemporary work migration. Here, I want to sketch the case of the Kven miners at the Alten Copper Works, in order to show how selective contemporary contextualisation is. The case is historically and sociolinguistically interesting not only because the mine employed many Kven workers, but also because it was in operation just at the time when the Norwegian state introduced assimilation policies.

The mine was in operation from 1826 to 1878, owned and managed by British industrialists and the first large industrial enterprise in a society that had made its living in traditional economies. During its first years, the directors had major difficulties to recruit and secure a sufficient, stable and at the same time cheap and flexible workforce in the sparsely populated periphery. Therefore, they saw great economic value in the Kven, who had escaped from misfortune in their home villages in Finland and Sweden and were willing to accept work for low wages. This is revealed in the directors' reports to their investors in London. Example 5 is an extract from a letter sent by the local directors of the Alten Copper Works to A.F. Nellen in London on 21 April 1834.

Example 5
[...] I have engaged and shall continue to engage as many Quans as we can advantageously employ, the difficulty we have hitherto laboured under, and which is inseparably connected with any Enterprise of magnitude in Districts so scantily populated as this but more particularly in an undertaking foreign to the habits of the inhabitants is now fast weaving away, and the probability of our succeeding in creating a mining population in a great measure from among our Quans is placed beyond a doubt [...]

In the mid-1800s, the mining population grew to over 1000 people. Nearly all of them were migrants, and more than half of them Kven. Language management in the workplace itself was not addressed in the original correspondence, probably because work in the mine was mainly physical. However, the company explicitly supported the use of Kven in the community. They offered school education in Kven to the workers' children (Nielsen, 1995), and argued politically against the linguistic and cultural assimilation policies of the Norwegian state (Hiss, 2017). The Kven were needed as workers, and the company would not risk anything that could cause them to leave the mine. The Kven workers were treated as a constitutive part of the mining population and a valuable economic resource. Simultaneously, the company had an interest in promoting the maintenance of the Kven's connections to their home villages (thus treating them as foreigners), in order to remain flexible when fewer workers were needed and to avoid being responsible for workers without employment (Hiss, 2017).

This treatment of the Kven workers as locals and foreigners at the same time only becomes visible when mapping the interplay of different relations and positions in the historical context. None of the examples of modern contextualisation includes such a nuanced perspective. The case of the Alten Copper Works and its Kven employees reveals more parallels with today's settings: when the Kven migrated to Norway in historical times, they were looking for better living conditions, just like many immigrants today; and just like today, migrants were needed as workers, and simultaneously considered a threat to national homogeneity.

Discussion: 'Red Threads' and the Contextualisation of the Past

In Example 1, High North Petroleum's account stated that 'communication and multicultural encounters run like a red thread through Northern Norwegian history'. I have pointed out that temporal contextualisation is diverse and multifaceted and that the ways in which we deal with the past in the present are necessarily selective. At the same time, any new present is an outcome of complex historical processes. The historical overview in the section 'Languages and Diversity in Northern Norway' showed close connections between multilingual and economic development in all historical phases. This relationship is, however, not constant but characterised by radical changes in the economic development, the languages and varieties used, and the valuation of linguistic diversity. This arouses questions about the construction of 'red threads' such as suggested in Example 1.

From all contemporary examples, it is clear that the past is mobilised in a here-and-now situation with a view to the present and future. The past is easily perceived as something fixed. But, as Blommaert (2018: 67) notes:

> ... even if the discourse itself remains apparently stable and unaltered, the material, social and cultural conditions under which it is produced and under which it emerges can change and affect what the discourse is and what it does.

This means that history does not merely exhibit continuity and changes; the past receives new meanings each time it is recontextualised in a new present and re-entextualised (Silverstein & Urban, 1996) in a new text. The result is an interplay between a perception of fixity and 'textual newness' (Silverstein & Urban, 1996: 13). Historical processes such as the Pomor Trade and Kven migration appear as fixed texts and serve as building blocks in the narrative construction of temporal continuity. However, both cases reveal a more multifaceted interplay of roles, relations and conditions than the contemporary examples suggest. Narration is an ideal tool to construct a sense of continuity and constancy in the face of change, but the one who narrates plays a critical role in the shape and content of the narrative (e.g. Bamberg *et al.*, 2011). The historical overview shows that linguistic diversity has been repeatedly reframed, valued and devalued in new political and economic discourses. A continual recontextualisation and re-entextualisation of the past is part of the historical process. A central motive in the present is the perception of a new centrality of the periphery (Pietikäinen & Kelly-Holmes, 2013) and regional belonging. All historical examples exhibit aspects of being located in the periphery. This renewed focus on the periphery might explain why these particular aspects of history are foregrounded.

Contextualising the past is selective. While foregrounded in Examples 1 and 2, linguistic and cultural diversity is backgrounded in Example 3. In none of the examples is the history of linguistic assimilation and the resulting discontinuities included in the construction of continuity; in other contexts, however, they are central to the narrative construction of community identities (Hiss, 2012). One explanation is that Norwegianisation policies are evaluated negatively today, which does not suit the positive messages of the examples. At the same time, new aspects of meaning are added in contemporary contextualisation, including future-orientation, corporate social responsibility, international collaboration and contemporary work migration. As a result, heritage becomes a commodity (e.g. Heller, 2010), which can be traded against other values.

To complete the picture, it is important to compare the examples with other contemporary perspectives on multilingual heritage. In Hiss (2019), I show that being confronted with the region's multilingual heritage arouses defensive reactions in many representatives of contemporary companies. Their explicit and implicit positioning vis-à-vis language ideologies and perceived societal expectations can only be understood in light of the historical development outlined here. The impact of the past is, thus, not only found in its creative use and recontextualisation, but likely more often in underlying experiences, ideologies and expectations, which can form a more complicated picture.

Conclusions

The past is interesting because it interacts with the present and future in many ways. Northern Norway hosts multiple examples of linguistic diversity, work and migration in historical time, which deserve more thorough investigation and can provide valuable insights when addressing contemporary diversity. But the past is not fixed. Understanding the role of the past in the present requires a view to past and present contexts and the multiple ways in which language builds connections over and across time. Unpacking the contemporary and historical contexts surrounding diversity, work and mobility reveals a high complexity of relations beyond contemporary and synchronic perspectives. The historical overview in this article has shown both continuities and radical changes across time, as well as recurrent motives at different points in time. Today, the past is mobilised creatively and selectively with a view to the present and future, but it also has a more implicit impact on decisions and reactions. The most important insight is that none of these perspectives stands alone. It is the interplay of different temporal perspectives that makes temporal contextualisation complex.

Acknowledgement

The present research was funded by the SAMKUL-programme of the Research Council of Norway (project 236865).

Notes

(1) Both counties have been merged from 1 January 2020. National and regional authorities have started a process to re-establish Troms and Finnmark as separate counties from 2024.
(2) Statistics Norway counted people who immigrated to Norway and people born in Norway to parents who had both immigrated to Norway (Dzamarija, 2008).
(3) The name of the company has been changed.

References

Aarsæther, N. (2015) Viable communities in the North? *Septentrio Conference Series* 1, 63–72.
Adam, B. (2004) *Time*. Cambridge: Polity.
Aguinis, H. (2011) Organizational responsibility. Doing good and doing well. In S. Zedeck (ed.) *APA Handbook of Industrial and Organizational Psychology. Vol 3: Maintaining, Expanding, and Contracting the Organization* (pp. 855–879). Washington, DC: American Psychological Association.
Auer, P., Couper-Kuhlen, E. and Muller, F. (1999) *Language in Time. The Rhythm and Tempo of Spoken Interaction*. Oxford: Oxford University Press.
Aure, M. (2012) Ny arbeidskraft, nye innbyggere – Nye nordlendinger. In S. Jentoft, J.-I. Nergård and K.A. Røvik (eds) *Hvor går Nord-Norge? Bind 2. Et institusjonelt perspektiv på folk og landsdel* (pp. 205–218). Stamsund: Orkana.
Bamberg, M., De Fina, A. and Schiffrin, D. (2011) Discourse and identity construction. In S.J. Schwartz, K. Luyckx and V.L. Vignoles (eds) *Handbook of Identity Theory and Research* (pp. 177–199). New York: Springer.
Blom, G.P. (1830) *Bemærkninger paa en Reise i Nordlandene og igjennem Lapland til Stockholm, i Aaret 1827 [Comments on a Journey to the Northlands and through Lapland to Stockholm in the year 1827]*. Christiania: Cammermeyer.
Blommaert, J. (2018) *Dialogues with Ethnography: Notes on Classics, and How I Read Them*. Bristol: Multilingual Matters.
Boutet, J. (2001) La part langagière du travail: Bilan et évolution [A review of the linguistic component of work and its evolution]. *Langage et société* 98 (4), 17–42.
Broch, I. and Jahr, E.H. (1984) Russenorsk. A new look at the Russo-Norwegian pidgin in Northern Norway. In P.S. Ureland and I. Clarkson (eds) *Scandinavian Language Contacts* (pp. 21–65). Cambridge: Cambridge University Press.
Broch, O. (1927) Russenorsk. *Archiv für slavische Philologie* 41, 209–262.
Broch, O. (1930) Russenorsk tekstmateriale. *Maal og Minne* 4, 113–140.

Duchêne, A. and Heller, M. (2012) Pride and profit. Changing discourses of language, capital and nation-state. In A. Duchêne and M. Heller (eds) *Language in Late Capitalism: Pride and Profit* (pp. 1–21). New York: Routledge.

Dzamarija, M.T. (2008) Definisjoner og betegnelser i innvandrerstatistikken: Hva skal "innvandreren" hete? [Definitions and terms in immigrant statistics: What should "the immigrant" be called?]. *Samfunnsspeilet* 4, 62–65.

Eidheim, H. (1969) When ethnic identity is a social stigma. In F. Barth (ed.) *Ethnic Groups and Boundaries* (pp. 39–57). Oslo: Universitetsforlaget.

Eriksen, K.E. and Niemi, E. (1981) *Den finske fare. Sikkerhetsproblemer og minoritetspolitikk i nord 1860–1940 [The Finnish Danger. Security Problems and Minority Politics in the North 1860–1940]*. Oslo: Universitetsforlaget.

Fabian, J. (1971) Language, history and anthropology. *Philosophy of the Social Sciences* 1 (1), 19–47.

Fishman, J.A. (1991) *Reversing Language Shift: Theoretical and Empirical Foundations of Assistance to Threatened Languages*. Clevedon: Multilingual Matters.

Friis, J.A. (1871) *En Sommer i Finmarken, Russisk Lapland og Nordkarelen. Skildringer af Land og Folk [A Summer in Finnmark, Russian Lapland and North Karelia. Descriptions of Country and People]*. Christiania: Cammermeyer.

Friis, J.A. (1891) *Skildringer fra Finmarken [Portrayals from Finnmark]*. Christiania: Cammermeyer.

Heller, M. (2010) The commodification of language. *Annual Review of Anthropology* 39 (1), 101–115.

Hewitt, R. (2012) Multilingualism in the workplace. In M. Martin-Jones, A. Blackledge and A. Creese (eds) *The Routledge Handbook of Multilingualism* (pp. 267–280). London: Routledge.

Hiss, F. (2012) Managing sociolinguistic challenges: Storytelling about language loss and continuity in the case of Sámi. In K.J.L. Knudsen, H.P. Petersen and K. á Rógvi (eds) *Four or More Languages for All: Language Policy Challenges of the Future* (pp. 36–54). Oslo: Novus.

Hiss, F. (2017) Workplace multilingualism in shifting contexts. A historical case. *Language in Society* 46 (5), 697–718.

Hiss, F. (2019) Responding responsibly: Ideological, interactional, and professional responsibilities in survey responses about multilingualism at work. *Journal of Applied Linguistics and Professional Practice* 12 (3), 289–312.

Hiss, F. (2022) Researching language at work in public and hidden domains. Historical time and temporal contextualization. In K. Gonçalves and H. Kelly-Holmes (eds) *Language, Global Mobilities and Blue-collar Workplaces*. London: Routledge.

Hiss, F. and Loppacher, A. (2021) "The working language is Norwegian, but that doesn't have anything to say, it seems": When expectations meet the new multilingual reality. *Acta Boarelia* 38 (1), 43–59.

Husebekk, A. (2016) En felles arktisk agenda. *UiT Norges arktiske universitet* [blogpost], 20 September 2016. https://uit.no/blogg/blogpost?blogg=185508&p_document_id=485867 (accessed 16 May 2017).

Huss, L. and Lindgren, A.-R. (2010) Scandinavia. In J.A. Fishman and O. García (eds) *Handbook of Language and Ethnic Identity: Disciplinary and Regional Perspectives* (pp. 255–268). Oxford: Oxford University Press.

Janson, K. (1874) *Skildringar fraa Nordland og Finnmorki [Reports from Nordland and Finnmark]*. Bergen: Giertsen.

Jensen, L.C. and Hønneland, G. (2011) Framing the High North. Public discourses in Norway after 2000. *Acta Borealia* 28 (1), 37–54.

Johansen, Å.M. (2013) Overcoming silence. Language emancipation in a costal Sámi-Norwegian community. *Sociolinguistic Studies* 7 (1/2), 57–77.

Lane, P. (2010) "We did what we thought was best for our children." A Nexus analysis of language shift in a Kven community. *International Journal of the Sociology of Language* 202, 62–78.

Lane, P. (2015) Minority language standardisation and the role of users. *Language Policy* 14 (3), 263–283.
Lane, P. and Räisänen, A.K. (2017) Kven in Norway. In C.A. Seals and S. Shah (eds) *Heritage Language Policies Around the World (pp.* 69–83). London: Routledge.
Lemke, J.L. (2000) Across the scales of time. Artifacts, activities, and meanings in ecosocial systems. *Mind, Culture, and Activity* 7 (4), 273–290.
Lønnsmann, D. and Kraft, K. (2018) Language in blue-collar workplaces. In B. Vine (ed.) *The Routledge Handbook of Language in the Workplace* (pp. 138–149). London: Routledge.
Marx, K. (1867) *Das Kapital. Kritik der politischen Oekonomi [Capital. Critique of Political Economy]*. Hamburg: Verlag von Otto Meissner.
Meeuwis, M. (2011) Bilingual inequality. Linguistic rights and disenfranchisement in late Belgian colonization. *Journal of Pragmatics* 43 (5), 1279–1287.
Nevalainen, T. (2015) What are historical sociolinguistics? *Journal of Historical Sociolinguistics* 1 (2), 243–269.
Nielsen, J.P. (1995) *Altas historie. Bind 2. Det arktiske Italia 1826–1920 [Alta's History. Volume 2. The Arctic Italy 1826–1920]*. Alta: Alta kommune.
Niemi, E. (2003) Kvenene i nord. Ressurs eller trussel? [The Kvens in the North. Resource or threat?]. In E. Niemi, J.E. Myhre and K. Kjeldstadli (eds) *Norsk innvandringshistorie. Bind 2. I nasjonalstatens tid 1814–1940* (pp. 128–146). Oslo: Pax.
Niemi, E. (2008) Kategorienes etikk og minoritetene i nord. Et historisk perspektiv [The ethics of categories and the minorities in the North. A historical perspective]. In F. Fagertun (ed.) *Veiviser i det mangfoldige nord. Utvalgte artikler av Einar Niemi* (pp. 169–182). Stamsund: Orkana.
Olsen, K. (2007) When ethnic identity is a private matter. *Journal of Ethnology and Folkloristics* 1 (1), 75–99.
Pietikäinen, S. and Kelly-Holmes, H. (eds) (2013) *Multilingualism and the Periphery*. Oxford: Oxford University Press.
Pietikäinen, S., Huss, L., Laihiala-Kankainen, S., Aikio-Puoskari, U. and Lane, P. (2010) Regulating multilingualism in the North Calotte: The case of Kven, Meänkieli and Sámi languages. *Acta Borealia* 27 (1), 1–23.
Rasmussen, T. and Nolan, J.S. (2011) Reclaiming Sámi languages: Indigenous language emancipation from East to West. *International Journal of the Sociology of Language* 209, 35–55.
Røvik, K.A., Jentoft, S. and Nergård, J.-I. (2011) Nord-Norge. Fra utkant til global arena [Northern Norway. From periphery to global arena]. In S. Jentoft, J.-I. Nergård and K.A. Røvik (eds) *Hvor går Nord-Norge? Tidsbilder fra en landsdel i forandring* (pp. 13–22). Stamsund: Orkana.
Scollon, R. (2008) Discourse itineraries: Nine processes of resemiotization. In V.K. Bathia, J. Flowerdew and R.H. Jones (eds) *Advances in Discourse Studies* (pp. 233–244). London: Routledge.
Scollon, R. and Scollon, S.W. (2004) *Nexus Analysis: Discourse and the Emerging Internet*. London: Routledge.
Sherover, C.M. (1991) Some dimensions of "heritage". *Research in Phenomenology* 21 (36), 36–47.
Silverstein, M. and Urban, G. (1996) The natural history of discourse. In M. Silverstein and G. Urban (eds) *Natural Histories of Discourse* (pp. 1–20). Chicago: The University of Chicago Press.
Simons, G.F. and Fennig, C.D. (eds) (2017) *Ethnologue: Languages of the World* (12th edn). Dallas: SIL International. http://www.ethnologue.com.
Statistics Norway (2022) StatBank Norway. https://www.ssb.no/en/statbank.
Thomas, N. (1994) *Colonialism's Culture. Anthropology, Travel and Government*. Cambridge: Polity Press.

3 'Doctor Johnny': The Discursive Construction of the Medical Doctor as an Immigrant

Nóra Schleicher

Introduction

The following case study analyses the televised representation of a migrant medical doctor of Nigerian origin, who is an L2 speaker of Hungarian. 'Doctor Johnny', working as a general practitioner (GP) in a village in Hungary, was introduced to viewers on 18 February 2015 on the evening newsmagazine of the most popular commercial TV channel of Hungary, RTL Klub.[1] The study aims to understand the construction of the figure of the migrant within the methodological framework of critical multimodal discourse analysis. It asks the question of why the migrant doctor was constructed as he was in the programme, with the aim of better understanding the use of the migrant figure in contemporary discourse and the ideological underpinnings influencing this usage.

Previous studies on the representation of migration and migrants in mediatised discourse often turned to theories of securitisation (Huysmans, 2006; Ibrahim, 2005; Rheindorf & Wodak, 2018; Vezovnik, 2018) and moral panic (Barlai & Sik, 2017; Morgan & Poynting, 2016) to make sense of the data. While these theoretical approaches informed my research in fruitful ways, the inclusion of media theories of agenda setting (McCombs & Shaw, 1972; McCombs et al., 2013) and framing (Entman, 2010) in the analytical framework offered a more complex understanding of my case.

In what follows, I first outline these theoretical underpinnings in more detail and offer a brief history of the societal background of my case. This is followed by a description of the methodological framework and the actual methods of data collection and analysis. I first offer a detailed multimodal analysis of the short video report. In the second part of the analysis, I place this televised piece into the wider social-discursive context to uncover the interconnection of meanings that influenced the production and possible interpretations of the programme. In the conclusion, I return to my research question and consider the possible role of the figure of the migrant in contemporary discourse.

Theoretical and Societal Background

The securitisation of migration is one of the dominant discourses across the western world today (see e.g. Buzan *et al.*, 1998; Huysmans, 2006). According to Buzan *et al.* (1998), securitisation acts require a securitising actor or agent, an existential threat, a referent object and an audience. Within the framework of securitisation, migrants, among others, can be identified as posing an existential threat. The nation appears as the threatened ideal that needs to be protected. The voters, who are often addressed as the audience in today's mediatised world, need to be convinced to support the securitising agent, usually the state, and its representatives. By overstating the threat, the aim is to justify any measures deemed necessary to fight migration.

The political campaign that preceded the 2018 Hungarian parliamentary elections was dominated by one issue: migration. The ruling right-wing party Fidesz, which consequently won the election by a two-thirds majority, successfully set the agenda for the political discourse. The threat of migration has been the key element of the Hungarian government's propaganda since the terrorist attack against the satirical weekly paper *Charlie Hebdo*, which took place on 7 January 2015 in Paris. The number of migrants in Hungary is much lower than in most European countries (Eurostat, 2018). Furthermore, since installing a fence around Hungary's southern border in the summer of 2015, it has been more difficult for migrants to enter the country. Nevertheless, Prime Minister Viktor Orbán and his government successfully convinced the majority of Hungarians that migration poses a threat to national security, a problem which can be combated only by him and his party (Wodak, 2021).

As part of a nationwide government campaign, the following billboard (among many) carried the message of the government to the people.

The billboard depicted in Figure 3.1 is a good example of how the securitisation of migration appears in practice. The message explicitly connects immigration with the threat of terrorism; designates the whole country as the target of the threat; and refers to 'the people' in general, who were 'consulted with' to legitimise actions of defence. The highly biased public service media (Freedom House, 2018) and government-sponsored media campaigns played crucial roles in the demonisation of migrants in Hungary (Barlai & Sík, 2017; Bernáth & Messing, 2015).

Cohen (2011), in his classic account of moral panic, called attention to the paramount role media can play in building up and spreading this

Translation: On top: Government information. Main body: The people decided: The country needs to be defended. On bottom: National Consultation about immigration and terrorism (all translations in this chapter are the author's).

Figure 3.1 Billboard of the Hungarian government

discourse of fear. According to Cohen, moral panics regularly emerge in societies when certain episodes, persons or groups appear to threaten certain social values or interests. Media build on these fears by stereotyping and exaggerating the presumed threat. The moral panic can lead to the demonisation of the given condition, person or group, hindering rational debate around the issue. Migrants from outside Europe, a group that the overwhelming majority of Hungarians had no first-hand experience with, proved to be an ideal object for the creation of moral panic. Due to Hungarians' lack of real experience, mass media could play an important role in the construction of the threatening migrant figure. Somewhat unusually, this specific moral panic was created from above. The agenda was set by the Prime Minister himself, and the majority of the media just followed suit (Bernáth & Messing, 2015).

The TV programme, which is the focus of this chapter, proves that there were attempts to resist this dominant discourse, to change the agenda and the frame set by the government propaganda, and to create a counter-discourse by reconstructing the migrant as a positive figure. The struggle to define the agenda and the frame of interpretation creates an important backdrop for my case. Agenda setting and framing theories, which consider mediatised discourse important in influencing people's mindsets, can serve as useful theoretical underpinnings for making sense of this struggle.

The agenda setting function of the media has already been highlighted by such early theorists as McCombs and Shaw (1972) (see also McCombs *et al.*, 2013). They claimed that while the media may not be successful in telling people what to think, they are successful in telling people what to think about by highlighting certain issues at the expense of others. Agenda setting theory also highlights the potential clash between the various interests of the politicians, the media and the public, which can result in a fight over setting the agenda. Framing theory, sometimes also called the second level of agenda setting (McCombs, 2004), is said to have originated from the ground-breaking work of Goffman (1974) on Frame Theory and goes a step further in claiming that the way a piece of news is framed influences the cognitive processing of the information it carries. Thus, the media have an influence not only on what the audience should think about but also on how they should think about the given issue. Frames are built on subtle cues that direct interpretation. It is thus not surprising that framing theory has been effectively used in discourse analysis (e.g. Tannen, 1993) and in media analysis (e.g. Entman, 2010) with the aim of understanding how reality is constructed. Within my field of interest, a similar approach has been used. Lupton and McLean (1998), for example, applied critical discourse analysis to study the representation of doctors in Australian newspapers and news magazines. Similarly, Lünenborg and Fürsich (2014) carried out intersectional analyses to study the representation of migrant women in German television.

Methodology and Methods

In order to gain an in-depth, holistic understanding of the mediatised construction of the migrant doctor, case study was chosen as a general research strategy. Robson (2002: 178) defines case study as a research strategy which examines a particular phenomenon within its real-life context and uses diverse sources of evidence to reveal the complexity of the case. Within this general research strategy, I used critical analysis of multimodal discourse (Van Leeuwen, 2013) in combination with the analysis of narrative networks (Gimenez, 2010).

In the first part of the analysis, I focus on a piece of televised representation of a migrant doctor working in Hungary. The story was broadcast on the 18 February 2015, on the evening newsmagazine Focus, which runs every weekday on the most popular commercial TV channel of Hungary, RTL Klub. Multimodal analysis was deemed necessary in order to gain an understanding of how language, visual images and music work together to create meaning. Kress and Van Leeuwen (2001) label language, images and music, among others, as *modes*. Modes are 'semiotic resources which allow the simultaneous realisation of discourses and types of (inter)action' (Kress & Van Leeuwen, 2001: 21). The semiotic choices made within the different modes interact with each other, resulting in intersemiosis, which creates a 'complex multidimensional semantic space' (O'Halloran, 2011: 126). Understanding this space is the first task of my analysis. To achieve that, I examine the choice of topics, interview subjects, semantic choices, as well as the choice of visual images and music as they work together to create meaning.

A close reading of the programme, focusing on the interplay of the different semiotic modes, can lead to an understanding of the manifest meaning, and shows us how the figure of the migrant doctor is constructed. However, as my aim is to uncover the ideological underpinnings of the examined media product and to understand not only the 'how' but also the 'why' behind the construction of the migrant, a critical discourse analytical approach was deemed appropriate. This meant moving from the actual programme towards the wider social-discursive context in which it was produced. Issues emerging from the analysis of the programme directed attention towards certain key elements of this social-discursive context.

Gimenez's (2010) concept of narrative networks provided a useful analytical framework for creating connections between the issues emerging from the analysis of the programme and the key issues of its social-discursive context. Gimenez (2010: 206–207) defines narrative network as 'a group of stories, texts and artefacts collected around the emerging issues in a core narrative'. He differentiates between two grand traditions of narrative analysis: the componential approach, looking at structural regularities of narratives; and the functional approach, which examines the purpose of narratives. He places his approach of narrative networks within the functional tradition, as it helps us understand the wider social function of narratives, and within the critical discourse analytical tradition, as his assumption is that stories always reflect more macro level social meanings which can be best understood if we analyse the relationship between the issues emerging from the core narrative with other stories, texts and artefacts reflecting these issues within the wider social context. The analysis of the emerging network helps us understand the more latent meaning of our key text. Thus, in the second part of the analysis I identify the key elements of the social-discursive context and choose such texts and artefacts that I consider to be representative examples of them. At the next step, I connect these texts and artefacts with the narrative that emerged from the programme and analyse the complex connections between them in order to gain a deeper understanding of the reasons behind the construction of the figure of the migrant medical worker.

Analysis, Part 1

RTL Klub, active in Hungary since 1997, is a member of the international media conglomerate RLT Group, which operates channels across Europe. Its newsmagazine, Focus, fits into the infotainment genres typical of the world of commercial television, with alternating lighter and more serious content presented to the viewers in an entertaining, easily accessible manner. In the examined programme, language, visual images and music work together to create meaning. The close reading and the multimodal analysis reveal how the programme constructs the figure of the migrant doctor. Doctor Johnny, a Black man of Nigerian origin and an L2 speaker of Hungarian, was introduced to the viewers by the anchor. While we hear the introduction, we can also see the doctor on the split screen. The lead captures the essence of the 5-minute 36-second piece:

Excerpt 1
In the poorest settlement of Hungary, patients are served by a doctor who came from Nigeria. Doctor Johnny has lived with us for 25 years. For 10 years he has been serving in Borsod, the poorest region of the country. He has four children and a wife. And, of course, plenty of patients, to whom he sometimes needs to give medicine on credit.[2]

Naming the protagonist *Doctor Johnny* can serve to capture the attention of the audience. The foreign first name labels the man as non-Hungarian, and its juxtaposition with the title *doctor* creates meaning through its unusualness. The positively polite act of naming the man Doctor Johnny is patronising and friendly at the same time, marking the doctor as different (foreign name), perhaps inferior (diminutive suffix), but also, with affection, one of us. The other, somewhat unusual and thus marked linguistic element here is that Dr Johnny does not simply work as a doctor, but he is *serving* his patients (*szolgálatot teljesít*). The choice of the phrase, with connotations of altruism and hardship, elevates the medical profession to a moral level.

Calling attention to the doctor's family, his wife and his children, and to the fact that he has lived *with us* (*nálunk*) for a long time, serves to emphasise his integration into the host community. In the lead, Dr Johnny is thus framed as Black, Nigerian, a settled family man, a doctor and a helper of the poor in Hungary. A little later he is also labelled as an economic migrant:

Excerpt 2
John xxx [full name is given in the original] is a Nigerian doctor. He has been curing patients here for 10 years. Today we would say that he came to the country as an economic migrant.

The term 'economic migrant' is mentioned with explicit reference to a relatively new political discourse in Hungary, which uses the term in an undifferentiated and pejorative way to refer to all recent refugees wanting to enter the country[3] (Bernáth & Messing, 2015). At the same time, the programme distances itself from this stance as attention is directed to the fact that this term, with all the negative connotations attached to it lately, was not even in use when the doctor arrived in the country a long time ago.

In the rest of the programme, the protagonist is constructed primarily through his profession. The visual construction of the medical doctor is straightforward, as symbolic signs of the profession are universally well

Figures 3.2–3.3 Visual construction of the medical profession[4]

known. We see Dr Johnny in a white coat while examining patients (see Figures 3.2 and 3.3), writing prescriptions, etc.

He is also constructed linguistically as a doctor. We can hear him diagnosing the sick children. He does not, however, talk to them, but addresses his words to the invisible reporter:

Excerpt 3

Dr Johnny: (s)he has constipation and sore- sore throat. Somehow (s)he must have caught a cold.
Image: prescriptions
Dr Johnny: S- so I'm prescribing medicines <incorrect suffix> and and eye eye drops bec-because (s)he has pink eyes <incorrect pronunciation of vowels> too.
Image: giving prescriptions to mother holding a child

Although we can rarely hear the doctor speaking in the programme (he speaks three times, never once saying more than two sentences), we can notice that he speaks fluent Hungarian with an audible non-standard accent and occasional minor grammatical mistakes. His speech is also characterised by frequent hesitations and false starts, suggesting he is searching for the right words. In the programme's narrative, Dr Johnny is thus constructed visually and linguistically as Black, coming from Nigeria; someone who would today be called an economic migrant, but also someone who speaks the language of the host community, and has established a family and settled down in the country. More importantly, he is a doctor who is here to help the poor, and especially the poor children, in Hungary.

The theme of poverty already appears in the lead (*And, of course, plenty of patients, to whom he sometimes needs to give medicine on credit*). Aside from the doctor, seven other people (the mayor, four men and a woman from the village, and the mother of a child patient of the doctor) are interviewed briefly. Five of them talk about poverty without any mention of the doctor at all. In spite of the title, it is not the doctor who plays the major role in the analysed piece. In fact, he is only on screen for 2:57 minutes out of the 5:36. Throughout the report, more time and thus more emphasis is given to the theme of poverty. Music, visual images, interviews with the locals and statistical information offered by the voice-over are all used to depict the depth of poverty in Hungary, and specifically in the two villages where the doctor works.

Visual signifiers of poverty appear from the very beginning of the programme (see Figures 3.4–3.6). We can see deserted villages where people can walk in the middle of the road, for lack of traffic. The trees cut down, as the voiceover explains, are the result of illegal logging for heating, suggesting that the inhabitants have no money for more expensive forms of energy. The written sign photographed in the mayor's office says that from the middle of the month one can apply for advance payment from next month's social benefit to the limit of maximum 5000 HUF (approximately 15 EUR). This extremely small amount, which is still clearly needed for survival, points to the depth of poverty experienced in this region of the country.

Slow, melancholic music accompanies the images signifying poverty. First, we can hear a few beats from the song 'Bajba, Bajba, Pélem' (I Got in Trouble) by Monika Miczura Juhász, a Hungarian Roma singer and previous member of the Roma music ensemble Ando Drom, which means 'on the road' in Romani language. Later, a few beats from 'Etno Camp', composed and played by Hungarian violinist Félix Lajkó, accompany images of poverty. Violin is a traditional musical instrument linked to Hungarian Roma culture, and Lajkó often turns towards Roma music for inspiration. The few audible lines from the Romani song and the violin music by Lajkó give emotional emphasis to the images. Both can also evoke Roma ethnicity. Roma is the largest ethnic minority in Hungary,[5] whose members are overrepresented among the poorest segments of the society.[6] Roma people are frequently used by Hungarian media as signifiers of poverty (Bernáth & Messing, 2012). Music linked to the community can unconsciously evoke images of this ethnicity and, through that, images of deep rural poverty.

The two settlements in which the doctor works are introduced to the viewers as being among the poorest ones in the country. Statistical data are given on unemployment and criminal activity rates and emigration:

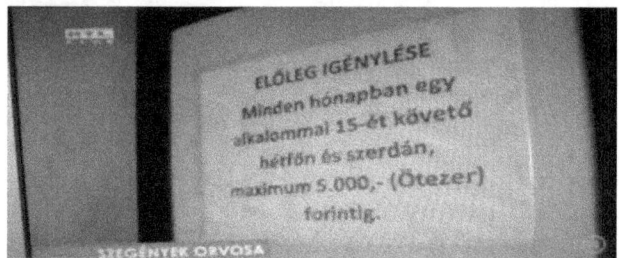

Figures 3.4–3.6 Visual signifiers of poverty

Excerpt 4

Voice over: Communal work is only available for 60–80 people. About 300 people are looking for a job, while 150 people are working abroad.

The issue of emigration from the villages is thematised further in short interviews in which inhabitants of the villages are asked what they do, how much they earn, and how they manage. We learn that those who go to work abroad can earn five times as much as those working in the village.

We now see the two topics connected; the Black African doctor is curing and helping the poor Hungarians who are ill. The subtitle *Doctor of the poor (szegények orvosa)* serves to emphasise this connection,

Figures 3.7–3.8 Visual signifiers of 'the doctor of the poor'

constructed visually by images where we can see the doctor in an emphatically poverty-ridden environment, walking with his assistant to visit his patients or inside the patients' crowded, poor homes, while examining them (see Figure 3.7). The shelf, for example, filmed in the home of a family visited by the doctor, signifies lack of sufficient nourishment (see Figure 3.8). The moral of the story is explicitly stated by the voice-over:

Excerpt 5
Voice-over: We meet a man[7].[strong emphasis]
Image: doctor from behind in white coat; patient entering the room
Voice-over: who helps people living on social assistance if they fall ill.
Music: few beats of trumpet music

Visual, linguistic and musical elements are used to emphasise that the doctor is a true human being with empathy, a real helper of the poor. He does not only cure people; he also gives medicine on credit, as we learn from an interview with the young mother of one of his patients. This element is used to depict the goodness of the doctor as well as to emphasise the depth of poverty in the village. Another interviewed patient says:

Excerpt 6
He is not a bad doctor. We are happy he is here, really.

The discourse marker *really* (*tényleg*) and the choice *not a bad* (*nem rossz*) instead of using the word 'good' signals that the interviewed subject believes the doctor is good in spite of the fact of being a foreigner and a Black immigrant.

The key moment arrives when Dr Johnny is filmed going by car from one of his villages to the other to visit his patients there. He is accompanied by the reporter who asks him the question which serves as the *raison d'être* of the whole programme:

Excerpt 7
Interview with doctor in car
Reporter: How could you compare Hungarian and Nigerian poverty?
Image: deserted landscape as seen from the car; doctor and reporter talking in the car.
Dr Johnny: The situation is similar (.) here and there too.

The similarity between poverty in Hungary and poverty in Nigeria is highlighted. The message is clear: Hungary has become so poor that we need the help of someone who, through his skin colour, origin and immigrant status, symbolises poverty itself. We are poorer than the poorest.

The image of the economic migrant, who is dangerous, parasitic, does not want to work or steals the work of Hungarians (as one of the billboards in the anti-migrant campaign claimed), is clearly refuted here (cf. Barlai & Sík, 2017). Instead, a very positive image of the useful economic migrant is being created, who not only speaks the language of his host country fluently but also performs a very important, much needed role in the community. Aside from introducing the migrant doctor, this short programme manages to raise the issues of poverty, emigration and the lack of doctors in the countryside.

Analysis, Part 2

In the second part of the analysis, I turn to the approach of narrative networks to study the wider social-discursive context of the programme. I start out from the issues raised in the analysed piece and identify key texts reflecting these issues. The texts below were found through a media search of the major online news portals around the period of the broadcast of the programme and were identified as examples of dominant discourses based on my familiarity with the social, political and cultural context; that is, my emic knowledge and insider status in the culture (Kirpitchenko & Voloder, 2014). The quotes from the texts that are analysed below represent patterns in the chosen texts. Next, I relate these key texts with the programme's narrative on Dr Johnny.

The first important text with explanatory power received wide coverage in Hungarian media. It is an example of a strongly anti-migrant discourse initiated from above, with heavy presence in the public service media, as documented by Bernáth and Messing (2015). Its first appearance in Hungary can be connected to an important pronouncement of the Hungarian prime minister, made after the Charlie Hebdo attack, about a month before the analysed film was broadcast. Very shortly after the attack, Prime Minister Viktor Orbán claimed that:

Excerpt 8
Economic immigration is a bad thing in Europe, we should not look at it as if it had any use, because it only brings trouble and evil to the European man, so immigration has to be stopped, this is the Hungarian position (...) We do not want to see significant minorities among us having different cultural characteristics and backgrounds from ours. We would like to keep Hungary as Hungary. (MTI, 2015)

The nation is defined as culturally homogenous, and anyone with a different cultural background poses a threat to nationhood itself. This narrative has proved to be so successful that, since then, it has dominated the agenda of the governing right-wing coalition. The anti-migrant discourse is consistently set within a securitisation frame. The analysed programme can be considered a response to this approach, questioning and resisting the interpretation of migration as threat.

The second text reflects on the issue of poverty raised by the programme. While the first text set the tone for government communication, this one characterises the agenda of the opposition. Poverty was thematised in relation to new statistical data published by Eurostat (2015), which came out a few months before the film, and which were widely covered by various Hungarian media outlets, including 444.hu where the excerpt below is taken from:

Excerpt 9
According to information from Eurostat, one-third of Hungarians have less than 65,000 Ft per month. Since the beginning of the crisis, in the last 5 years poverty has continuously increased. There are half a million more poor people living in the country now than in 2008; last year, too, the number of poor people grew by 100,000.

Both the source of the information and the hard numbers quoted frame the issue as objective and unquestionably real. The government does not, however, want to see this issue on the political agenda and treats it as taboo. This is well exemplified by an email sent by the Ministry of Human Resources to its employees, which was leaked to the media on the same day when the analysed television programme was broadcast. The email, quoted by vs.hu, forbade employees to use specific words and phrases, including poverty, deep poverty and child poverty:

Excerpt 10
Employees of the Ministry of Human Resources (...) received an internal e-mail: in the e-mail (...) words and phrases are listed, page after page, which 'cannot be used in communication with each other or with beneficiaries'. (...) Among the objectionable phrases we can find (...) words like poor, poverty, deep poverty, child poverty (...).

The two examples above represent the political fight over setting the discursive agenda. Discussion of poverty within Hungary is clearly uncomfortable for those in power, who try to make the problem disappear by simply not talking about it. Opposition parties, some civil organisations, and journalists, on the other hand, try to keep the issue on the agenda. The analysed television programme takes a clear stand in this fight by depicting the depth of poverty in the Hungarian countryside. What is more, the programme frames the issue with the symbolic help of the figure of the migrant, who is used by government propaganda with exactly the opposite objective, to distract attention from deprivation.

Finally, the third important issue raised by the programme is the shortage of doctors in Hungary, resulting in the fact that Dr Johnny has to serve in two different villages at the same time, and occasionally treats more than 100 patients in one day. This fits into a narrative describing the continuing emigration of Hungarian doctors and nurses. Opposition parties and some media outlets, including RTL Klub, keep this issue on the agenda, often incorporated within a wider discussion of the dire situation of the Hungarian health care sector; meanwhile, government representatives attempt to deny this. Just two weeks before the analysed programme was broadcast, the emigration of Hungarian doctors made its way into the headlines of the evening news of RTL Klub,[8] and into international news too.[9] On the 30 January 2015, one of the leading political weeklies, HVG.hu, placed the issue into political context, giving the following headline for an article on emigrating doctors:

Excerpt 11
Although Viktor Orbán announced already last year that they had stopped doctor-emigration, in reality the number of emigrating doctors has not decreased.

The strange compound word, *doctor-emigration* (*orvoselvándorlás*) frames the issue as a stabilised, thus grave, phenomenon and not simply a momentary, minor problem.

The continuous emigration of Hungarians, including Hungarian doctors, in hopes of a better life abroad, can be used to contest discourses condemning economic immigration. It is thus connected to both the issue of immigration through opposition and the issue of poverty through causality.

The mediatised construction of Doctor Johnny can only be fully understood within this social-discursive context exemplified by the network of narratives described above. The figure of the Black doctor is useful in enabling the TV channel to question, challenge and refute the anti-immigrant discourse of the government, and to remind people about the problem of the emigration of Hungarian doctors, who are themselves economic migrants just like Dr Johnny. It creates an opportunity to visualise deep poverty in Hungary with the help of strong symbolic elements evoking associations between Nigeria and Hungary.

The picture would not be complete, however, without understanding the political economy influencing the situation of the internationally-owned commercial TV channel within the Hungarian media landscape. Profit-oriented commercial media aiming for high ratings to achieve high revenues from advertisements do not typically take sides in political debates, as they do not want to alienate members of their audience (Hardy, 2008). However, even neutral infotainment can be considered hostile in an environment which requires a government-friendly approach from all journalists. In 2014, a new law (Lex RTL) levied taxes on the advertisement revenues of commercial media. Soon after its ratification, the law was modified in a way which singled out RTL Klub as its main target. The channel (RTL Klub, 2014) termed the law 'Lex RTL Klub' and interpreted

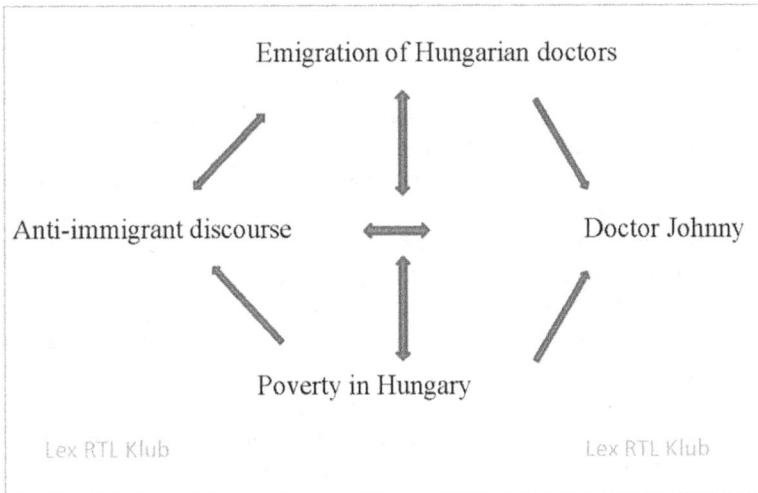

Figure 3.9 The network of narratives surrounding the programme in focus

it as a government attack against freedom of speech. The channel resisted the economic pressure and became visibly more focused on political issues.

Figure 3.9. illustrates the complex connections among the earlier-described narratives. One-way arrows represent unidirectional connections. Anti-immigrant discourse is used to divert attention away from discourses of poverty. The mediatised representation of Doctor Johnny calls attention to the shortage of Hungarian doctors caused by their emigration and symbolises the depth of poverty in the Hungarian countryside besides creating a counter-narrative to the anti-immigrant discourse of the government. Two-way arrows are used to represent mutual connections. Anti-immigrant discourses and discourses on the emigration of Hungarians are in conversation with each other through their similarity and difference. The emigration of the Hungarian doctors can be framed both as a result and consequence of and a contributing factor to the poverty of the country. Lex RTL Klub serves as a backdrop to the case influencing the TV channel's take on the issues.

In sum, the analysis of the programme and its social-discursive context revealed a manifest message of the report which refuted the bad and dangerous migrant image by constructing the good and helpful figure of the medical doctor, and a latent message which used the same figure to emphasise the depth of poverty in Hungary.

Conclusion

In recent years the topic of migration has dominated the agenda of the interconnected political and media landscape of Hungary. The study presented here has posed the question of how the figure of the migrant is constructed in this context. The dominant discourse presents migration within the framework of securitisation. A growing body of literature has recognised and analysed this phenomenon. The programme in focus seemingly fits in the agenda by presenting a counter discourse, focusing on the economically useful migrant figure who linguistically integrated into the host community and also represents such general human values as goodness and empathy.

The in-depth analysis that intertwined the programme's narrative with other key texts, however, revealed that the figure of the migrant was used in order to highlight a different issue: the depth of poverty in Hungary. The choice of a Black immigrant from Nigeria was not accidental, as it offered the opportunity for comparison through associations. Poverty, runs the subliminal message of the programme, is as bad in Hungary as in Sub-Saharan Africa.

The choice of the profession of the migrant is not accidental either. The figure of the doctor can play multiple roles. On the one hand, it implicitly highlights the issue of emigration from Hungary and the resulting lack of medical workers in the country. The programme conveys that the situation in the Hungarian health care sector is so bad that the country needs doctors from Africa to cure the ill in the impoverished countryside. On the other hand, the choice of the doctor is also helpful in constructing a figure of authority and knowledge whose word can be trusted, but at the same time is a loveable and relatable figure whose main job is to help and cure, and whose altruism and empathy can thus be highlighted. The positive migrant figure is much easier to construct through the figure of the doctor than, for example, through the figure of the unskilled migrant labourer or the rich entrepreneur migrant (cf. Allan, 2013; Kerekes, 2017). The intersecting ethnic, professional and migrant identity of Doctor Johnny thus serves the ideological aim of the programme perfectly. By framing the migrant doctor as a symbol of poverty, it successfully changes the agenda and resists the moral panic built around the issue of migration. But what makes the migrant figure so suitable for this role? Georg Simmel (1950: 402), in his classic essay, defines *The Stranger* as follows:

> The stranger is thus being discussed here, not in the sense often touched upon in the past, as the wanderer who comes today and goes tomorrow, but rather as the person who comes today and stays tomorrow.

The Stranger – Simmel argues – is characterised by closeness and remoteness at the same time. These characteristics make him especially fit for certain roles. He is an ideal recipient of confessions, which he understands through his closeness to the host community and can guard through his remoteness from it. This same closeness and remoteness make him ideal for forming objective and trusted opinions of the host community. Doctor Johnny, who has lived in Hungary for 25 years and speaks and understands Hungarian, but whose origin and skin colour will always mark him as different, is a perfect representation of the Stranger. His profession and his knowledge of the local language make him a recipient of confessions of illness and deprivation; he can see into the depth of poverty and form objective opinions about the situation. But, as Simmel highlights, the Stranger is never marked with his individual characteristics. He is similar to us, sharing with us the collective human identity, and different from us, sharing with other groups collective identities of race, language or religion. He is never just himself. He represents either humankind (cf. 'We meet a man') or the general Other (cf. 'having different cultural characteristics and backgrounds from us'). It is exactly this lack of personal characteristics that renders this figure so suitable for use in various signification processes.

In the analysed programme, the doctor is not asked to tell his story to the viewers; hardly anything is known about his life and experience. His figure is used in an attempt to change the political agenda, by calling attention to the issue of poverty and the situation of health care. The more frequently used and well-described securitisation frame also uses the figure of the migrant, although with a different aim (Huysmans, 2006; Ibrahim, 2005; Rheindorf & Wodak, 2018; Vezovnik, 2018): it is used to represent a general existential threat against which only the present rulers can defend the nation. While the two agendas are not equally valid and not equally anchored in reality, they are similar in the ways they use the figure of the migrant and the issue of migration in order to achieve various aims that are not at all connected to the complex empirical reality of the individual migrant workers' lives and experiences. The archetypal figure of the Stranger, which is best represented in today's world by the figure of the migrant, is ideal for this role. This study shows how various general characteristics of the Stranger (e.g. his profession, ethnicity or origin) can be used as signs in an attempt to frame issues and guide interpretation.

The case study, which served as a general framework for the research, offers an in-depth understanding of a phenomenon, but also has its limitations. These are mainly related to the generalisability of the findings and the subjectivity of sample choice. While results from this study suggest that discourses on migration simply use migrants as a pretext in order to focus attention on other issues, further research based on a wider and more representative sample of mediatised discourse is needed to confirm that. Further research is also needed to reveal how, in contexts different from the one described here, the figure of the migrant is constructed, and for what purposes it is used.

Appendix: Original Excerpts

Excerpt 1
Magyarország legszegényebb településén egy Nigériából jött orvos látja el a betegeket. Doktor Johnny 25 éve él nálunk. 10 éve az ország legszegényebb régiójának számító Borsodban teljesít szolgálatot. 4 gyereke van és egy felesége. Na meg rengeteg betege, akiknek néha hitelbe kénytelen adni a gyógyszert.

Excerpt 2
John xxx [teljes név] nigériai orvos. 10 éve gyógyítja itt a betegeket. Ma úgy mondanánk, annak idején gazdasági bevándorlóként jött az országba.

Excerpt 3
Dr. Johnny: székrekedése van meg a tork- torokgyulladása van. Valahogy megfázhatott.
Dr Johnny: az- azért írok a gyógyszerekt, meg a szem szemcseppet is mer kotohártya gyulladása is van.

Excerpt 4
Bemondó: Közmunka csak 60-80 embernek jut. Körülbelül 300 keres munkát, 150 pedig külföldön dolgozik.

Excerpt 5
Voice-over: Találkozunk egy emberrel.
Voice over: aki segít, ha a segélyből élő emberek megbetegednének.

Excerpt 6
Nem rossz orvos. Örülünk, hogy itt van, tényleg.

Excerpt 7.
Riporter: Hogy tudnád összehasonlítani a magyar szegénységet és a nigériai szegénységet?
Dr Johnny: hasonló a helyzet (.) itt is meg ott is

Excerpt 8
'A gazdasági bevándorlás rossz dolog Európában, nem szabad úgy tekinteni rá, mintha annak bármi haszna is lenne, mert csak bajt és veszedelmet hoz az európai emberre, ezért a bevándorlást meg kell állítani, ez a magyar álláspont. (...) Nem akarunk tőlünk különböző kulturális tulajdonságokkal és háttérrel rendelkező jelentős kisebbséget látni magunk között, Magyarországot szeretnénk Magyarországként megtartani' (MTI, 2015)

Excerpt 9.
'Bár Orbán Viktor már tavaly bejelentette, hogy megállították az orvoselvándorlást, a kivándorló orvosok száma valójában nem csökkent'. *HVG.hu*, 30th Jan. 2015 https://hvg.hu/itthon/20150130_Kozel_ezer_magyar_orvos_ment_kulfoldre_ta

Excerpt 10
'Az Eurostat tájékoztatása szerint a magyarok harmadának havi 65 ezer forintja sincs. A válság kitörése óta, az elmúlt öt évben folyamatosan nő a szegénység. Most félmillióval több szegény él az országban, mint 2008-ban, tavaly is százezerrel nőtt a szegények száma'.
Király András, *444.hu*, 3rd Oct. 2014 https://444.hu/2014/10/03/nincs-penze-a-ksh-nak-a-szegenysegi-statisztikara

Excerpt 11
'Belső e-mailt kaptak az Emberi Erőforrások Minisztériumának (...) munkatársai: a levélben (...) oldalakon keresztül sorolják azokat a szavakat és kifejezéseket, amelyek "nem használhatók az egymás közötti, illetve a kedvezményezettekkel folytatott kommunikációban". ... A nemkívánatos kifejezések között (...) vannak, mint szegény, szegénység, mélyszegénység, gyermekszegénység ...' *vs*.hu, 18th Febr. 2015. https://vs.hu/kozelet/osszes/az-emmi-dolgozoinak-tilos-kimondaniuk-hogy-stadion-es-szegenyseg-0218

Notes

(1) Fókusz: Nigériából jött, a legszegényebbeknek segít. (He came from Nigeria and helps the poorest). A report by Géza Polgár. *RTL Klub*, 18 February 2015. http://rtl.hu/rtlklub/fokusz/nigeriabol-jott-a-legszegenyebbeken-segit.
(2) All the original (before translation) Hungarian excerpts are available in the Appendix. If not marked otherwise, excerpts are from the analysed video report.
(3) The terms most often used in government propaganda and government-friendly media to describe the people who arrived at the Hungarian border following the 2015 refugee

crisis are: '*gazdasági bevándorló*' and '*megélhetési bevándorló*' (both usually translated into English as economic migrant, but the first is seemingly neutral and only contextual usage renders it pejorative, while the second is clearly pejorative due to its complicated intertextual history); '*migráns*' (migrant) which, due to its foreign sounding and contextual use, is also highly pejorative; and '*illegális bevándorló*' (illegal migrant). The terms '*menekült*' (refugee) and '*menedék kérő*' (asylum seeker) were avoided in these contexts. (For a detailed analysis see Bernáth & Messing, 2015.)

(4) All the screenshots are from the analysed video report which is available in the online archive of RTL Klub at http://rtl.hu/rtlklub/fokusz/nigeriabol-jott-a-legszegenyebbeken-segit.

(5) The Hungarian Roma people do not form a unified, homogeneous group; there are at least three linguistically and culturally different Roma groups living within the geographical borders of the country.

(6) According to population statistics, 35% of the population of the first village and 94% of the population of the second village appearing in the programme are of Roma origin. Sources: https://hu.wikipedia.org/wiki/Als%C3%B3vad%C3%A1sz#Népcso portok; https://hu.wikipedia.org/wiki/Cseny%C3%A9te#Népcsoportok.

(7) The Hungarian word 'ember' translated here as 'man', is gender neutral.

(8) Híradó Még több orvos ment külföldre (Even more doctors went abroad). *RTL.hu*, 30 January 2015. http://rtl.hu/rtlklub/hirek/meg-tobb-orvos-ment-kulfoldre.

(9) On the 28 January 2015, *The Guardian* was also discussing the emigration of Hungarian doctors: '"Every day, for six years, three doctors and two nurses have left Hungary," János Bélteczki, head of the Hungarian Doctors' Association, says of the uphill struggle all the EU's central and eastern European countries face in trying to keep hold of their highly trained health workers'. Source: http://www.theguardian.com/society/2015/jan/28/-sp-hungary-india-doctors-nhs-recruitment-drive-effect.

References

Allan, K. (2013) Skilling the self: The communicability of immigrants as flexible labour. In A. Duchêne, M. Moyer and C. Roberts (eds) *Language, Migration and Social Inequalities: A Critical Sociolinguistic Perspective on Institutions and Work* (pp. 56–78). Bristol: Multilingual Matters.
Barlai, M. and Sík, E. (2017) A Hungarian trademark (a "Hungarikum"): The moral panic button. In M. Barlai, B. Fähnrich, C. Griessler and M. Rhomberg (eds) *The Migrant Crisis: European Perspectives and National Discourses* (pp. 147–169). Berlin: Lit Verlag.
Bernáth, G. and Messing, V. (2012) Szélre tolva [Pushed to the edge]. *Médiakutató* 2, 18–28.
Bernáth, G. and Messing, V. (2015) Bedarálva. A menekültekkel kapcsolatos kormányzati kampány és a tőle független megszólalás terepei [Crushed. The government campaign about refugees and the fields for independent speech]. *Médiakutató* 6 (4), 7–17.
Buzan, B., Waever, O. and de Wilde, J. (1998) *Security. A New Framework for Analysis.* Boulder, CO: Lynne Rienner.
Cohen, S. (2011) *Folk Devils and Moral Panics.* Abingdon: Routledge.
Entman, R.M. (2010) Media framing biases and political power: Explaining slant in news of Campaign 2008. *Journalism* 11 (4), 389–408.
Eurostat (2015) The risk of poverty or social exclusion affected 1 in 4 persons in the EU in 2014. http://ec.europa.eu/eurostat/documents/2995521/7034688/3-16102015-CP-EN.pdf.
Eurostat (2018) Migration and migrant population statistics. http://ec.europa.eu/eurostat/statistics-explained/index.php/Migration_and_migrant_population_statistics.
Freedom House (2018) Country report: Hungary. https://freedomhouse.org/country/hungary/freedom-world/2018.

Gimenez, J.C. (2010) Narrative analysis in linguistic research. In L. Litosseliti (ed.) *Research Methods in Linguistics* (pp. 198–215). New York: Continuum.
Goffman, E. (1974) *Frame Analysis*. New York: Harper & Row.
Hardy, J. (2008) *Western Media Systems*. London: Routledge.
Huysmans, J. (2006) *The Politics of Insecurity: Fear, Migration and Asylum in the EU*. New York: Routledge.
Ibrahim, M. (2005) The securitization of migration: A racial discourse. *International Migration* 43 (5), 163–187.
Kerekes, J. (2017) Language mentoring and employment ideologies: Internationally educated professionals in search of work. In J. Angouri, M. Marra, and J. Holmes (eds) *Negotiating Boundaries at Work. Talking and Transitions* (pp. 11–28). Edinburgh: Edinburgh University Press.
Kirpitchenko, L. and Voloder, L. (2014) Insider research method: The significance of identities in the field. In P. Brindle (ed.) *Sage Research Methods Cases* (pp. 1–18). Thousand Oaks, CA: SAGE.
Kress, G. and van Leeuwen, T. (2001) *Multimodal Discourse: The Modes and Media of Contemporary Communication*. London: Arnold.
Lex RTL - Az RTL Magyarország közleménye. *RTL Klub*, 30 June 2014. http://rtl.hu/rtlklub/hirek/belfold/cikkek/2014/06/30/lex_rtl_az_rtl_magyarszag_kozlemenye (accessed 21 June 2018).
Lupton, D. and McLean, J. (1998) Representing doctors: Discourses and images in the Australian press. *Social Science & Medicine* 46 (8), 947–958.
Lünenborg, M. and Fürsich, E. (2014) Media and the intersectional other: The complex negotiation of migration, gender, and class on German television. *Feminist Media Studies* 14 (6), 959–975.
Magyar Kormány [Hungarian Government] (2015) Official website of the national consultation on migration and terrorism. http://nemzetikonzultacio.kormany.hu/.
McCombs, M. (2004) *Setting the Agenda: The Mass Media and Public Opinion*. Cambridge: Polity.
McCombs, M. and Shaw, D.L. (1972) The agenda-setting function of mass media. *Public Opinion Quarterly* 36 (2), 176–187.
McCombs, M.E., Shaw, D.L. and Weaver, D.H. (2013) *Communication and Democracy: Exploring the Intellectual Frontiers in Agenda-setting Theory*. New York: Routledge.
Morgan, G. and Poynting, S. (2016) Global islamophobia: Muslims and moral panic in the West. New York: Routledge.
MTI (2015) Orbán: gazdasági bevándorlóknak nem tudunk menedéket adni. *HVG*, 11 January 2015. http://hvg.hu/itthon/20150111_Orban_gazdasagi_bevandorloknak_nem_tudunk (accessed 8 May 2018).
O'Halloran, K.L. (2011) Multimodal discourse analysis. In K. Hyland and B. Paltridge (eds) *The Bloomsbury Companion to Discourse Analysis* (pp. 120–137). London: Bloomsbury.
Rheindorf, M. and Wodak, R. (2018) Borders, fences, and limits – Protecting Austria from refugees: Metadiscursive negotiation of meaning in the current refugee crisis. *Journal of Immigrant & Refugee Studies* 16 (1–2), 15–38.
Robson C. (2002) *Real World Research* (2nd edn). Hoboken, NJ: Blackwell.
Simmel, G. (1950) The stranger. In K. Wolff (ed.) *The Sociology of Georg Simmel* (trans. K. Wolff) (pp. 402–408). New York: Free Press.
Tannen, D. (ed.) (1993) *Framing in Discourse*. Oxford: Oxford University Press.
Van Leeuwen, T. (2013) Critical analysis of multimodal discourse. In C. Chapelle (ed.) *Encyclopedia of Applied Linguistics* (pp. 1–5). Oxford: John Wiley and Sons, Inc.
Vezovnik, A. (2018) securitizing migration in Slovenia: A discourse analysis of the Slovenian refugee situation. *Journal of Immigrant & Refugee Studies* 16 (1–2), 39–56.
Wodak, R. (2021) *The Politics of Fear: The Shameless Normalization of Far-right Discourse* (2nd edn). Thousand Oaks, CA: Sage Publishing.

4 Multilingual Professionals, Monolingual Contexts and Multicultural Mindsets: Towards an Intercultural Mindset

Fiona O'Neill

Introduction

The question of how people may live and work together equitably in increasingly complex configurations of linguistic and cultural diversity has generated debate (Blommaert, 2013; Kraus, 2012; Pavlenko, 2019; Vertovec, 2010) and become a focus for professional education (Glaser *et al.*, 2007; Spencer-Oatey & Franklin, 2009). In migrant-receiving countries, including the UK, USA, Canada and Australia, where English is the dominant language, responses to such diversity have sought to promote the notion of living and working together in a multicultural mosaic of many cultures. The Australian Government's Multicultural Statement (Australian Government, 2017) exemplifies a positive attitude on diversity, but tends to essentialise cultures and downplay the contribution of languages. Multilingualism is understood by some as a problem for which monolingualism is a logical solution (McNamara, 2011). Clyne (2005: xi) described this as a 'monolingual mindset', a way of thinking such that the potential of multiple languages is undervalued.

Interculturality has provided alternative ways of thinking about living and working together in contexts of growing linguistic and cultural diversity. However, this notion can also underplay the role of languages and emphasise differences amongst cultures, conceptualised as static and bounded to ethnic or national identities (Ferri, 2018; Holmes & Dervin, 2016). In the fields of education, professional training or the contemporary world of work, interculturality is often understood in terms of *competence* – the skills, knowledge and qualities that people can acquire to effectively navigate contemporary linguistic and cultural diversity (Byram,

1997; Deardorff, 2006; Kramsch, 2011). This view has, however, come under critique (Phipps, 2010).

The narrative study on which this chapter is based has taken an intercultural orientation to explore how multilingual, mobile professionals make sense of their experience of relocating to live and work in 'multicultural Australia' (Australia Government, 2017), with a focus on their experience of language use in workplace interactions. The findings contribute to our understanding of how such people use their multilingual resources to negotiate their professional selves and to manage ways of working together. Taking a dialogic approach to narrative inquiry (Riessman, 2008), I draw on Bakhtin (1981) and Ricoeur (1984) to argue that these multilingual professionals engage in ongoing processes of reflection and reflexivity in interactions with others. In doing so, they navigate 'multicultural mindsets' that overlook and undervalue their multiple languages, to create professional selves that go beyond notions of competence. As intercultural professionals (O'Neill, 2020), they draw on an intercultural mindset or orientation (Scarino, 2020) that informs how they make sense of their experience and respond in interactions with others. The discussion of the findings is illustrated with extracts from interviews with four of the 12 participants. Below I first briefly outline previous empirical studies that explore the intercultural experience of multilingual professionals in today's workplaces, and explain the design of the study, before turning to the discussion and concluding thoughts.

Multilingual Migrants in Working Life

The contemporary workplace is increasingly becoming a multilingual reality (Angouri, 2013), presenting a growing need to better understand the role language and multilinguality play in professional identities and ways of working together (Hazel, 2015). Socio- and applied linguistic studies have explored the phenomenon of human mobility in relation to working life, highlighting themes of identity, trust, acceptance and belonging (Angouri & Marra, 2011; Blommaert, 2013; Canagarajah, 2017; Duchêne et al., 2013; Kerekes et al., 2013; Roberts, 2010, 2011; Sarangi & Roberts, 2002; Tranekjaer, 2015). These studies have been conducted in a variety of contexts, revealing issues of adaptation and experiences of marginalisation for multilingual migrants. Findings indicate that people who relocate to live and work frequently experience gatekeeping (Sarangi & Roberts, 2002) as a 'linguistic penalty' (Roberts, 2010: 218), and 'exclusionary practices' (Heller, 2013: 191). Often, scholars explicitly or implicitly draw on Bourdieu's (1991) notion of the symbolic power of language to include and exclude. For Bourdieu, language is a form of cultural capital (Bourdieu, 1986). Fields exist in which there are forms of linguistic capital that are highly sought, and people develop dispositions in relation to language practices that enable them to make sense of themselves and their fit in the world, while also sustaining and reproducing a privileged 'legitimate language' (Bourdieu, 1991: 170) and linguistic norms that support the field (Bourdieu & Passeron, 1977). These dispositions become taken for granted, an internalised logic (Bourdieu, 1990), habitus (Bourdieu, 1977) or 'socialised subjectivity' (Bourdieu & Wacquant, 1992: 126) that informs how people make sense of themselves, and themselves in relation to others.

These key ideas can be found in applied linguistic research that explores the ways in which language plays out in workplace contexts in which a dominant language may be privileged, with consequences for how people may work together equitably (Angouri & Miglbauer, 2014; Søderberg & Holden, 2002; Virkkula-Räisänen, 2010). In the context of internationalisation, some workplaces may encourage migrant professionals to openly make use of their multilingual resources (Angouri, 2013; Angouri & Miglbauer, 2014; Lønsmann, 2017; Lønsmann & Kraft, 2018; Räisänen, 2013; Risager, 2016; Virkkula-Räisänen, 2010). Even when multilingual approaches are in place, however, studies show that a hierarchy may still exist in which some languages have greater currency than others, impacting on communication and perceptions of roles and relationships in the workplace (Lønsmann & Kraft, 2018). Again, Bourdieu's (1991) idea that language is never neutral and carries a symbolic power continues to be relevant in developing understandings of the role language plays in multilingual migrants' working lives, regardless of whether workplaces favour the use of one or multiple languages.

Increasingly, researchers use an intercultural lens to consider the ways in which people, mobility, languages and work intersect, in terms of such challenges and also the potential affordances. For example, Hobman *et al.* (2004) sought to better understand intercultural encounters and develop workplace training which could harness the creative opportunities that linguistic and cultural diversity may provide. Guilherme *et al.* (2010) brought together contributions based on a three-year study that scoped intercultural training for professional mobility in Europe. Mada and Saftoiu (2012) also investigated the role of language in workplace identities and relationships with a focus on intercultural competence. Such examples prioritise understandings of interculturality in terms of competence, but may overlook other affordances (Phipps, 2010). Moving away from the idea of intercultural competence, Scarino *et al.* (2017) explored the personal experiences and perspectives of professionals through their narrative accounts of working together in linguistically and culturally diverse settings, describing them in terms of intercultural *capabilities*. The study provides an example of how narrative inquiry can reveal tacit understandings and workplace practices related to language use that go beyond notions of competence, and go to the heart of being and becoming.

A Dialogic Approach to Narrative

The study on which this chapter is based draws on Riessman's (2008) approach to narrative inquiry, which attends to the dialogic nature of narrative texts, and on Ricoeur's (1984) notion of narrative identity. Ricoeur (1984: 65) considers how people 'emplot' their lives, such that time becomes an interpretive resource in their narratives to create a meaningful and coherent sense of self. This involves reflective and reflexive processes in which narrators make sense of their experiences over time, creating plots, casts and coherent trajectories to reach logical 'endpoints' (Ricoeur, 1984: 66). An endpoint provides a moral of the story; a rationale for who the narrators understand themselves to be. For Ricoeur (1984, 1988), narrative is fundamental to the constitution of the self. Narrative texts do not arise in isolation; they are created in, and contribute to, contexts. In taking a dialogic approach to narrative inquiry, Riessman (2008) draws on Bakhtin's (1981) notions of 'heteroglossia' and 'dialogism'. For Bakhtin, language is more than just words and grammar; it is a resource for creating and interpreting meaning that is 'ideologically saturated' and imbued with 'a world view' (1981: 271). While it may appear unified, language is always subject to an 'ongoing process of linguistic stratification and differentiation' (1981: 67) brought about by competing 'centrifugal' and 'centripetal' forces (1981: 271–272). This leads to heteroglossia, or 'a multiplicity of social voices' (1981: 263), in both literary texts and everyday talk; voices that interact with one another in dynamic, responsive relationships over time and space. This interrelationship of text and context enables 'a dialogue between points of view' in every utterance (1981: 76). In this sense, the dialogue is not only between people but also simultaneously includes 'the internal dialogism of the word' (1981: 279). From this perspective, as researcher, I was attentive to my role in co-creating the participants' narratives in interaction with them, and the significance of our language choices in creating and interpreting diverse meanings, and shared understandings, together.

Thus, all texts, including the narratives of the participants in this study, can be understood as made up of multiple social, temporal, spatial and historical voices that interact; a process in which words and language come into contact and competition with each other to yield multiple possible meanings (Bakhtin, 1981). For Bakhtin (1986), experience, thought, words and text come together in meaningful ways, but these meanings must never be taken at face value. From this orientation to narrative text, my analysis required careful attention to language and context, to understand how people construct a 'dialogic or narrativized self' (Riessman, 2008: 37). Vitanova (2005: 144) also draws on Bakhtin to argue that narratives can be understood as 'zones of dialogic constructions' in which authorship of oneself occurs. Keeping this dialogic self in view requires attending to the interaction between the participants and the researcher, and the 'conceptual horizon' (Bakhtin, 1981: 282) each brings to making and interpreting meaning.

Therefore, according to Riessman (2008), it is important for the researcher to explore who, and also how, when, where, and with whom the narrator constructs the self. Interrogating the relationship between personal experience, narrative text and context, and focusing on the role of language in this way, opens up possibilities for more in-depth understandings of how people make sense of and manage working together when there are diverse understandings in play. While Riessman (2008) identifies and describes this framework for narrative inquiry in relation to three studies, only one of them investigates the experience of work and identity (Riessman, 2004), and none considers the complexity that arises for multilingual migrants.

The Study

Twelve multilingual professionals from diverse professions and with tertiary education in English participated in semi-structured interviews with the researcher (author), who collected data in the form of narrative accounts and reflections on their experiences of living and working in Australia. Participants were recruited through French cultural and professional organisations in Australia and the researcher's own networks. The selection criteria were that they had relocated from a francophone country to live and work in Australia for a minimum of six months and that they self-identified as having French as a primary language and English (studied at a tertiary level) as an additional language. While they were all francophone, this was a heterogeneous group of professionals who reflected diversity in their countries of origin, multilingual repertoires, migration and employment trajectories, ages and genders. The participants self-identified with a variety of ethnicities including European, Iberian and Asian, with one participant self-identifying as 'Black'. Such self-identifications were particularly marked when they felt that Australians questioned their claim to 'frenchness'. A summary of participant profiles is provided in Table 4.1, with the pseudonyms of the key participants featured in this chapter indicated by an asterisk.

Two interviews of at least one hour duration with each participant took place approximately six weeks apart. During the interviews, participants were invited to talk about and reflect on their experiences of relocating to live and work in Australia. The focus of these semi-structured interviews was on how they interpreted and managed themselves in workplace interactions; in other words, how did they make sense of others making sense of them as multilingual, migrant professionals? The participants reported that time between the first and second interviews enabled them to recall anecdotes and reflect more deeply on their experiences, and also gave them a unique opportunity to consider how the use of their linguistic resources had become routine.

During the interviews, the participants were invited to use both French and English according to their preference, and I responded by continuing the conversation in whichever language they used in a given moment. This was

Table 4.1 Summary of participant profiles

Name	Country of origin	Linguistic repertoires	Profession	Time in Australia
*Alain	France	French, English	Architect	35 years
*Benjamin	Luxembourg	French, English	Scientist	7 years
Charlotte	France	French, Spanish, English	Business administration	20 years
David	France	French, English	Business	25 years
Eliane	France	French, English, Spanish, Italian	Event management	2 years
Félix	France (La Réunion)	French, English	Information technology	10 years
Gérard	France	French, Polish, Italian, English	Scientist	5 years
Hervé	France	French, German, Latin, Greek, English	Information technology	1 year
Isobel	Vietnam	French, Vietnamese, English	Scientist	1 year
*Juliette	France	French, Spanish, English	Marketing	4 years
*Katherine	France	French, German, Spanish, English	Health and welfare	30 years
Laurent	France	French, English	Business	6 months

a conscious choice to draw on the multilingual resources available to both the participants and me to create and interpret meaning collaboratively in the interviews. The narrative accounts were transcribed verbatim in the languages spoken at interview (French-English translations are my own), and the analysis attended closely to linguistic features that kept multiple languages, multiple voices and competing perspectives in play (Riessman, 2008). The process of analysis therefore involved multiple passes in which the data were coded and analysed for instances of direct and reported speech, intertextuality and indexicality (Bakhtin, 1981; Hanks, 1992). This approach to the capture of data and analysis has kept my own voice as an Australian researcher in view (English is my primary language and French an additional language), to acknowledge my part in shaping the accounts collaboratively with the participants (Mishler, 1991; Riessman, 2008).

The findings are discussed in three sections which explore the following aspects: monolingual contexts, multicultural mindsets and intercultural mindsets, with the discussion illustrated with interview extracts from four of the participants: Alain, Benjamin, Juliette and Katherine. Given the focus of this chapter, their accounts exemplify ways of making sense of their experience that were identified as similar across the participants' narratives.

Monolingual Contexts

The participants experienced attitudes and practices in monolingual contexts which framed their multilingualism as problematic. This is a surprising phenomenon when we consider that Australia's multilingual profile is rapidly growing due to migration, with the Australian Bureau of Statistics showing an almost 25% increase in the number of people speaking a language other than English at home between 2011 and 2016 (id, 2018). Despite having studied English at a tertiary level, all of the participants experienced moments in which their English language proficiency was questioned, and mutual comprehension was thought to be at risk. However, the solution to communication problems was not seen to be a mutual responsibility or accomplishment. The following interview extract from Juliette, who self-identifies as French-Australian and works in marketing, illustrates this point:

Juliette: donc il m'appelle pour me dire en fait que j'ai le poste par téléphone et il me dit par contre « il faut travailler un peu sur votre accent parce que je ne le voudrais pas qu'on perde des clients parce qu'ils ne vous comprennent pas » ... et du coup j'ai refusé le poste ... parce que ... je sais que les gens comprennent et que je pense que quand les gens font un remarque comme ça c'est ... ça ne va pas marcher parce que ça veut dire qu'on n'est pas très très ouvert ... et si je dois tous les jours être pétrifiée de dire un mot parce que ... on vous juge là-dessus ... ce n'est pas la peine

Translation: ... so they called me to say I had the job on the phone and he said, though, 'You'll have to work a bit on your accent because we don't want to lose clients because they don't understand you'... and straight away I refused the job ... because ... I know people understand and I think that when people make a remark like that it's ... it's not going to work because it shows that they're not really very open ... and if I have to be petrified every time I say a word because ... I'm going to be judged on it ... it's not worth it (translated by the author)

Here Juliette ventriloquises (Bakhtin, 1981; Riessman, 2008) the Australian employer who frames her multilinguality as a risk, not an asset. The process of ventriloquising here involves using direct speech to revoice the employer's words, drawing attention to a significant aspect of her experience, and highlighting that beneath his lack of trust in her language ability lies his lack of trust in her professional competency. Her revoicing highlights the employer's perception of risk to the business, and his expectation that it is incumbent on her to mitigate this risk. In Bakhtin's (1981) terms, this reveals her understanding to me, an Australian researcher, of the potential for political discourses to position multilingual migrants as a potential threat to economic progress, a problem for which monolingualism is the solution (Acharya, 2017; McNamara, 2011). The point Juliette makes for my benefit is to show that she does not feel constrained by the 'monolingual mindset' (Clyne, 2005: xi) that informs such discourses, as she promptly takes the initiative and declines the job. Drawing on Ricoeur's (1984) notion of narrative identity, Juliette uses this anecdote to portray her professional trajectory in such a way that highlights her agency. This is one of many *peripeteia* (Ricoeur, 1984: 66) or setbacks found across the participants' narratives, with which they overcome unexpected difficulties in terms of who they are and how they might participate professionally. This allows them to construct narrative selves that positively frame being multilingual, despite the negative evaluations they may encounter (Ruuska, 2016).

Even in backstage (Goffman, 1959) conversations between colleagues, being multilingual can be judged negatively and seen as a threat to workplace cohesion. In an extended anecdote, Ben, a scientist who self-identifies as European, Swiss and French Swiss, recounts a moment when he spoke in French in an aside to an African francophone colleague before a meeting:

Benjamin: I sat next to her and said in French to her and she replied in French and the person running the meeting … really perceived … to make fun of her … and then she really cracked it in front of everyone … and she said 'What are you guys talking about?' … and I was taken aback because it was nothing about her work for me it was … she was showing some information from other areas and she thought I was we were having a laugh because we were speaking another language talking about her … her work … but it wasn't the case so at first I was confused I said 'Why are you upset? It wasn't important' and she said 'But yeah the fact that I couldn't understand it really upset me' … and it took a few days just to get over it and … so she's very sensitive as well … um yeah so I'm a bit more careful now

Here Benjamin uses direct speech to ventriloquise (Bakhtin, 1981; Riessman, 2008) the exchange between a colleague and him, highlighting how he was sanctioned in front of his colleagues for drawing on his multilingual resources. In Bakhtin's (1981) terms, historical, social and political voices are being revoiced here; voices that intend to reinforce the dominance of one language – English in this context – as a shared expectation and value (Australian Government, 2017; Clyne, 2005). From this perspective, multilingualism is framed as disrespectful, unprofessional and even un-Australian (see Morgan, 2018). As a consequence of such a mindset, multilingualism can become increasingly invisibilised in the workplace, not just because of concerns about mutual comprehension or working together for economic gain, but in the pursuit of workplace cohesion. The endpoint (Ricoeur, 1984) of this anecdote highlights how this was a formative experience for Benjamin that has shaped his professional sense of self and logic of practice (Bourdieu, 1990). Reflecting on his account in conversation with me, he makes the point that it has now become routine to be circumspect about when, where and with whom he engages in multilingual practices. This anecdote resonates with Bourdieu's (1991) notion of the power of language to include and exclude. There are also broader social consequences when people's multilingual resources are not valued and used in the workplace. Mutual understandings can be put at risk, and perceptions of what is at stake in professional interactions, and of roles and relationships, are evaluated through the lens of only one language and the limits of one's conceptual outlook (Bakhtin, 1981). This in turn can impact on how information is shared and decisions are made when working together (Scarino *et al.*, 2017).

Multicultural Mindsets

Despite Australian society appearing to orient itself positively to multiculturalism, the Multicultural Statement (Australian Government, 2017) exemplifies a 'multicultural' mindset that tends to essentialise cultures, invisibilise languages, and overlook the role language plays in constituting people's sense of self. The analysis of the narratives highlights how these multilingual professionals encounter, reflect on and respond to such ways of thinking.

The extract below from an interview with Alain, an architect who self-identifies as a 'world citizen' born in France and educated in France, South Africa and Australia, illustrates how the relationship between languages and cultures can be 'divided and conquered' by a 'multicultural' mindset which he experiences in interactions with colleagues and clients when they detect a French accent or learn that he is francophone:

Alain:	I think multilinguals are not seen as … multilinguals … they're seen as multicultural … that's the thing … and so invariably you're not a French speaker, you are a francophile … or you're a peon … or you are … an immigrant … or you are … but somehow it's never just simply …. 'You speak French well' that's for me because of my … origin is French … that's interesting … I wonder if the question was asked of someone Australian who has learnt French, maybe they would have a different answer to that
Interviewer:	But for you personally?
Alain:	My … it's always inseparable to this notion of multiculturalism … and that's the polemic attached to it in Australia … there's the sort of … the smug well-to-do middle class which likes the fact that it brings out a whole bunch of culinary options … but not really anything beyond

Here Alain revoices and interrogates (Bakhtin, 1981; Riessman, 2008) social and political discourses to highlight their limited ways of thinking about linguistic and cultural diversity. As Clyne (2005: 151) argues, although multilingualism is 'part and parcel of Australia's multicultural demography', Australia's multicultural policies and practices have done little to support linguistic diversity, leaving Australian society's language potential critically underexploited. Alain's reflection highlights how his multilingual francophone identity is subsumed by labels such as 'francophile', 'peon' or 'immigrant', appropriating (Bakhtin, 1981) 'middle class' Australian discourses that foreground and essentialise perceptions of migrant cultural repertoires at the expense of recognising the value of their multilingual resources. He reinforces his point by keeping the relationship between text and context in play, alluding to the fact that while both he and I speak French, we are differentially positioned by such discourses. His playful dig at the 'multicultural', 'middle class' mindset resonates with Bakhtin's (1981; Vitanova, 2005) notions of heteroglossia and revoicing through parody and irony, and challenges attitudes and practices that lead to categorisations and stereotyping of multilingual migrants. According to Bakhtin (1981: 293):

> The word in language is half someone else's. It becomes one's own only when the speaker populates it with his own intention, his own accent, when he appropriates the word, adapting it to his own semantic and expressive intention.

In appropriating the words of others, Alain also demonstrates his understanding that such labels do more than simply identify people as belonging to the same category. Lumping people together and categorising them also involves making assumptions and associations between groups of people and particular ways of being and doing (Sacks, 1992; Scollon *et al.*, 2012). The power of these words can trigger presuppositions, and position people beyond the mainstream; but, in the context of Alain recounting this narrative to me as an Australian researcher, he is calling into question their usual meaning and associations (Riessman, 2008). This is the construction of a narrative self (Ricoeur, 1984) that resists being restricted or marginalised by a 'multicultural' mindset. Through such anecdotes of social and workplace interactions, each of the participants develops plots and brings together casts which provide a rationale for the kind of person and professional they are and aspire to be. In doing so, they explore and contest both the positive and negative categorisations and stereotypes they encounter, and the many different meanings that 'French', 'foreign', 'migrant', and 'multicultural' can have.

Positive categorisations tend to reduce being multicultural to exotic, non-threatening, 'sentimental stereotypes' (Kramsch, 2011: 355) that revolve around food, wine, romance and luxury goods, particularly in relation to French people. The following excerpts from interviews with Katherine, a social worker who self-identifies as someone who 'used to be French', illustrate how these multilingual professionals not only interpret but also reflexively manage 'multicultural' mindsets in face-to-face interactions in the workplace:

> Katherine: Well sometimes you know I make a joke and I say oh you know I say things like 'Oh gee ... I don't drink coffee ... so I can't be French ... and I don't wear jewellery ... so I can't be a woman'... because the logic is all French women love jewellery and roses and romance and sexy and all the rest of it ... so that's the cliché

And here, referring to a conversation with a male Anglo colleague at work:

> Katherine: We were talking about I can't do exercise and he made a comment like 'Well you really miss it because French women like to be hot and sweaty'
> Interviewer: Oh no ...really? (laughs)
> Katherine: (laughs) you know ... it's like ... so you know I have choice to either say 'How do you know that?' or to say 'Yes you're right' ... you know ... in that particular instance I just didn't say anything ... but ... yes so there are stereotypes ... and sometimes I use it
> Interviewer: Yes ... how do you use it?
> Katherine: I will say 'Oh yes I'm always right ... of course ... I'm arrogant' ... 'Of course that's me because I'm always right' ... 'I'm arrogant ... you can't be arrogant you're English and you're always wrong'

Here Katherine revoices (Bakhtin, 1981; Riessman, 2008) popular discourses often found in the media related to what it means to be French and female, contesting the stereotypes she frequently encounters and subverting the multicultural mindset that reproduces them. Again, this is accomplished through the use of parody (Bakhtin, 1981), to challenge and redefine what it means to be French, foreign and female, and to propose an alternative logic and construct a 'dialogic self' (Riessman, 2008; Vitanova, 2005) that does not conform to received ideas of who and how she 'should' be in the eyes of others. Across the participants' narratives, the analysis of such moments reveals how these multilingual professionals frequently use humour and irony in conversations (Kramsch, 2009), in Katherine's words, to 'educate' local colleagues (and the researcher) by disrupting ways of thinking about differences as foreign or alien. Drawing on Ricoeur's (1984) notion of narrative self, these illustrative examples demonstrate how, rather than being constrained by limiting stereotypes, they can *use* them in interactions to construct a coherent, authentic sense of self over time. This is important when we consider the findings of other studies that highlight how multilingual professionals can feel constrained and excluded in the workplace (Duchêne *et al.*, 2013; Kerekes *et al.*, 2013; Roberts, 2011; Sarangi & Roberts, 2002; Tranekjaer, 2015).

Negative categorisations around being multicultural are often associated with concerns about social cohesion and security, based on perceptions of what is normal, and a person's capacity to play by the rules, where the rules are created by the dominant culture and centripetal forces that cultivate a singular take on language and meaning (Bakhtin, 1981). The following excerpt from Alain's narrative serves to further illustrate this point:

> Alain: ... as I was gaining facility in English it wasn't simply about fluency it was also about making the adjustments in the expression to fit in with the contextual culture ... and so ... and there's something that the Australians are very sensitive to is that people make references to the old country or the recent immigrants and ... they don't seem for a culture which has so much immigration ... they don't understand that for these new immigrants this is the only frame of reference they have so they will make those backwards references and it's not because they're finding a deficit in Australia ... which is what is interpreted by the Australians and usually elicits the response 'Oh well ... if you don't like it why don't you just go back'

Here Alain signals a recognition that while the dominant culture sets the rules for the ways language can take on particular meanings in particular contexts (Blommaert, 2013; Bourdieu, 1991), as a multilingual speaker he is aware that meaning is always a process of interpretation, in which an understanding of the relationship between language, culture and context is crucial (Bakhtin, 1981). Multilingual people who have relocated to live and work may not immediately have at hand the contextualisation cues (Gumperz, 1982) that locals assume are shared knowledge. Knowing who can say what to whom, when, and being aware that there are therefore multiple possible interpretations, has become part of his narrative self (Ricoeur, 1984; Riessman, 2008). In revoicing the anti-migration slogan, 'If you don't like it why don't you just go back', Alain calls up discourses from popular media and politics, with which we are familiar, to underline the point that they categorise migrants as 'them' and the mainstream as 'us' (Issa, 2017), while at the same time situating himself beyond categorisation (neither Australian nor a recent immigrant). Such discourses conceptualise diversity as a problem caused by others (Crichton & O'Neill, 2017; Scarino *et al.*, 2015; Scarino *et al.*, 2017). In placing the perceived problem of diversity with others, such a mindset can see the solution as something required of 'them', not 'us'. While categorisation (Sacks, 1992) is fundamental to how humans make sense of the world and create meaning, people are mostly unaware of the role that language plays and the extent to which they draw on categories in their daily lives to construct particular perspectives. Examples such as this from the participants' narratives highlight the insight they have as multilingual speakers of how language and context matter to the way membership categories (Sacks, 1992) are reproduced, sustained and interconnected through social, political and historical voices (Leudar & Nekvapil, 2004).

In the Australian context, 'multicultural' mindsets are evident in the label 'Culturally and Linguistically Diverse' or 'CALD'. In public and policy documents, including the Australian Government's Multicultural Access and Equity Action Plan (DSS, 2017), multilingual migrants are placed in the category 'CALD', setting them apart from an imagined monolingual, monocultural mainstream (Anderson, 1983). This situates diversity with 'multicultural others' rather than acknowledging that everyone brings their own 'conceptual horizon' (Bakhtin, 1981: 282) that informs how they interpret and create meaning, and therefore everyone contributes to the diversity of a given context. The term 'CALD' tends to emphasise difference, frame diversity as problematic and reproduce discourses of marginalisation in the workplace (Scarino et al., 2017). There are consequences for migrants in working life as this extract from Katherine's interview illustrates:

> Katherine: I think it's that misunderstanding ... that people make judgement about ... you know I always say people are quite happy for me to be a foreigner as long as I behave like them ... that's a very direct thing to say and I think it can be quite critical and that's where there is this problem

Despite having lived and worked in Australia for over 20 years, Katherine emphasises that she will continue to be regarded as 'foreign' and subject to negative evaluations by others, particularly if she does not meet cultural expectations in regard to language and communication in the workplace. 'Multicultural' mindsets do not recognise cultures and communicative norms as dynamic and changing with time and context. There are implications for how people live, learn and work together in diversity when people are not enabled to participate on a level playing field, and this can impact on the quality of workplace interactions (Lévy, 2011; Scarino et al., 2017; Suni, 2017). Speaking up can pose risks, and being heard can also be complicated for multilingual people, particularly when voicing alternate understandings could reinforce the very misunderstandings and stereotypes embedded in social and professional discourses. Nevertheless, the analysis reveals the strategic processes by which these multilingual professionals play with the language of others to create understandings of self that are not subject to an ongoing sense of marginalisation.

Towards an Intercultural Mindset

In constructing their dialogic, narrative selves (Riessman, 2008; Vitanova, 2005), the participants resist and challenge attitudes that discourage and devalue multilingual practices, essentialise cultures, and potentially marginalise them in everyday interactions in the workplace. In drawing on Riessman's (2008) dialogic approach to narrative inquiry, an 'intercultural mindset' has emerged, seen in the participants' internalised dispositions to use their multilingual resources strategically, both to resist and challenge a 'multicultural' mindset, and to develop dynamic, creative options for being, thinking and interacting in their social and professional worlds.

In the first instance, an intercultural mindset is seen in their dispositions to routinely use their linguistic resources to resist and challenge a 'multicultural' mindset. This has already been demonstrated in the analysis of illustrative examples earlier in the chapter in which these people ventriloquise and appropriate social and historical voices in interactions with others (Bakhtin, 1981). Take, for example, Katherine, in the interview extracts presented earlier in the chapter, where she appropriates the words that others frequently use in association with French people – 'romance', 'sexy', 'arrogant' – to revoice (Bakhtin, 1981) and redefine them on her own terms. This strategy is not quite the same as the recontextualising (Linell, 1998) that all speakers routinely practice in interactions to confirm understandings. Rather, this is sophisticated language play, in which the rules of the activity type (Levinson, 1992), as set by the mainstream, are contested, not within one language but across multiple languages. In this way, intercultural mindsets routinely reflect on and reflexively play with the potentiality of meanings in interactions, exploring and capitalising on competing meanings, testing the limits and at times strategically breaking linguistic norms. These multilingual professionals experience language, not as a singular reality, but as an interpretive lens and a creative resource for meaning-making (Liddicoat & Scarino, 2013).

In reflecting on their narrative accounts, the participants commented on their observations that others were not always aware that language will settle on different meanings, as they are uttered in diverse, dynamic contexts; or, in Bakhtin's (1981) terms, heteroglossia. The following excerpt from Alain's interview illustrates this:

> Alain: I think if you've only got one way of expressing yourself ... you're completely blindsided to the fact that that language is actually imperfect ... that the mono language person and the mono cultural person ... doesn't have the insight ... because that's all they know.

Here, Alain constructs a narrative self (Ricoeur, 1984) as a multilingual professional who is insightful, expressive and knowledgeable about the limitations of taking words at face value.

In the next extract, Alain provides further detail on what constitutes an intercultural mindset, as he describes his disposition to use his multilingual resources as a creative resource in the workplace:

Alain: La façon de voir ... la façon de ... comment ... d'entrer dans la matière ... est difèrente ... qu'en anglais ou en français ... oui (*The way you look at things ... the way ... how ... you get into the subject ... it's different ... whether in English or in French ... yes*) [...] you do approach the subject in a different way ... slightly ... I mean it's not black and white ... it's not as if you are having a diametrically opposed sort of opinion because you are choosing one language over another but it does give you a slightly different emphasis I think it does ... that's the key there it's the emphasis that changes and then from that you then branch out into other connections that you may not have reached ... I think in that way it is creative ... or for me I find it's useful in creativity [...] if you have a conversation and try to convey a point and you know you're not getting through or you have a sense that you're not getting through ... then often if you have one language only one way of thinking and you're not aware that language is actually a tool ... then you'll repeat the argument ... and you'll repeat the argument and you'll repeat the argument and ... so you've tried and you get your point across by sheer brute force of repetition ... whereas then ... I will then run through that possibility and say 'OK how would that sound in French?' ... does that give me an insight into ... a different set of words a different approach a different way of ... of bringing this concept forward ... and then that might reshape that second iteration and then I might use a different way of expressing the same idea and then that might go tilt with the audience and they might go 'Oh yes OK ... that's what you really mean' ... so I think that's in that way what I find quite useful as a tool ... as a shortcut to really generating different options ... for communication

Here Alain reflects on how his multilingual resources provide him with novel, alternate ways of communicating and working with others. This multilingual *savoir faire* evokes Byram's (1997) notion of *savoirs*, ways of knowing and doing required for intercultural competence. Similarly, Kramsch (2011: 355) describes a 'symbolic competence', a capacity to mediate or 'interpret one's own and the others' culture, each in terms of the other' as a skill much needed in the contemporary world. Taking Alain's anecdote as an illustration, an intercultural mindset routinely disposes him to reflection and reflexivity (Ricoeur, 1984; Schön, 1983), and enables him to rethink and repurpose language, to persuade and problem solve, to connect and create meaning, and to mediate understandings between himself and others. Alain is not unaware of the power that lies just beneath the surface of words (Bakhtin, 1981; Bourdieu, 1991; Riessman, 2008). Drawing on Ricoeur (1984), Alain constructs a narrative self that is accomplished not despite, but *because* he is multilingual. Where a 'multicultural' mindset undervalues languages other than that of the dominant culture, an intercultural mindset values multilingual repertoires and deploys them even when communicating in a shared language such as English.

Nevertheless, the notion of an intercultural mindset extends beyond notions of skills, knowledge and competence. The following extract from Juliette's interview serves to illustrate:

> Juliette: Je crois que quand on a vécu dans un seul endroit toute sa vie, quand on a parlé avec une seule langue et on rencontre les mêmes types de gens c'est difficile dans le marketing de se mettre à la place d'un autre client ou d'une autre audience ... peut-être que ça nous aide en fait de nous mettre dans la place d'autres ou dans un autre contexte ou dans un autre environnement puisqu'on le fait tous les jours
> Interviewer: Vous êtes française et australienne ... est-ce qu'il y a un peu de mouvement ?
> Juliette: Tout le temps ! Tout le temps il y a du mouvement en fait ... en fonction de ... avec qui je suis ... de ce que je fais ou de ce que je suis en train de faire.
> Translation
> Juliette: I think that when you've lived in only one place all your life when you've only spoken one language and you meet the same type of people it's difficult in marketing to put yourself in the place of another client or audience ... perhaps it helps us actually to put ourselves in other people's place or in another context or in another environment since we're doing it every day
> Interviewer: You're French and Australian ... is there a bit of movement?
> Juliette: All the time! All the time there's movement in fact ... in terms of ... who I'm with ... what I'm doing or in the process of doing
> (Translated by the author).

In her role as a marketing professional, Juliette draws on her experience of attending to the multiple possible ways other people may interpret and respond in a given interaction. To see the world as others see it requires actively and continuously orienting to others in interactions and the 'conceptual horizons' (Bakhtin, 1981: 282) they draw on to create and interpret meaning. This involves stepping out of one's own received understandings and becoming an outsider to consider the different perspectives that diverse horizons may afford. In Bakhtin's (1981) terms, this is to become 'alien' in every encounter, not in the sense of being marginalised or foreign, but of simply reconsidering the familiar as unfamiliar. Here Juliette's understanding of her narrative self extends notions of interculturality beyond the acquisition of competence or knowledge of other cultures, to who she *is* – contemporaneously insider and outsider and, as such, an intercultural mediator of diverse understandings.

Here, an intercultural mindset can be understood as a reflective and reflexive process of exploring and knowing oneself as other (yet not *othered*) in every encounter. The narrative selves (Ricoeur, 1984) seen in these accounts experience, but are not constrained by, discourses of marginalisation that inform gatekeeping attitudes (Roberts, 2011; Sarangi & Roberts, 2002) and practices that could serve to exclude them (Bourdieu, 1991). Where multicultural mindsets tend to group people together, reproducing dominant voices that rely on categories of 'us' and 'them', and creating associations between such categories and stereotypical ways of being and doing, these illustrative examples highlight dispositions to consider and engage productively with the multiple perspectives in play in every utterance. In this sense, while every interaction has the potential to be a gatekeeping moment, an intercultural mindset affords possibilities to resist and challenge being excluded by those who appear to have the upper hand, to expand one's own and others' horizons by mediating meanings beyond the limitations of a single language and culture (Kramsch, 2011; Scarino, 2014), and to create new ways of working together in linguistic and cultural diversity (Zarate *et al.*, 2003, 2011). For the participants, it is not possible to be the same person or professional who they might have been in a single language, as these dispositions become routine and internalised, and ultimately understood as transforming of the self.

Discussion and Concluding Thoughts

Through their narratives, these multilingual professionals articulated and reflected on their evolving understandings of how their languages came into play in what are often perceived to be monolingual contexts, contexts that they understand are not pre-existing, but created moment by moment in interaction. In this chapter I have argued that the reflectivity and reflexivity evident in the ways they conceptualise diversity, draw on their multilingual resources, and develop intercultural ways of thinking, responding and being, point to a need to rethink perceptions of multilingual professionals as 'multicultural others' or emerging monolinguals; truly monolingual contexts are becoming increasingly hard to find in the social and professional worlds in which we move (Blommaert, 2008). The participants' reflective accounts reveal how they pick up on the social and historical voices that could be limiting, and invoke and revoice them in everyday workplace interactions. In reflecting on and recounting their experiences in conversation with me, an Australian researcher, they constructed narrative, dialogic selves (Riessman, 2008; Vitanova, 2005) in which setbacks and challenges that could be understood as gatekeeping became an integral part of the plot, neither tangential nor the final word in their stories. Their narratives have arrived at endpoints (Ricoeur, 1984) in which they are not marginalised or delimited in an ongoing sense, yet the risk is always present. For this reason, they have internalised dispositions over time to reflect on and interrogate language, to reflexively resist categorisations, and to draw on the creative potential their multilingual resources afford them. Drawing on Bourdieu's notion of 'socialised subjectivity' (Bourdieu & Wacquant, 1992: 126), these dispositions can be understood as a *socialised intersubjectivity* (O'Neill, 2015) which enables them to routinely reflect on and reflexively manage how others are making sense of them in interactions, to consider the multiple perspectives in play, and to transform their sense of self.

Bringing together Bakhtin's (1981) notions of heteroglossia and dialogism and Ricoeur's (1984) notion of narrative self to the analysis has highlighted the awareness and agency of these multilingual professionals, and the powerful, and at times playful, ways they draw on intercultural thinking and practices. In the interviews with these multilingual professionals, my voice and perspectives as a local, Australian-born professional were present, and so contributed to how and why the narratives were constructed in particular ways. Keeping the subjectivities of both the participants and the researcher in play can be understood as a strength, not a limitation, as it acknowledges and foregrounds the relationship between context and text, experience and thought, languages and cultures (Bakhtin, 1981; Riessman, 2008). The participants' multilingual voices and my own voice as a local researcher have been woven together to create a unique, overarching narrative. This new text is a story of being, knowing and doing, revealed in an intercultural mindset which sees linguistic and cultural diversity for its creative and transformative potential. Such understandings are important if we are to reconsider ways of living and working together equitably in increasingly complex contexts of diversity, generated by professional mobility, not only in terms of challenges but also possibilities.

References

Acharya, M. (2017) 6 new requirement to acquire Australian citizenship. *SBS Hindi*, 23 June. http://www.sbs.com.au/yourlanguage/hindi/en/article/2017/04/21/6-new-requirements-acquire-australian-citizenship (accessed 7 July 2017).

Anderson, B. (1983) *Imagined Communities. Reflections on the Origin and Spread of Nationalism*. London: Verso.

Angouri, J. (2013) The multilingual reality of the multinational workplace: Language policy and language use. *Journal of Multilingual and Multicultural Development* 34 (6), 564–581.

Angouri, J. and Marra, M. (eds) (2011) *Constructing Identities at Work*. Houndsmills: Palgrave Macmillan.

Angouri, J. and Miglbauer, M. (2014) "And then we summarise in English for the others": The lived experience of the multilingual workplace. *Multilingua* 33 (1–2), 147–172.

Australian Government (2017) Multicultural Australia: United, strong, successful. Australia's multicultural statement. http://mccsa.org.au/wp-content/uploads/2017/10/multicultural_policy_2017.pdf.

Bakhtin, M.M. (1981) *The Dialogic Imagination: Four Essays*. Austin, TX: University of Texas Press.

Bakhtin, M.M. (1986) The problem of speech genres (trans. V. McGee). In C. Emerson and M. Holquist (eds) *Speech Genres and Other Late Essays* (pp. 60–102). Austin, TX: University of Texas Press.
Blommaert, J. (2008) Bernstein and poetics revisited: Globalization and education. *Discourse and Society* 19 (4), 425–451.
Blommaert, J. (2013) Citizenship, language and superdiversity: Towards complexity. *Journal of Language, Identity and Education* 12 (3), 193–196.
Bourdieu, P. (1977) *Outline of a Theory of Practice* (trans. by R. Nice). Cambridge: Cambridge University Press.
Bourdieu, P. (1986) The forms of capital. In J.G. Richardson (ed.) *Handbook of Theory and Research for the Sociology of Education* (pp. 241–258). New York: Greenwood.
Bourdieu, P. (1990) *The Logic of Practice*. Cambridge: Polity Press.
Bourdieu, P. (1991) *Language and Symbolic Power*. Cambridge: Polity Press.
Bourdieu, P. and Passeron, J.-C. (1977) *Reproduction in Education, Society and Culture* (2nd edn, trans. R. Nice). London: Sage Publications.
Bourdieu, P. and Wacquant, L. (1992) *An Invitation to Reflexive Sociology*. Cambridge: Polity Press.
Byram, M. (1997) *Teaching and Assessing Intercultural Communicative Competence*. Clevedon: Multilingual Matters.
Canagarajah, S. (2017) *The Routledge Handbook of Language and Migration*. New York: Routledge.
Clyne, M. (2005) *Australia's Language Potential*. Sydney: UNSW Press.
Crichton, J. and O'Neill, F. (2017) Risk and safety in linguistic and cultural diversity: A narrative intervention in residential aged care. In J. Crichton, C.N. Candlin and A.S. Firkins (eds) *Communicating Risk* (pp. 51–66). Basingstoke: Palgrave Macmillan.
Deardorff, D.K. (2006) Identification and assessment of intercultural competence as a student outcome of internationalization. *Journal of Studies in International Education* 10 (3), 241–266.
DSS (2017) Multicultural access and equity action plan 2016–2017. https://www.dss.gov.au/our-responsibilities/settlement-and-multicultural-affairs/programs-policy/multicultural-access-and-equity.
Duchêne, A., Moyer, M. and Roberts, C. (eds) (2013) *Language, Migration and Social Inequalities: A Critical Sociolinguistic Perspective on Institutions and Work*. Bristol: Multilingual Matters.
Ferri, G. (2018) *Intercultural Communication: Critical Approaches and Future Challenges*. Cham: Palgrave Macmillan.
Glaser, E., Guilherme, M., del Carmen Méndez García, M. and Mughan, T. (2007) *ICOPROMO, Intercultural Competence for Professional Mobility*. Strasbourg/Graz: Council of Europe Publishing.
Goffman, E. (1959) *The Presentation of Self in Everyday Life*. New York: Anchor Books.
Guilherme, M., Glaser, E. and del Carmen Méndez García, M. (2010) *The Intercultural Dynamics of Multicultural Working*. Bristol: Multilingual Matters.
Gumperz, J. (1982) *Discourse Strategies*. Cambridge: Cambridge University Press.
Hanks, W.F. (1992) The indexical ground of deictic reference. In A. Duranti and C. Goodwin (eds) *Rethinking Context: Language as an Interactive Phenomenon* (pp. 43–76). Cambridge: Cambridge University Press.
Hazel, S. (2015) Identities at odds: Embedded and implicit language policing in the internationalized workplace. *Language and Intercultural Communication* 15 (1), 141–160.
Heller, M. (2013) Language and dis-citizenship in Canada. *Journal of Language, Identity and Education* 12 (3), 189–192.
Hobman, E.V., Bordia, P. and Gallois, C. (2004) Perceived dissimilarity and workplace involvement: The moderating effects of group openness to diversity. *Group and Organization Management* 29 (5), 560–587.

Holmes, P. and Dervin, F. (2016) Introduction - English as a lingua franca and interculturality: Beyond orthodoxies. In P. Holmes and F. Dervin (eds) *The Cultural and Intercultural Dimensions of English as a Lingua Franca* (pp. 1–30). Bristol: Multilingual Matters.

id (2018) Australia community profile: Language spoken at home. http://profile.id.com.au/australia/language.

Issa, A. (2017) 'Go back to where you came from' is an ugly trademark of Australian racism. *The Guardian*, 12 July. https://www.theguardian.com/commentisfree/2017/jul/12/the-rightwing-rampage-against-our-multicultural-society-is-30-years-too-late (accessed 23 May 2018).

Kerekes, J., Chow, J., Lemak, A. and Perhan, Z. (2013) Trust or betrayal: Immigrant engineers' employment seeking experiences in Canada. In C.N. Candlin and J. Crichton (eds) *Discourses of Trust* (pp. 269–284). Basingstoke: Palgrave Macmillan.

Kramsch, C. (2009) *The Multilingual Subject: What Foreign Language Learners Say About their Experience and Why it Matters*. Oxford: Oxford University Press.

Kramsch, C. (2011) The symbolic dimensions of the intercultural. *Language Teaching* 44 (3), 354–367.

Kraus, P.A. (2012) The politics of complex diversity: A European perspective. *Ethnicities* 12 (1), 3–25.

Leudar, I. and Nekvapil, J. (2004) Media dialogical networks and political argumentation. *Journal of Language and Politics* 3 (2), 247–266.

Levinson, S.C. (1992) Activity types and language. In P. Drew and J. Heritage (eds) *Talk at Work. Interaction in Institutional Settings* (pp. 66–100). Cambridge: Cambridge University Press.

Lévy, D. (2011) Introduction: Languages and the self (trans. by N. Pierdominici). In G. Zarate, D. Lévy and C. Kramsch (eds) *Handbook of Multilingualism and Multiculturalism* (pp. 63–76). Paris: Editions des Archives Contemporaines.

Liddicoat, A. and Scarino, A. (2013) *Intercultural Language Teaching and Learning*. Chichester: Wiley-Blackwell.

Linell, P. (1998) *Approaching Dialogue: Talk, Interaction and Contexts in Dialogical Perspectives*. Amsterdam: John Benjamins.

Lønsmann, D. (2017) A catalyst for change: Language socialization and norm negotiation in a transient multilingual workplace. *Journal of Linguistic Anthropology* 27 (3), 326–343.

Lønsmann, D. and Kraft, K. (2018) Language policy and practice in multilingual production workplaces. *Multilingua* 37 (4), 403–427.

Mada, S. and Saftoiu, R. (2012) *Professional Communication Across Languages and Cultures*. Amsterdam: John Benjamins.

McNamara, T. (2011) Multilingualism in education: A poststructralist critique. *The Modern Language Journal* 95 (3), 430–441.

Mishler, E.G. (1991) Representing discourse: The rhetoric of transcription. *Journal of Narrative and Life History/Narrative Inquiry* 1, 255–280.

Morgan, R. (2018) Queensland hospital confirms staff told to speak only English in 'unofficial' email. *SBS News Australia,* 16 January. https://www.sbs.com.au/news/queensland-hospital-confirms-staff-told-to-speak-only-english-in-unofficial-email (accessed 23 May 2018).

O'Neill, F. (2015) Multilingual francophone professionals' experience of moving between languages and cultures: a narrative study. PhD thesis, University of South Australia.

O'Neill, F. (2020). *The Intercultural Professional*. Basingstoke: Palgrave Macmillan.

Pavlenko, A. (2019) Superdiversity and why it isn't: Reflections on terminological innovation and academic branding. In B. Schmenk, S. Breidbach and L. Küster (eds) *Sloganization in Language Education Discourse: Conceptual Thinking in the Age of Academic Marketization* (pp. 142–168). Bristol: Multilingual Matters.

Phipps, A. (2010) Training and intercultural education: The danger in 'Good citizenship'. In M. Guilherme, E. Glaser and M. del Carmen Méndez García (eds) *The Intercultural Dynamics of Multicultural Working* (pp. 59–73). Bristol: Multilingual Matters.

Räisänen, T. (2013) Processes and practices of enregisterment of business English, participation and power in a multilingual workplace. *Sociolinguistic Studies* 6 (2), 309–331.

Ricoeur, P. (1984) *Time and Narrative* (trans. K. McLaughlin and D. Pellauer) (Vol. 1). Chicago: Chicago University Press.

Ricoeur, P. (1988) *Time and Narrative* (trans. K. McLaughlin and D. Pellauer) (Vol. 3). Chicago: Chicago University Press.

Riessman, C. (2004) A thrice told tale: New readings of an old story. In T. Greenhalgh and V. Skultans (eds) *Narrative Research in Health and Illness* (pp. 309–324). London: British Medical Journal Books/Blackwell Publishing.

Riessman, C. (2008) *Narrative Methods for the Human Sciences*. Thousand Oaks, CA: Sage Publications.

Risager, K. (2016) Lingua francas in a world of migrations. In P. Holmes and F. Dervin (eds) *The Cultural and Intercultural Dimensions of English as a Lingua Franca* (pp. 33–49). Bristol: Multilingual Matters.

Roberts, C. (2010) Language socialization in the workplace. *Annual Review of Applied Linguistics* 30, 211–227.

Roberts, C. (2011) Gatekeeping discourse in employment interviews. In C.N. Candlin and S. Sarangi (eds) *Handbook of Communication in Organisations and Professions* (pp. 407–432). Berlin: De Gruyter Mouton.

Ruuska, K. (2016) Between ideologies and realities: Multilingual competence in a languagised world. *Applied Linguistics Review* 7 (3), 353–374.

Sacks, H. (1992) *Lectures on Conversation*. Cambridge, MA: Blackwell.

Sarangi, S. and Roberts, C. (2002) Discourse (mis)alignments in professional gatekeeping encounters. In C. Kramsch (ed.) *Language Acquisition and Language Socialization: Ecological Perspectives* (pp. 197–227). London: Continuum.

Scarino, A. (2014) Teaching foreign languages in an era of globalization. *The Modern Language Journal* 98 (1), 386–401.

Scarino, A. (2020). Mediation in the assessment of language learning within an interlingual and intercultural orientation: The role of reciprocal interpretation. In M.E. Poehner and O. Inbar-Lourie (eds) *Toward a Reconceptualization of Second Language Classroom Assessment* (pp. 43–60). Cham: Springer Nature.

Scarino, A., Crichton, J., O'Keeffe, V., O'Neill, F. and Dollard, M. (2015) Communicating work health safety in the context of cultural and linguistic diversity in aged care. https://linguisticandculturaldiversityinagedcare.wordpress.com/2015/04/communicating_safety_in_cald_in_aged_care_report_web_isbn_978-1-922046-14-7.pdf (accessed 18 May 2020).

Scarino, A., O'Neill, F. and Crichton, J. (2017) Communicating safety and care in the context of linguistic and cultural diversity in aged care: An intercultural approach to training. https://www.unisa.edu.au/PageFiles/199171/Communicating%20safety_an%20intercultural%20approach%20to%20training_Final%20Report_2017.pdf (accessed 18 May 2020).

Schön, D.A. (1983) *The Reflective Practitioner: How Professionals Think in Action*. New York: Basic Books.

Scollon, R., Scollon, S. and Jones, R.H. (2012) What is a discourse approach? In R. Scollon, S. Scollon and R.H. Jones (eds) *Intercultural Communication: A Discourse Approach* (3rd edn, pp. 1–24). Oxford: Wiley-Blackwell.

Spencer-Oatey, H. and Franklin, P. (2009) *Intercultural Interaction: A Multidisciplinary Approach to Intercultural Communication*. Baskingstoke: Palgrave Macmillan.

Suni, M. (2017) Working and learning in a new niche: Ecological interpretations of work-related migrations. In J. Angouri, M. Marra and J. Holmes (eds) *Negotiating Boundaries at work: Talking and Transitions* (pp. 197–215). Edinburgh: Edinburgh University Press.

Søderberg, A.-M. and Holden, N. (2002) Rethinking cross cultural management in a globalizing business world. *International Journal of Cross Cultural Management* 2 (1), 103–121.

Tranekjær, L. (2015) *Interactional Categorization and Gatekeeping: Institutional Encounters with Otherness*. Bristol: Multilingual Matters.

Vertovec, S. (2010) Towards post-multiculturalism? Changing communities, conditions and contexts of diversity. *International Social Science Journal* 61 (199), 83–95.

Virkkula-Räisänen, T. (2010) Linguistic repertoires and semiotic resources in interaction: A Finnish manager as a mediator in a multilingual meeting. *Journal of Business Communication* 47 (4), 505–531.

Vitanova, G. (2005) Authoring self in a non-native language: A dialogic approach to agency and subjectivity. In J.K. Hall, G. Vitanova and L.A. Marchenkova (eds) *Dialogue with Bakhtin on Second and Foreign Language Learning: New Perspectives* (pp. 138–158). Mahwah, NJ: Lawrence Erlbaum Associates.

Zarate, G., Gohard-Radenkovic, A., Lussier, D. and Penz, H. (2003) *Médiation culturelle et didactique des langues*. Graz: Conseil de l'Europe.

Zarate, G., Lévy, D. and Kramsch, C. (eds) (2011) *Handbook of Multilingualism and Multiculturalism*. Paris: Édition des Archives Contemporaines.

5 'Getting the job done': Conventional Expressions as Shibboleths in Multilingual Job Interviews

Marta Kirilova

Introduction

Increased mobility and migration around the world have created both opportunities and challenges for linguistic and cultural integration of newcomers. Some of the challenges are particularly visible in cases in which refugees and migrants need to up-skill or re-skill their professional as well as linguistic competences. In Scandinavia, for instance, although English is widely accepted as a 'default' language and a lingua franca in academic contexts (Bolton & Kuteeva, 2012; Mortensen & Haberland, 2012; Thøgersen, 2010) and in high-paying specialist jobs (Lønsmann, 2014; Øhrstrøm, 2016), studies have documented the glass ceiling effect of Danish when it comes to career progression and engagement in the society (Kirilova & Lønsmann, 2020; Lønsmann, 2015). At the same time, linguistic requirements for low-paying jobs in the service sector have been oriented towards developing competences in the local language (for Danish, see Bramm & Kirilova, 2018; Sørensen & Holmen, 2004; for Swedish, see Sandwall, 2013; for Finnish, see Strömmer, 2016; Suni, 2017).

Denmark in particular has for some years now developed various tailor-made integration initiatives in which crash courses in Danish are combined with mentoring activities and courses focusing on cultural socialisation and language learning through employment (e.g. workplace Danish, doctor-patient Danish, Danish for truck-drivers). Such courses and programmes are designed to facilitate quick and targeted linguistic advancement of the newcomers for the needs of the local labour market. Many of these initiatives, however, are often managed by peers and colleagues with little or no training in how to support the newcomers linguistically. Bramm and Kirilova (2018) have documented that sporadic peer-to-peer training is rarely beneficial for the migrant learner's linguistic production and could even have a negative effect on their motivation to learn. Among politicians in Denmark, however, there is a broad consensus that Danish language is the way to employment and integration. Newcomers, especially refugees and migrants from less developed countries, are expected to become 'good' at Danish in order to be 'productive' and to 'participate' in the Danish society. From a sociolinguistic point of view, it is obvious that what counts as 'productivity', 'societal engagement' and being 'good' at Danish depends on numerous factors such as job type, time spent learning Danish, employers' attitudes towards foreign workers, as well as local policies and a range of societal and individual factors.

In this chapter, I present and discuss data from Denmark. More specifically, I analyse a selection of job interviews from an integration initiative for refugees and migrants in Copenhagen (2006–2016). The initiative was called 'Integration and Training positions' (IO Positions, 2007) and was targeted as a starter kit for newcomers to Denmark considered to have the required professional qualifications for the given job but relatively limited knowledge of Danish. The job positions spanned from kitchen helpers without formal education to business managers or IT specialists with a graduate degree. A requirement for all IO positions was that the job interview had to be conducted in Danish. According to the IO guidelines, though, the applicants' level of Danish was not supposed to have an effect on the decision for selection as long as their professional qualifications met the set criteria. In practice, however, the applicants' linguistic and communicative skills were much more in focus than their professional skills. Even though the intention behind the IO positions was to draw on the applicants' job-related qualifications (regardless of Danish language competence), knowledge of Danish played an important role in the actual selection of candidates and was a central theme during many of the job interviews (see e.g. Kirilova, 2013).

The job interview data I analyse here illustrate how applicants and assessment committees negotiate understanding through Danish as a shared linguistic resource. The chapter consists of four parts. First, I present examples from previous research on job interviews where linguistic and cultural assessments take place (Kirilova, 2013; Roberts & Campbell, 2006). I draw on language ideology (Irvine & Gal, 2000; Silverstein, 2006) as a theoretical framework and discuss the notions of *gatekeeping*, *membership ascription* and *shibboleths* to operationalise language ideology and illustrate the processes of inclusion and exclusion through language. Second, I address the use of conventional expressions as shibboleths in the negotiation of lingua-cultural co-membership. I suggest that when language users at a beginner's level use conventional expressions in the communication with language users at a more advanced linguistic level (or when L2 beginners communicate with L1 users), conventional expressions may help L2 users to communicate more effectively. In the third part, I present data and methods, and analyse extracts of one job interview where the applicant communicates through a large number of conventional expressions. I argue that conventional expressions may not only enable linguistic understanding, but also support the social relationship between the interlocutors thus playing an important role for their mutual affiliation, especially in high-stakes gatekeeping contexts. In the last part, I return to the language ideological framework for a broader discussion and directions for future research.[1]

Job Interviews from the Perspective of Language Ideology

The overall purpose of a job interview is to find the best person for a given job. In addition to possessing knowledge and skills in a professional field, the applicant has to be a person whom the employer likes and wants to keep in the workplace. Establishing and negotiating likability is a complex process that rests on numerous factors. From a linguistic point of view, however, it is evident that language plays a major role in negotiating a relationship between the interlocutors in an interaction since they use language to position themselves and each other in relation to different social actions. Clearly, what people say, and how they say it, influences the way other people perceive and judge them. These perceptions and judgements are based on certain ideologies of what we consider 'appropriate' within a given social or cultural frame.

To conceptualise the relationship between language use and ideology, Silverstein (1985) developed the notion of 'the total linguistic fact'. He argued that when we analyse language from a sociolinguistic point of view, we must consider not only *language structure* but also *contextualised language use* (i.e. where is language used and by whom) and *ideologies* about language users and use. These three components are 'irreducibly dialectic in nature' (Silverstein, 1985: 220) which means that linguistic practices are shaped by ideologies and vice versa.

The link between linguistic practice and (societal) ideologies can be further explained through the notion of *indexicality*. In linguistic anthropology (e.g. Blommaert, 2007; Silverstein, 1976, 2003), indexicality is central for illustrating how language in use points to a particular identifiable and socially-regulated context. Indexicality is powerful in job interviews and has direct consequences for many of the decisions and assessments recruiters make. For example, the linguistic behaviour of the applicants in a job interview is often seen as indexical of the way in which these applicants will perform in the job because the linguistic resources they make use of are directly linked to professional competences and evaluated on that basis. The way interlocutors use language to agree and disagree with each other in a job interview is also crucial to the decision of whom the job will be given to.

In a comprehensive study of job interviews in the UK, Roberts and Campbell (2006) have shown that linguistic performance and professional competence are interrelated as if there was a one-to-one relationship between the way an applicant interacts with the recruitment committee and the way in which an applicant is going to be in the job. How candidates and interviewers relate to each other during the interview is also regarded as indicative of how candidates will relate to future colleagues and superiors in the job. Roberts and Campbell (2006) have also pointed out that newcomers and less fluent speakers may suffer a *linguistic penalty* (see also Roberts, 2021), which means that candidates who do not communicate according to native speaker norms (linguistic, cultural, professional) will be judged not only as 'poor' language users but also as incompetent workers (see also Chapter 7 in this volume).

Kerekes (2003, 2006), Kirilova (2017), Lundmann (2015) and Scheuer (2001) have likewise shown that successful candidates are particularly skilful at showing commitment at both a professional and a personal level. However, if the candidates only present themselves through professional discourse, employers may find it difficult to identify the person behind the discourse. On the other hand, if candidates draw extensively on their private life in the job interview, they might be perceived as 'too much' which could result in a candidate not being taken seriously in a future work task.

In Kirilova and Angouri (2018), we analysed an example in which an applicant with a Middle Eastern background suddenly expressed a liberal attitude towards alcohol and gender equality by declaring that he drank vodka, while his wife drank wine. With this positioning he probably wanted to take a step away from a widespread ethnic stereotype of Muslims as religiously fanatical and self-denying. In the course of the conversation, however, this statement seemed to achieve the opposite effect: instead of bridging presumed cultural differences, it actually widened the gap between the applicant and the assessment committee, who used the statement as an opportunity to emphasise ethnic differences (see also Angouri, 2018, on identity politics). It is difficult to say whether cultural stereotypes had an impact on why this particular applicant did not get the job, but I have shown elsewhere (Kirilova, 2017) that candidates who fail to maintain a socially equal positioning with the assessment committee are often assessed negatively. Another applicant in the data (Kirilova, 2013) said that she was not sure whether making coffee for everybody was part of her duties as a newcomer as she was used to doing so at her former workplace in Asia. When the recruitment committee later described this applicant, they considered it a problem that she might not be able to maintain an equal status among her new colleagues. A third applicant started negotiating a lower salary for himself just to get the job.

Again, the recruitment committee was unwilling to hire him because they felt the applicant was too quick to occupy a subordinate position, which they interpreted as a lack of independent thinking.

These examples replicate the deeply-rooted ideology of the job interview as indexical for what happens in the job afterwards and feed into a broader discussion of what it means to fit into a particular workplace context (Angouri, 2018; Kirilova & Angouri, 2018; Roberts, 2021).

Ideologies are not always *brought along* in the conversation as a general attitude or a stereotype towards a particular cultural group. They can also be *brought about* in the course of the talk (e.g. Baynham, 2014). Especially brought along ideologies could be based on common sense ideas of what people consider well-known 'facts'. However, if these 'facts' are inconsistent with an already established ideological design, they might 'go unnoticed' or 'get explained away' (Irvine & Gal, 2000: 38). Irvine and Gal provide an interesting insight into how ideological arguments are developed, maintained and eventually erased if they do not fit into a particular scheme. If perceptions deviate from an already established (ideological) understanding, they will be 'rendered invisible' from the general pattern. When Danish politicians claim that 'in Denmark we speak Danish', it is an example of erasure. It fits into a neoliberal political agenda of Denmark as a nation state, but does not consider the multilingual practices in society, where many people have access to and speak different languages. These linguistic practices are 'erased' in favour of the overall (political) ideology. It is difficult to distinguish whether the assessments in job interviews are based on already established stereotypes or occur spontaneously in the conversation, but the processes of brought along, brought about and erasure are equally essential for understanding the complex interplay between ideology, interactional positioning and assessments.

Operationalising Ideology through *Gatekeeping, Membership Ascription* and *Shibboleth*

To elaborate further on linguistic ideology and its mechanisms, I will discuss three concepts that point to different ways in which language and social evaluation intertwine: *gatekeeping, membership ascription* and *shibboleth*.

Gatekeeping denotes an ideological practice in which, based on certain implicit or explicit criteria for appropriate linguistic, cultural or social behaviour, some people are included while others are excluded (see also Chapter 7 in this volume). Erickson (1975) coined the notion of gatekeeping in interactional sociolinguistics, arguing that gatekeeping occurs in settings where one person usually has the authority to make decisions that potentially affect the other person's future (see also Erickson &

Schultz, 1982; Gumperz, 1982; Jupp *et al.*, 1982; Kirilova, 2014; Komter, 1991; Roberts, 1985; Roberts & Sayers, 1987; Tranekjær, 2015). Job interviews, citizenship tests and examinations are prototypical examples of gatekeeping events, but as Tranekjær and Kappa (2016) point out, the interlocutors constantly evaluate each other's performance, which means that gatekeeping takes place all the time and in every interaction, regardless of context and situation. In the analysis, I use gatekeeping at a more general level as a key process in understanding job interviews as linguistic events that swing between inclusion and exclusion.

Membership ascription and *membership negotiation* (Baker, 2000; Day, 2012; Sacks, 1972; Schegloff, 2007; Stokoe, 2012; Tranekjær, 2015; Tranekjær & Kappa, 2017) are processes that deal with how people negotiate identities and ascribe each other's membership categories. Through these categories, people gain understanding of how a specific social context is organised and how norms and deviations are produced and reproduced within that particular social context. For example, an ascription to the category 'second language user' (L2 users) implies that second language users are typically assessed from the point of view of first language users (L1 users) (see Davies, 2003) which leads to a hierarchical subdivision between L1 and L2 users. Although such ascriptions are widely accepted and unquestioned, they have consequences for how second language users are positioned and treated in relation to work and integration.

Shibboleth is interrelated with gatekeeping and membership ascription. The notion of shibboleth has been used in various contexts to describe the exclusion and inclusion processes where language plays a role in how people are perceived and judged. Shibboleth is a word, a phrase and, in a broader sense, a way of communicating that indicates an attachment to a particular group. Book of Judges (12: 4–6) describes a historical event in which the pronunciation of either [ʃ] or [s] in shibboleth was used to determine whether a person belonged to the Gileadites or the Efraimites, two Semitic tribes that were fighting each other. In the biblical narrative, those who could not pronounce shibboleth as a Gileadete were identified as the enemy and slaughtered. Although the consequences of deviant pronunciation today might not be terminal for the users in the same way, assessing belonging on the basis of a particular linguistic feature is widely applied in asylum interviews (Blommaert, 2009; Kolinksy, 2016; McNamara, 2012; Spotti, 2015), citizenship interviews (Fogtmann, 2007) and internship recruitment (Tranekjær, 2015). Shibboleth has gained popularity in contemporary sociolinguistic studies, especially through scholarship on testing (McNamara, 2005, 2012) and securitisation (Khan, 2014; Khan & McNamara, 2017). Clearly, the increasing attention on boundary crossing, and the need for constant assessment of linguistic and cultural belonging and non-belonging, call for a tangible concept that can capture and illustrate the relationship between language and cultural identity. Derrida (2005: 23) also draws on the notion of shibboleth in several contexts, referring to it as 'a password', 'a rallying cipher', 'a sign of membership' and a 'political watchword' – all terms that illustrate the powerful ideology and vulnerability of linguistic and cultural belonging.

In this chapter, I use shibboleth as an index for linguistic and cultural belonging to a particular group and with a certain effect (e.g. inclusion or exclusion). Shibboleths can appear at different linguistic levels (phonological, morphological, semantic and discursive), but these levels are impossible to separate from each other. Genres and discourses can also act as shibboleths, so that a particular style or a discourse may become associated with a particular group and indexical for the possession of a particular cultural capital (Bourdieu, 1977; see also Silverstein, 2006, on 'wine talk'; and Eckert, 1989, on identity ascription among high school adolescents). Shibboleth summarises Silverstein's (1985) 'total linguistic fact': if a phonological feature, a lexical expression or a style is to be perceived as an index for belonging or non-belonging, it must hold a specific linguistic structure that certain language users are able to identify in a certain context as either excluding or including. Gumperz's (1982) contextualisation cues, i.e. the verbal and nonverbal mechanisms of signalling how a particular meaning should be inferred from an utterance, are also shibboleths in this sense. But while Gumperz primarily focuses on lack of understanding, I use shibboleth to explore moments of understanding that lead to inclusion and membership ascription. Shibboleth seems a more tangible notion for conceptualising the interrelation between language structure, context and ideology as it points more directly to how belonging and fitting in are potentially indexed through language.

Conventional Expressions as Shibboleths

Conventional expressions are short phrases that are routinised in certain cultures or communities. They have a relatively fixed phonetic, morphological and syntactic structure, for example, 'that's all right' or 'for sure'. Such expressions are usually frequent, immediately recognisable and support the social aspect of communication (see Wray, 2002, for an overview).

In language teaching with an emphasis on communicative competence, conventional expressions are often introduced relatively early in the learning activities (Bardovi-Harlig, 2012; Ellis, 1983; Eskildsen & Wagner, 2015). Conventions may function independently as 'islands of reliability' (Dechert, 1983), 'zones of safety' (Boers *et al.*, 2006) or code-switching strategies in less well-developed L2 speech. Thus, they both relieve the cognitive burden of language learning (Schmitt, 2010) and create a linguistic and cultural connection between the new speaker and the speakers of the target language community (e.g. Tannen, 1990). In a study of communicative competence of English-language users, Yorio (1980) found that conventional forms (as he calls them) serve a number of sociolinguistic functions such as regulating inconvenient moments and facilitating linguistic choices by reducing the complexity in L2 communicative exchange:

> ....saying the wrong thing or reacting unconventionally in a certain situation can create the wrong impression. Second language speakers have often been called too aggressive or too timid, impolite or too polite, loud and pushy or wishy-washy, for this very reason. Conventionalised forms make communication more orderly because they are regulatory in nature. They organise reactions and facilitate choices, thus reducing the complexity of communicative exchanges. They are group identifying. They separate those who belong from those who don't. They do this by serving as instruments for establishing rapport, reinforcing awareness of group membership, perpetuating goals, values, and norms of the group, indicating speakers' readiness to conform to group norms, and defining social relations and the relative status of the different communicators. (Yorio, 1980: 438)

Yorio's approach to conventional expressions and their group-identifying function captures the gatekeeping and evaluative aspect of multilingual interaction. In order to be evaluated positively as being 'one of us' (which is the core of institutional gatekeeping), an L2 speaker needs to negotiate affiliation to the group they want to be accepted by. For any L2 speaker at a beginner's level, the accurate use of conventional expressions in the course of the conversation may not only facilitate better understanding, but also build a social relationship with an interlocutor from a particular group (national, cultural, linguistic), thus enabling the L2 speaker to become a part of this group. Of course, it is not a given that any L2 speaker will automatically gain recognition to a local cultural community by only using conventional expressions, but there might be situations in which L2 users – especially at a beginner's level – would gain some lingua-cultural acknowledgement when they communicate through conventional expressions. This would depend, however, on how co-membership is established and negotiated. Erickson and Shultz (1982) have argued that shared background, experience and interests may facilitate a common referential frame, which may foreground a desire among the interlocutors to communicate and develop a relationship in the encounter. It may be easier to demonstrate – and easier to understand – that participants are collaborating if they have a common background. Successfully negotiated co-membership will then lead to what Erickson and Shultz call 'comfortable moments' and a state of 'conversational synchrony' which ideally takes place when the interlocutors are able to effectively navigate the different roles and frames in the conversation (Goffman, 1981).

It is important to highlight that conventions often function at the level of phatic communication and take on a 'bonding' function (Coulmas, 1981; Malinovski, 1923; Senft, 1995) between people who are brought together and either need to or want to cooperate. Laver (1975: 236) argues that the information exchanged in phatic communication is not referential, but rather is indexical information about 'aspects of the participants' social identity relevant to structuring the interactional consensus of the present and future encounters'. This particular indexicality is highly relevant to the use of conventional expressions as markers of successful cooperation and their function as shibboleths for linguistic and cultural belonging to a lingua-cultural target community.

To sum up, conventional expressions might facilitate successful cooperation between L1 and L2 speakers because they enable not only linguistic understanding but also a co-membership within a particular lingua-cultural group in the gatekeeping process. As Yorio (1980: 438) put it, the use of conventions might indicate an awareness of group membership, as well as a desire to perpetuate group goals, values and norms. In this sense, conventional expressions could be indexical for who is going to be accepted as a member of a particular group. This is what I hope to show in the next sections.

Data and Method

The examples in this article derive from a corpus of 41 audio-recorded job interviews with applicants who speak Danish as an L2 and assessment committees (interviewers) who speak Danish as an L1. Data also include follow up dialogues with six assessment committees and individual interviews with 39 job applicants. I analyse excerpts from one job interview as an illustrative case study of conventional expressions as shibboleths in the negotiating of a common lingua-cultural frame. The interview is characteristic of how successful job interviews are conducted (e.g. in terms of structure and topics) and highlights in particular how conventional expressions function as a successful communicative strategy at a beginner's level of Danish.

I use interactional sociolinguistics (IS) (Gumperz, 1982; Gumperz & Roberts, 1991; Gumperz et al., 1979; Roberts & Campbell, 2006) to draw parallels to similar analyses of multilingual job interviews. I also include tools and notions from conversation analysis (CA) (Heritage, 1984; Pomerantz, 1984; Sacks et al., 1974; Steensig, 2001) to evaluate how the individual contributions are perceived and negotiated by the interlocutors at the sequential level as well as at the supra-segmental level (pauses, intonation) and paralinguistic levels (laughter, murmur). In addition, I draw on *alignment* and *affiliation* as two different activities in the interaction (Steensig, 2012; Stivers, 2008; Stivers *et al.*, 2011). While alignment takes place at the sequential level and describes the structural turn-taking collaboration in the conversation, *affiliation* (Pomerantz, 1984; Tannen, 1990) is rather about engaging in the conversation through actions (comments, assessments, questions, initiatives) that illustrate a higher level of commitment than merely keeping one's turn. Affiliation is thus useful in describing phatic communication and co-membership negotiation.

Both IS and CA draw on a methodology that engages with the participants' perspectives, but IS and CA differ in some important aspects. While CA considers every interaction more or less independent of the wider context, a sociolinguistic approach is typically open to interpretation within a broader social perspective and often includes several data sources collected through ethnography. Since my focus is on language ideology, I draw not only on the job interview data, but also on field notes and follow up interviews with the assessment committees. In these interviews, for example, the members of the assessment committee account for their preferences of applicants for the positions they wish to fill. These accounts provide important background information that contributes to the understanding of the specific interactional moves in the job interviews, and I will draw on them in the analysis, which I present in the next section.

The Case of Ruben

Ruben is the pseudonym of a 25-year-old applicant for the job of kitchen assistant at a boarding school for autistic children. Ruben was born and raised in Cuba, where he studied art. At the time of the job interview, Ruben had lived in Denmark for one year and had taken some Danish classes. Altogether, four candidates were invited for a job interview, and the job was given to Ruben as he was considered the best candidate. The assessment committee consisted of two female employees: a manager (MAN) and a kitchen assistant employee (EMP).

In the following analysis, I present three excerpts from Ruben's interview and a list of conventional expressions that he uses throughout the interview. In Example 1, the manager asks Ruben about his plans for the future. This is a typical job interview question illustrating the notion of indexicality. The story that Ruben produces will be related to a certain professional identity (e.g. 'goal-oriented', 'independent', 'able to make decisions'), which the interviewers will try to infer from what Ruben says and the way he says it (see also Roberts & Campbell, 2005). I use Example 1 as a showcase of Ruben's communicative competence in Danish after one year of language classes as well as an illustration of how he responds to questions posed by the manager. I will later contrast Example 1 with two other examples, in which the interviewers are managing the interaction while Ruben only provides supplementary feedback. Now let us consider Example 1 first:

Example 1

		English translation	Danish original
01.	RUB:	åh (.) ↑guitar normally	øh (.) ↑guitar normalt
02.		åh (.) ah I can	øh (.) ah jeg kan godt
03.		xxx or if you ah (.)	xxx eller når man æ: (.)
04.		I will begin again because	jeg skal starte igen fordi
05.		for a long time I have not	i lang tid har ikke prøve
06.		tried again (0.7) a guitar	igen (0.7) en guitar ella:
07.		o:r (.)↑a:h o:h I don't	(.)↑nå:h ø:h jeg vil ikke
08.		want when I xxx just study	når jeg xxx bare studere
09.		(.) study waiter and I	(.) studerer tjener og jeg
10.		would like but	vil også gerne men
11.		psychology but oh it	psykologi men øh det
12.		the problem wa:s oh (.)	problemet va:r øh (.)
13.		my finances	min økonomi
14.	EMP:	yes	EMP: ja

The above transcript makes it easier to follow Ruben's rather disrupted narrative about playing guitar and studying, but it is important to point out that the large number of breaks, repairs, hesitancies and non-standard pronunciation and intonation pose a serious challenge to understanding him. Ruben sounds slightly more fluent in the English translation I have provided than in the original Danish recording, as the translation cannot represent all deviations in the same way as in the original. However, the excerpt shows clearly that the two interviewers do not participate in the conversation for 24 seconds (lines 1–13), although Ruben's many pauses and mumblings are, in principle, transition-relevant points. The lack of verbal participation could be interpreted as a lack of understanding,[2] and I assume that both the employee and the manager listen intently to try and make sense of Ruben's account. When Ruben states 'I also want to start but psychology but the problem was my finances' (lines 9–13), a sudden breakthrough occurs and the employee immediately reacts (yes, line 14). Once the storyline becomes clearer and displays a causality that makes sense in relation to the employee's original question about Ruben's plans for the future, she immediately confirms understanding.

Let us look at two other examples in which the kitchen employee is the primary speaker while Ruben and the manager listen to her. In Example 2, the kitchen employee gives details about the number of children at the boarding school and explains how the children's day-to-day life is organised:

Example 2

	English translation	Danish original
1.	EMP: and in here <u>twelve</u> ↑children ↑live	EMP: og i heroppe ↑bor <u>tolv</u> ↑børn
2.	RUB: yeah-	RUB: ja-
3.	EMP: -whe:re six children live in	EMP: -hvo:r der bor seks børn i
4.	↑one end of the house	↑dne:n ende af huset
5.	<RUB: okay> and six children	<RUB: okay> og seks børn i
6.	in the ↓other end	↓dn<u>anden</u> ende
7.	RUB: <u>o-kay</u>	RUB: <u>o-kay</u>
8.	EMP: and in each end there is a	EMP: og i hver ende er der en
9.	↑group mom	↑gruppe.mor
10.	RUB: o-↑kay	RUB: o-↑kay
11.	EMP: like a mom or a dad	EMP: lissom en mor eller far
12.	at home-	derhjemme-
13.	RUB: that's quite all right	RUB: det er helt i orden
14.	MAN: ha ha	MAN: ha ha

In Example 2, Ruben produces five different types of feedback, and we see a continuous upgrade of feedback forms. In line 2, he aligns with the employee with a 'yeah'. In line 5, he overlaps with a quick 'okay'. In line 7, he produces a stretched 'o: kay', and in line 10, he comes with a longer and stretched o:↑ka:y with a rising intonation. The second and third 'okay' sound slightly exaggerated because of the intonation and the prolonged vowels. They also fall a bit earlier than what might be expected as a relevant turn-transition point. The fifth feedback in line 13 (det er helt i orden/it's quite all right) also comes quickly and suddenly and triggers a muted laugh from the manager (line 14).

I will now focus on the conventional expression 'det er helt i orden'. Functionally, the expression is used in Danish primarily to assure one's interlocutor in a conversation that what he or she has said is perfectly acceptable. It is idiomatic in Danish because 'i orden' (meaning 'in order') has nothing to do with 'order' but is merely an expression of alignment. It occurs typically after either a commissive ('I would like to ask you to do X') or an interrogative ('can I do Y?' or 'we should not do Z') when one of the interlocutors seeks approval. The person who says 'it's quite all right' has either granted a permission or approved of what the other person has suggested or asked for. There is a hierarchical relation in the act of approving. The person who says 'it's all right' has typically a higher status or an authority to make decisions (at least in that particular context). When Ruben says 'it's quite all right', it goes slightly awry in relation to his participant role as a job applicant in front of an employment committee because the employee is not seeking permission to explain, but is in the process of giving an account of how the workplace is run. On the other hand, 'it's quite all right' could be seen as an upgrade of the previous feedback Ruben has produced in the extract (yes, okay, o:kay and o:↑ka:y). The reaction to 'it's all right' is laughter – the manager and the employee notice the expression and treat it as humorous, possibly because of the hierarchical bias. Regardless of the wryness of the utterance (or perhaps because of it), the conventional expression creates an opportunity for mutual affiliation. Let us consider Example 3:

Example 3

	English translation	Danish original
1.	MAN: could you just eat	MAN: kunne du bare spise
2.	↑chocolate ↑as you wanted	↑chokolade som du ↑ville
3.	RUB: yeah	RUB: ja
4.	MAN: ↑yeah	MAN: ↑ja
5.	RUB: yeah for sure	RUB: ja helt sikkert
6.	MAN: ha ha	MAN: ha ha
7.	RUB: yeah loads of chocolate	RUB: ja masser af chokolade

In Example 3, the manager enquires about previous work experience and Ruben explains that he used to work at a chocolate factory. When the manager asks him if he could eat as much chocolate as he wanted, Ruben responds positively, and then he produces two conventional expressions, first 'helt sikkert' ('for sure' or 'you bet') and then 'masser af chokolade' (loads of chocolate). These two expressions serve the same supportive function as the expression in Example 2 and invoke the same type of laughter (see also Tranekjær, 2017, on laughables as a resource for negotiating shared identities). It is difficult to decide whether the manager laughs because of the situation (the good thing about eating chocolate every day) or because of Ruben's acute use of that particular expression. Either way, these conventional expressions provide an opportunity for mutual affiliation. Of course, there might be numerous factors contributing to creating a positive environment, but it is notable that the number of conventions in this particular interview is high compared to other job interviews in the data (see Kirilova, 2013). This might explain the manager's positive reaction and the affiliative pattern that is established in Examples 2 and 3 and in the rest of the interview. The list below shows that Ruben predominantly uses evaluative expressions that support phatic communication and have an affiliative function in the structuring of consensus:

	English translation	Danish original
1.	it's really hard	det er rigtig svært
2.	for sure/you bet	helt sikkert
3.	yeah precisely	ja præcis
4.	that's a good one	den er god
5.	that's exciting	det er spændende
6.	that's quite all right	det er er helt i orden
7.	hard work	hårdt arbejde
8.	it's a good workout	det er god træning
9.	I'm tired of chocolate	jeg er træt af chokolade
10.	it was a good conversation	det var en dejlig samtale
11.	totally terrible	helt vidt forfærdeligt
12.	totally annoying all the time	vildt irriterende hele tiden
13.	I love barbecue	jeg kan godt lide grill
14.	traditions – that's nice	traditioner - det er dejligt
15.	*not a problem	*ikke nogen problem
16.	*I love horse	*jeg elsker hest

Most of these expressions are frequent in Danish (1–7) and can be recognised as conventions (e.g. I'm tired of X, I like X). I have also included 15 and 16 despite minor morphological deviations, which in fast-rate speech are difficult to notice ('heste' instead of 'hest' and 'noget' instead of 'nogen'). Common to the 16 expressions is that they are short and recognisable. In contrast to Example 1, which illustrated how Ruben tackles an answer to an abstract question when he is left on his own, it seems that when the interviewers do the talking, Ruben's affiliative use of conventional expressions in Danish is particularly interesting and noteworthy. I argue that through these expressions, Ruben becomes a more fluent user of Danish and a more trustworthy job applicant. Apart from serving as 'zones of safety' (Boers *et al.*, 2006) and 'islands of reliability' (Dechert, 1983), these expressions not only display an understanding of the topic and a well-developed pragmatic competence in Danish, but also an in-group relation with the two members of the assessment committee. I would like to argue that through these conventional expressions, Ruben gains a voice in a language that he is still struggling with and manages to establish himself as a future employee who is enthusiastic, committed, able to take a stand and also 'ready to conform to group norms' (Yorio, 1980: 438). For the assessment committee, it is obvious to see this particular linguistic behaviour as indexical for the way in which he will be able to carry out the tasks in the job: independently, critically, committedly and in a (culturally) recognisable manner.

Finally, I include the manager's comments about Ruben from a brief session conducted after the job interview. In this session, the manager explained that the committee had decided to hire Ruben rather than other applicants because Ruben was someone who, in her words, 'fitted into the environment' and was 'easy to communicate with, despite his Danish'. The second statement comprises an interesting contradiction, which I will discuss briefly. Clearly, the manager acknowledged the fact that Ruben was easy to communicate with, but on the other hand, she drew attention to his Danish, which she evaluated as not being satisfactory ('despite his Danish'). In comparison, she explained that one of the other applicants was 'fluent', another was 'academic' and a third one was simply 'good at Danish'. Therefore, when she acknowledged Ruben for being easy to communicate with, she was probably referring to his interactive competence. In this case, interactive competence relates to good listening skills, pragmatic awareness and use of conventional expressions. However, according to her this is not sufficient for being good at Danish. Thus, the manager displayed a dual attitude where she first expressed her contextualised understanding of effortless communication and interactive competence based on the job interview interaction. At the same time, she also articulated a decontextualised normative view of what 'good' Danish is, or should be (clearly different from the way Ruben speaks). So what made Ruben a good candidate then? I suggest that Ruben 'passed' the job interview because he competently used conventional expressions through which he successfully negotiated co-membership to the in-group (Danish) community. The conventional expressions came to function as in-group shibboleths that helped Ruben position himself as someone who 'fitted into the environment'. When co-membership had been negotiated and established and Ruben was accepted as 'one of us' (i.e. someone who fits into the environment), it overshadowed (or 'erased' in Irvine and Gal's (2000) terminology) the decontextualised (political) requirement to speak 'good' Danish in Denmark. In this sense it is an effective strategy if second language users (even with a limited command of the second language) are able to negotiate cultural membership (through e.g. conventional expressions). Particularly in gatekeeping contexts, the use of conventional expressions might also indicate that the applicant had perhaps worked hard to acquire linguistic and cultural knowledge of Danish and might thus be willing to adapt to new norms and expectations. The effort that Ruben had put into learning Danish over a relatively short period of time became yet another indexical feature for general engagement, determination and commitment.

Conclusion

From the perspective of linguistic ideology (e.g. Irvine & Gal, 2000; Silverstein, 1985), this chapter discusses data from multilingual job interviews in Denmark. To specify and operationalise the processes of indexicality, inclusion and exclusion, I use the notions of gatekeeping, co-membership and shibboleth. In the analysis, I focus particularly on one job applicant's use of conventional expressions in Danish. The applicant, Ruben, was a new speaker of Danish at a beginner's level, but his skilful use of conventional expressions seemed to play a role for the successful outcome of the interview. Although the data are limited, the case of Ruben is illustrative of how the use of conventional expressions might strengthen the social relation between language users with different levels of shared linguistic resources. Especially in high-stakes gatekeeping interactions, conventional expressions might help new speakers to obtain linguistic and cultural in-group status, and, as in the case of job interviews, conventions might help L2 applicants to communicate more successfully, which eventually might lead to a job offer. While L1 speakers of Danish are able to use conventional expressions more or less unnoticed, conventions trigger a 'marked' effect when new speakers use them, especially those at a beginner's level. One reason for this might be that certain conventions are less expected in a beginner's vocabulary. Therefore, conventions might create not only a positive environment, but also a common lingua-cultural context that could allow membership into the target community. Ruben's job interview is a showcase of co-membership in which the conventional expressions function as shibboleths for becoming part of the group, but the interview is not unique in terms of how cultural identities are negotiated in order to fit in with the gatekeepers' expectations. In this regard, my analysis feeds into a broader discussion of what it means to fit into a particular linguistic and cultural context (see also Kirilova & Angouri, 2018). Fitting in is clearly about negotiating co-membership; those applicants who are able to negotiate an equal positioning and a membership status within a gatekeeper's community (through e.g. common linguistic resources, cultural values and other group similarities) might very well be the preferred applicants. Because of the gatekeeping element of the job interview, applicants will often strive to negotiate an in-group identity with the assessment committee in the hope of getting a job. Whether they position themselves as skilful users of Danish through conventional expressions, modest workers in terms of salary expectations or husbands that support gender equality in the family, candidates show awareness of the highly ideological imagery of the job interview. The shibboleths they use (successfully or unsuccessfully) confirm the existence of a monolingual and monocultural ideology according to which the preferred future employees are those with whom the employers can identify themselves with (culturally as well as linguistically). Studying conventional expressions as markers of interactional affiliation might give new insights into the multi-layered relationship of language, culture and ideology. It requires more data and more studies to further map the interplay between the use of particular phrases, conventions, words or discourses and cultural recognition. It is also evident that we need to study other types of interactions and contexts where institutional gatekeeping plays a role in the dynamics and outcomes of the conversation.

Appendix: Transcription Conventions

(.)	short pause
(4.0)	4 sec pause
<hallo>	overlap
hallo	stressed word or part of a word
ha:llo	stretched vowel
↑hallo	rising pitch
↓hallo	falling pitch
xxx	incomprehensible passage

Notes

(1) Parts of the theoretical framework and the analysis of conventional expressions are also described in a Danish version of this article (Kirilova, 2018).
(2) There are no indications of verbal feedback/repair, but it is possible that video-recordings would have shown non-verbal agreement (e.g. nodding) which I cannot see in the audio-data.

References

Angouri, J. (2018) *Culture, Discourse, and the Workplace*. New York: Routledge.
Baker, C.D. (2000) *Locating Culture in Action: Membership Categorisation in Texts and Talk*. St. Leonards, NSW: Allen & Unwin.
Bardovi-Harlig, K. (2012) Formulas, routines, and conventional expressions in pragmatics research. *ARAL* 32, 206–227.
Baynham, M. (2014) Identity: Brought about or brought along? Narrative as a privileged site for researching intercultural identities. In F. Dervin and K. Risager (eds) *Researching Identity and Interculturality* (pp. 73–92). New York: Routledge.
Blommaert, J. (2007) Sociolinguistics and discourse analysis: Orders of indexicality and polycentricity. *Journal of Multicultural Discourses* 2 (2), 115–130.
Blommaert, J. (2009) Investigating narrative inequality: African asylum seekers' stories in Belgium. *Discourse & Society* 12 (4), 413–449.
Boers, F., Eyckmans, E., Kappel, J., Stengers, H. and Demecheleer, M. (2006) Formulaic sequences and perceived oral proficiency: Putting a lexical approach to the test. *Language Teaching Research* 10 (3), 245–261.
Bolton, K. and Kuteeva, M. (2012) English as an academic language at a Swedish university: Parallel language use and the 'threat' of English. *Journal of Multilingual and Multicultural Development* 33 (5), 429–447.
Bourdieu, P. (1977) Cultural reproduction and social reproduction. In J. Karabel and A.H. Halsey (eds) *Power and Ideology in Education* (pp. 487–511). Oxford: Oxford University Press.
Bramm, E. and Kirilova, M. (2018) "Du skal bare sætte hende i gang, du skal ikke gå og passe hende" – Om sprog i praktikforløb for flygtninge og indvandrere. *Sprogforum* 66, 85–94.
Coulmas, F. (ed.) (1981) *Conversational Routine: Explorations in Standardized Communication Situations and Prepatterned Speech*. Berlin: Walter de Gruyter.
Davies, A. (2003) *The Native Speaker: Myth and Reality*. Clevedon: Multilingual Matters.
Day, D. (2012) Conversation analysis and membership categories. In C.A. Chappelle (ed.) *The Encyclopedia of Applied Linguistics* (pp. 1050–1055). Oxford: John Wiley & Sons.

Dechert, H.W. (1983) How a story is done in a second language. Strategies in interlanguage communication. In C. Faerch and G. Kasper (eds) *Strategies in Interlanguage Communication* (pp. 175–195). London: Longman.
Derrida, J. (2005) Shibboleth: For Paul Celan. In T. Dutoit and O. Pasanen (eds) *Sovereignties in Question: The Poetics of Paul Celan* (pp. 1–64). New York: Fordham University Press. (Originally published as Schibboleth: Pour Paul Celan by Éditions Galilé, 1986).
Eckert, P. (1989) *Jocks and Burnouts: Social Categories and Identity in the High School*. New York: Teachers College Press.
Ellis, R. (1983) Formulaic speech in early classroom second language development. In D. Handscombe (ed.) *The Question of Control. Selected Papers from the 17th Annual Convention of Teachers of English to Speakers of Other Languages* (pp. 53–65). Washington, DC: Teachers of English to Speakers of Other Languages.
Erickson, F. (1975) Gatekeeping and the melting pot: Interaction in counseling encounters. *Harvard Educational Review* 45 (1), 44–70.
Erickson, F. and Shultz, J. (1982) *The Counselor as Gatekeeper: Social Interaction in Interviews*. New York: Academic Press.
Eskildsen, S.W. and Wagner, W. (2015) Sprogbrugsbaseret læring i en tosproget hverdag. En forskningsoversigt over sprogbrugsbaseret andetsprogstilegnelse og sprogpædagogiske implikationer. *NyS, Nydanske Sprogstudier* 48, 71–104.
Fogtmann, C. (2007) Samtaler med politiet: Interaktionsanalytiske studier af sprogtestning i danske naturalisationssamtaler. PhD thesis, Københavns Universitet.
Goffman, E. (1981) *Forms of Talk*. Oxford: Blackwell.
Gumperz, J.J. (1982) *Discourse Strategies*. Cambridge: Cambridge University Press.
Gumperz, J.J. and Roberts, C. (1991) Understanding in intercultural encounters. In J. Blommaert and J.J. Verschueren (eds) *The Pragmatics of Intercultural and International Communication* (pp. 51–90). Amsterdam: John Benjamins.
Gumperz, J.J., Roberts, C. and Jupp, T.C. (1979) *Crosstalk: A Study of Cross-Cultural Communication*. London: National Centre for Industrial Language Training in association with BBC.
Heritage, J. (1984) A change-of-state token and aspects of its sequential placement. In J.M. Atkinson and J. Heritage (eds) *Structures of Social Action* (pp. 299–345). Cambridge: Cambridge University Press.
IO Positions (2007) Vejledning om integration og oplæringsstillinger (2007). *KL, Danske Regioner and KTO Kommunale Tjenestemænd of Overenskomstansatte*. https://www.kl.dk/media/8910/io-stillinger-praesentation.pdf (accessed 16 June 2021).
Irvine, J.T. and Gal, S. (2000) Language ideology and linguistic differentiation. In P. Kroskrity (ed.) *Regimes of Language* (pp. 35–83). Santa Fe, NM: School of American Research Press.
Jupp, T.C, Robertsand, C. and Cook-Gumperz, J. (1982) Language and disadvantage: The hidden process. In J. Gumperz (ed.) *Language and Social Identity* (pp. 232–256). Cambridge: Cambridge University Press.
Kerekes, J. (2003) Distrust: A determining factor in the outcomes of gatekeeping encounters. In G. House, G. Kasper and S. Ross (eds) *Misunderstanding in Social Life* (pp. 227–257). London: Longman.
Kerekes, J.A. (2006) Winning an interviewer's trust in a gatekeeping encounter. *Language in Society* 35 (1), 27–59.
Khan, A.W. (2014) Asylum-seeking migration, identity-building and social cohesion: Policy-making vs. social action for cultural recognition. *Contemporary Social Science* 9 (3), 285–297.
Khan, K. and McNamara, T. (2017) Citizenship, immigration laws, and language. In S. Canagarajah (ed.) *The Routledge Handbook of Migration and Language* (pp. 451–467). London: Routledge.

Kirilova, M. (2013) All dressed up and nowhere to go: Linguistic, cultural and ideological aspects of job interviews with second language speakers of danish. PhD thesis, University of Copenhagen.

Kirilova, M. (2014) 'Det kan være svært' – Om sprog og kultur i andetsprogsdanske ansættelsessamtaler. *Nordand – Nordisk tidsskrift for andetsprogsforskning* 9 (1), 9–36.

Kirilova, M. (2017) 'Oh it's a DANISH boyfriend you've got'– Co-membership and cultural fluency in job interviews with minority background applicants in Denmark. In J. Angouri, M. Marra and J. Holmes (eds) *Negotiating Boundaries at Work* (pp. 29–49). Edinburgh: Edinburgh University Press.

Kirilova, M. (2018) 'Det er helt i orden': Kulturelle shibboletter i jobsamtaler med andetsprogsbrugere af dansk. *NyS, Nydanske Sprogstudier* 1 (55), 40–69.

Kirilova, M. and Angouri, J. (2018) You are now one of us – Negotiating 'fitting in' in the workplace. In A. Creese and A. Blackledge (eds) *The Routledge Handbook of Language and Superdiversity* (pp. 345–360). London: Routledge.

Kirilova, M. and Lønsmann, D. (2020) Dansk–nøglen til arbejde? Ideologier om sprogbrug og sproglæring i to arbejdskontekster i Danmark. *Nordand* 4 (1), 37–57.

Kolinsky, H. (2016) The shibboleth of discretion: The discretion, identity, and persecution paradigm in American and Australian LGBT asylum claims. *Berkeley Journal of Gender Law & Justice* 31 (2), 206–40.

Komter, M. (1991) *Conflict and Co-operation in Job Interviews*. Amsterdam: John Benjamins.

Laver, J. (1975) Communicative functions of phatic communion. In A. Kendon, R. Harris and M. Key (eds) *Organization of Behavior in Face-to-face Interaction* (pp. 215–238). The Hague: De Gruyter.

Lundmann, L. (2015) Basic assumptions when assessing people: Studies of job interviews and personality testing. PhD thesis, University of Copenhagen.

Lønsmann, D. (2014) Linguistic diversity in the international workplace: Language ideologies and processes of exclusion. *Multilingua – Journal of Cross-Cultural and Interlanguage Communication* 33 (1–2), 89–116.

Lønsmann, D. (2015) Language ideologies in a Danish company with English as a corporate language: 'It has to be English'. *Journal of Multilingual and Multicultural Development* 36 (4), 339–356.

Malinowski, B. (1923) The problem of meaning in primitive languages. In C.K. Ogden and I.A. Richards (eds) *The Meaning of Meaning* (pp. 296–336). London: K. Paul, Trench, Trubner & Co.

McNamara, T. (2012) Language assessments as shibboleths: A poststructuralist perspective. *Applied linguistics* 33 (5), 564–581.

McNamara, T. (2005) 21st century shibboleth: Language tests, identity and intergroup conflict. *Language Policy* 4 (4), 351–370.

Mortensen, J. and Haberland, H. (2012) English – The new Latin of academia? Danish universities as a case. *International Journal of the Sociology of Language* 216, 175–197.

Pomerantz, A. (1984) Agreeing and disagreeing with assessments: Some features of preferred/dispreferred turn shapes. In J.M. Atkinson and J. Heritage (eds) *Structures of Social Action* (pp. 57–101). Cambridge: Cambridge University Press.

Roberts, C. (1985) *The Interview Game: And How It's Played*. London: British Broadcasting Corporation.

Roberts, C. (2021) *Linguistic Penalties and the Job Interview*. Bristol: Equinox Publishing.

Roberts, C. and Sayers, P. (1987) Keeping the gate: How judgements are made in interethnic interviews. In K. Knapp, W. Enninger and A. Knapp-Potthof (eds) *Analyzing Intercultural Communication* (pp. 111–135). Berlin: Mouton de Gruyter.

Roberts, C. and Campbell, S. (2005) Fitting stories into boxes: Rhetorical and textual constraints on candidates' performances in British job interviews. *Journal of Applied Linguistics* 2 (1), 45–73.

Roberts, C. and Campbell, S. (2006) *Talk on Trial: Job Interviews, Language and Ethnicity* (Research report 344). London: Department for Work and Pensions (DWP).
Sacks, H. (1972) An initial investigation of the usability of conversational data for doing sociology. In D. Sudnow (ed.) *Studies in Social Interaction* (pp. 31–74). New York: Free Press.
Sacks, H., Schegloff, E.A. and Jefferson, G. (1974) A simplest systematics for the organisation of turn-taking for conversation. *Language* 50 (4), 696–735.
Sandwall, K. (2013) *Att hantera praktiken. Om sfi-studerandes möjligheter till interaktion och lärandepå praktikplatser*. Göteborg: Ineko.
Schegloff, E.A. (2007) A tutorial on membership categorization. *Journal of pragmatics* 39 (3), 462–482.
Scheuer, J. (2001) Recontextualization and communicative styles in job interviews. *Discourse Studies* 3 (2), 223–248.
Schmitt, N. (2010) *Researching Vocabulary: A Vocabulary Research Manual*. Berlin: Springer.
Senft, G. (1995) Phatic communion. In J. Verschueren, J.O. Östman and J. Blommaert (eds) *Handbook of Pragmatics* (pp. 1–10). Amsterdam: John Benjamins.
Silverstein, M. (1976) Shifters, linguistic categories, and cultural description. In K. Basso and H. Selby (eds) *Meaning in Anthropology* (pp. 11–55). Albuquerque: University of New Mexico Press.
Silverstein, M. (1985) Language and the culture of gender: At the intersection of structure, usage, and ideology. In E. Mertz and R.J. Parmentier (eds) *Semiotic Mediation: Sociocultural and Psychological Perspectives* (pp. 219–259). Orlando, FL: Academic Press.
Silverstein, M. (2003) Indexical order and the dialectics of sociolinguistic life. *Language & Communication* 23 (3–4), 193–229.
Silverstein, M. (2006) Old wine, new ethnographic lexicography. *Annual Review Anthropology* 35, 481–496.
Spotti, M. (2015) Sociolinguistic shibboleths at the institutional gate. In K.K. Arnaut, J. Blommaert, B. Rampton and M. Spotti (eds) *Language and Superdiversity* (pp. 261–279). New York: Routledge.
Steensig, J. (2001) *Sprog i virkeligheden. Bidrag til en interaktionel lingvistik*. Århus: Aarhus Universitetsforlag.
Steensig, J. (2012) Conversation analysis and affiliation and alignment. In K. Mortensen and J. Wagner (eds) *The Encyclopedia of Applied Linguistics: Conversation Analysis*. Cambridge: Wiley–Blackwell. https://doi.org/10.1002/9781405198431.wbeal0196.
Stivers, T. (2008) Stance, alignment, and affiliation during storytelling: When nodding is a token of affiliation. *Research on Language and Social Interaction* 41 (1), 31–57.
Stivers, T., Mondada, L. and Steensig, J. (2011) Knowledge, morality and affiliation in social interaction. In T. Stivers, L. Mondada, and J. Steensig (eds) *The Morality of Knowledge in Conversation* (pp. 3–26). Cambridge: Cambridge University Press.
Stokoe, E. (2012) Moving forward with membership categorization analysis: Methods for systematic analysis. *Discourse Studies* 14 (3), 277–303.
Strömmer, M. (2016). Affordances and constraints: Second language learning in cleaning work. *Multilingua* 35 (6), 697–721.
Suni, M. (2017) Working and learning in a new niche: Ecological interpretations of work-related migration. In J. Angouri, M. Marra and J. Holmes (eds) *Negotiating Boundaries at Work: Talking and Transitions* (pp. 197–215). Edinburgh: Edinburgh University Press.
Sørensen, M.S. and Holmen, A. (2004) *At blive en del af en arbejdsplads: Om sprog og læring i praksis*. Copenhagen: Institut for Pædagogisk Antropologi, Danmarks Pædagogiske Universitet.
Tannen, D. (1990) Gender differences in topical coherence: Creating involvement in best friends' talk. *Discourse Processes* 13 (1), 73–90.

Thøgersen, J.M. (2010) Coming to terms with English in Denmark: Discursive constructions of a language contact situation. *International Journal of Applied Linguistics* 20 (3), 291–326.
Tranekjær, L. (2015) *Interactional Categorization and Gatekeeping: Institutional Encounters with Otherness*. Bristol: Multilingual Matters.
Tranekjær, L. (2017) Laughables as a resource for foregrounding shared knowledge and shared identities in intercultural interactions in Scandinavia. In D. Van de Mieroop and S. Schnurr (eds) *Identity Struggles: Evidence from Workplaces Around the World* (pp. 185–206). Philadelphia: John Benjamins.
Tranekjær, L. and Kappa, K. (2016) The interactional establishment of the membership category 'nonnative speaker' in gatekeeping encounters. In K. Bardovi-Harlig and J.C. Félix-Brasdefer (eds) *Pragmatics and Language Learning* (vol. 14, pp. 93–122). Honolulu, HI: National Foreign Language Resource Center.
Wray, A. (2002) *Formulaic Sequences and the Lexicon*. Cambridge: Cambridge University Press.
Yorio, C.A. (1980) Conventionalized language forms and the development of communicative competence. *TESOL Quarterly* 14 (4), 433–442.
Øhrstrøm, C. (2016) L2 listening at work. A qualitative study of international employees' experiences with understanding Danish as a second language. PhD thesis, University of Copenhagen.

6 Assessing and Analysing Health Care Finnish: Test Performance and Lived Experiences

Marja Seilonen and Minna Suni

Introduction

The question of what constitutes sufficient language skills is often raised in relation to migrants and working life. Different stakeholders may decide what is sufficient for each purpose and what is not, and individuals are to show that their language proficiency meets the given requirements (see also Chapters 5, 7 and 10 in this volume). The language proficiency level required for employment specifically in the health sector and for ensuring patient safety is under public debate worldwide. In Finland, which is the setting for our study, this topic has come under scrutiny, as the number of health professionals with tertiary degrees obtained abroad is continually increasing. Approximately 600 internationally educated health care professionals obtain professional practice rights annually, and already in 2014, 9% of medical doctors, 7.7% of dentists, and 3.5% of nurses were from outside Finland (NIHW, 2021), representing larger proportions than in many other EU countries.

We approach the question of sufficient language skills by presenting the background, development process, and research outcomes of a language assessment experiment implemented in the *Health care Finnish* project (*Health care Finnish: Developing and assessing Finnish proficiency among health care professionals*, University of Jyväskylä, Finland). The general aim of the project was to explore how the language education and language proficiency assessment of health care professionals with tertiary qualifications could be developed. As part of the project, a tailor-made language assessment module was developed in order to find out how professional language skills could be meaningfully assessed in a less widely taught language – Finnish – and what kind of added value, if any, such assessment could bring if seen against the existing assessment procedures.

The study was motivated by the nationally recognised need to meet the new educational needs and to update the language policies applied in the licensure (legalisation, authorisation) processes that concern professional practice rights in the health sector (Ministry of Education and Culture (MEC), 2014). Neither prior empirical research on this topic in Finland nor comparative evidence from other corresponding contexts, for instance in other Nordic countries, was available for the ministries and national authorities as a resource in decision-making yet. Therefore, a project containing an assessment experiment with a well-established test of general language proficiency in Finnish (Finnish National Certificate for Language Proficiency (FNCLP)) and a tailor-made field-specific language assessment module was funded by the Ministry of Education and Culture and conducted by our research team.

In this chapter, we aim to show what language skills the research participants were able to demonstrate in the language assessment experiment as a whole, and in its tailor-made professional language assessment module in particular. We also exemplify how their work experience manifested itself in their test performances and in their reflections in post-test interviews.

We will first introduce Finnish language policies concerning the language requirements established for internationally educated professionals in health care, and then give an overview of the *Health care Finnish* project, including its aims, implementation and quantitative findings. In the empirical part of this chapter, qualitative findings on test performances will be reported, and feedback received in post-test interviews will be analysed. Finally, we discuss the relevance of our research findings by setting them in a broader societal framework of labour migration, the positioning and employability of a mobile workforce, and language and education policies.

International Mobility and Language Policies in the Health Sector

The global mobility of the workforce has been present in health care for a long time, but this has become even more intense and visible in recent years, and is also widely criticised due to brain drain and other features related to recruitment ethics (see e.g. Marcus *et al.*, 2014). In Finland, internationally educated health professionals may get recruited in two ways: through regular migration processes by which health professionals move to Finland for various reasons and seek employment in their new country of residence, or through tailor-made recruitment programmes in which intensive language instruction is provided in the country of origin (e.g. in the Philippines or in Spain) for some months before the participants migrate to begin their work in Finland (see Raunio, 2013; Schleicher & Suni, 2021). What is common for both cases is that learning Finnish typically starts only after the decision to move has been made, or after arrival in Finland.

Working in such a less widely taught second language (L2) is inherently different from working in one's native language or in English, which one has usually learnt at school and developed further during university studies, and thus knows relatively well before making employment and relocation decisions. For those whose L2 proficiency is still rather limited when starting a new job, reconstructing self-confidence as a professional takes time (Schleicher & Suni, 2021; Suni, 2017). Exacerbating these challenges, overt mistrust towards internationally recruited health workers is sometimes exhibited by clients, colleagues and the general public (Virtanen, 2017). In turn, for those who come from outside the European Union/European Economic Area (EU/EEA) region, accessing work in one's own field may take several years due to lengthy licensure processes. For these workers, there is a risk of losing touch with the field before getting a related job in a new country, as they usually need to develop their L2 skills outside the health care context first.

Patient safety is key to understanding why language requirements play a special role in the health care sector, both locally and globally. Language policies for medical and health care professionals ensure that patients are in safe hands in all circumstances; precise legislation concerns such issues as patient rights and medical records, which regulate certain aspects of language use in the workplace (Valvira, 2021). The policies and their implementation vary greatly. However, while national policies are rooted in local historical and societal contexts, they are also affected by global trends such as the increasing international mobility of the workforce.

In Europe, a change in the EU directive 2005/36 ensuring free mobility of the workforce within the EU was introduced in 2015, which allowed national authorities to set language requirements for health professionals who previously could freely seek employment in other EU countries without having their language knowledge documented. This brought changes in national-level language policies concerning health care worker recruitment in Finland too.

Proficiency in a national language is a central requirement for migrants entering the labour market in a new country. In Finland, internationally educated health care professionals demonstrate their Finnish (or Swedish) language proficiency through the Finnish National Certificates of Language Proficiency (FNCLP) intermediate-level test; they need a minimum level of 3 (equivalent to level B1 according to the Common European Framework of Reference for Languages (CEFR)), irrespective of their place of origin. However, the issue has been raised as to whether this minimum level (3, or B1) demonstrated in a test of general Finnish (or Swedish) is sufficient for a health care professional to work in Finland (see Kela & Komppa, 2011; MEC, 2014; Tervola, 2019).

The change in the EU directive has already resulted in aligning the language requirements for health care professionals who received their degrees in the EU/EEA with those for individuals who received their degrees outside the EU/EEA area. The change, which was proposed in 2014 (MEC, 2014), came into effect in 2016. In parallel, ministry-level suggestions were made to raise the required proficiency level from FNCLP level 3 to level 4 (CEFR level B1 to B2) and to complement the standardised Finnish National Certificates for Language Proficiency (FNCLP) test with a test module that assesses *professional* language skills. This proposal has not yet come into effect, but indications of such assessment were already analysed in our assessment experiment designed in line with these suggestions and reported in this chapter (see also Seilonen *et al.*, 2016).

It should be noted that employers play a key role as gatekeepers, since they are responsible for ensuring that the language skills of hired employees meet the needs of their tasks at work (see also Chapter 5 in this volume; Roberts, 2021). In Finland, this means that employers in the health sector have the right to require a higher proficiency level than FNCLP 3 (CEFR B1), which is the threshold level only for the licensure process and not for the work itself. In addition, an employer's statement that the applicant demonstrates sufficient L2 proficiency can be taken into account during the licensure process; in certain cases, an FNCLP test is therefore not considered necessary (Valvira, 2021). Employers can thus be seen as key actors in language policy and assessment even if evaluating language proficiency is not their area of expertise.

Degrees obtained in other EU/EEA countries are accepted in Finland. For example, after showing level-3 Finnish (or Swedish) knowledge, a medical doctor, dentist or nurse from a country such as Estonia, Poland or Germany can freely access the labour market in Finland. In turn, medical doctors who have obtained their qualifications in a country outside of the EU/EEA must complete a licensure procedure which consists of approval of the degree, an internship, a Finnish or Swedish language test, and a three-part medical licensure examination to obtain professional practice rights in Finland (Valvira, 2021). The examination, which must be carried out in Finnish or Swedish (Valvira, 2021), is organised by the University of Tampere in cooperation with the National Supervisory Authority for Welfare and Health. It consists of three examinations: clinical examination, examination on the Finnish health care system and practical patient care examination. From 2022 onwards, the language requirement to be met in the last part (practical patient care examination) has been higher than the current legislation prescribes (FNLCP); the university has taken an active role in language policy here, but it has also received overt support for this change from the national authority (Mikkonen, 2021; Toikkanen, 2021). Dentists also have to do an internship and pass a language test (FNLCP 3) and competency examinations organised by the University of Helsinki or Turku (Valvira, 2021).

The failure rates in the examination have been relatively high among internationally educated medical doctors (Tervola *et al.*, 2015). Furthermore, passing all three parts of it and attaining a sufficient level of Finnish (or Swedish) proficiency can be time-consuming. The examination context can also be seen as contradictory: while B1-level knowledge is officially sufficient for licensure, with only that level of proficiency it is not possible to demonstrate abstract and academic knowledge effectively. There is, in addition, a risk of covert dual assessment: while an applicant's language proficiency is overtly measured through the official (FNCLP) test, additional language assessment is embedded in the linguistic demands of passing the examination. The new policy, with a higher language requirement, can be seen as a way to resolve this contradiction.

In addition to prescribing official language requirements and examinations, language policy is present in a migrant health care employee's daily life through legislation concerning issues such as the ways of handling patient information, documentation practices (medical records), and patient rights (information to be available in a comprehensible manner; also interpretation arranged if necessary). As Virtanen (2017) has shown in her study of international nursing students doing their practical training in Finnish, learning to manage electronic patient record practices, for example, is an important step in the socialisation process toward attaining a position as an independent professional. The texts on these records are multi-voiced and socially constructed, and it is essential to learn to formulate them in accordance with convention.

In the next section, we will give an overview of field-specific language assessment. The needs, means and challenges of this kind of assessment are briefly discussed in the context of international mobility of health care workers. Then we will describe the design of the field-specific assessment module that was developed and used as part of our assessment experiment and created for research purposes only.

Developing a Field-Specific Language Assessment

Test development and research focusing on work-related second language skills of health care professionals have generally concentrated on English-language contexts. For workplaces using other languages, only a general language test (such as FNCLP in Finland) is typically used, without separate field-specific language assessment. This is understandable, since developing and maintaining a valid high-stakes test system is both demanding and expensive. It is worth noting that English is a common medium of instruction in many degree programmes outside of English-speaking countries. In Finland alone, several nursing programmes are in English; they were originally designed to prepare Finnish students for international careers, but now they attract mainly international students who wish to gain admission to a free, high-quality education (see Virtanen, 2017). In East-Central

Europe, similarly, tertiary qualifications in medicine can be obtained in English at several universities; there, student fees are crucial for university finances. Such programmes are attractive to students coming from countries where competition is very tight or medical programmes are not as highly ranked. Some countries also educate nurses in English explicitly for export purposes: the Philippines is the best-known example of such an explicit nurse export policy (see Marcus *et al.*, 2014). It is thus no wonder that professional health care language tests have focused on English proficiency.

The most widely used language test is the Occupational English Test (OET), which consists of four parts representing four skill areas (listening, reading, writing and speaking), with an emphasis on communication in health care environments. OET is widely accepted in English-speaking countries (e.g. Australia, New Zealand, the United Kingdom, Ireland, the US, Canada, Singapore and Dubai). As Elder and McNamara (2016) have noted regarding OET development and research, some of the key challenges are to create assessment criteria which reflect the language needs of real working life, are reliable, and easy to operationalise.

As mentioned above, high-stakes test systems similar to OET are not available for non-English contexts. Therefore, our experiment included intensive development work even though the tasks were not meant for wider use beyond this project. One of the key challenges in field-specific language assessment is to achieve sufficient authenticity as concerns language practices at work, while keeping the assessment procedures feasible (see McNamara & Ryan, 2011). In any health care work, professionals speak and write on the basis of what they have read, heard and observed, and graphical and numerical information is also present in these interactions. To replicate real-life communicative practices as much as possible, we designed a professional language assessment module comprising integrated tasks that challenged traditional ways of assessing speaking, writing and comprehension skills separately. The assessment module was used for research purposes only.

The use of integrated tasks or thematic links is common practice in many English as a Second Language (ESL) tests (e.g. International English Language Testing System (IELTS), TOEFL iBT) (Esmaeili, 2002; McNamara, 2009), and a remarkable breakaway from the four skills tradition which has dominated the language assessment field since Lado (1961). However, official tests focusing on field-specific language and utilising integrated tasks have not yet been established or examined. According to Hamp-Lyons (1991), real skills in an L2 can be shown better in a field-specific test than in a general language test. Integration of sub-skills reflects real-life situations at work (see McNamara, 2009), so by developing integrated tasks we aimed to approximate real-life communicative situations. Since it was not feasible to include authentic face-to-face interactions in the experiment, we instead used simulated tasks.

A tailored professional language assessment module with integrated tasks was designed to complement the FNCLP. The module featured the use of material-based integrated tasks, where two or more receptive and productive sub-skills were combined (e.g. writing based on spoken video material and speaking based on written documents). The six integrated tasks focused on domain-specific communicative functions, such as giving advice, providing information, requesting action and reporting. The simulated tasks contained interaction with colleagues, patients and the relatives of the patients, and required continuous shifts between professional and colloquial language use, and between written and spoken modalities (see, for instance, Komppa et al., 2014; Moore et al., 2015).

The research setting was expected to provide information on how a performance-based assessment of professional language skills could complement the FNCLP language proficiency profile of a health care professional. Much of the professional language learning takes place on the job, so the test construct and criteria have to be designed to reflect this (e.g. Elder et al., 2012).

In the next sections, we first present the research participants and their test scores, and then report the qualitative observations based on the test performances and post-test interviews that formed the core of our analysis.

Data Sets and Test Performance

The data consist of two data sets: test performances and post-test interviews. The key participants of the project were 34 internationally educated health care professionals. All participants had tertiary qualifications from outside Finland: they were medical doctors (code DR, n = 9), dentists (DT, n = 2) or nurses (N, n = 24). At the time of the experiment, the participants were working, applying for a license to work in Finland's health sector, or participating in in-service training to qualify to work in their original professions in Finland. Many of them had obtained other types of work experience in Finland while waiting for their licenses. Most typically, nurses had been employed as care assistants in elderly homes, i.e. they had worked in the same field but in lower-status positions where professional practice rights are not required.

The participants came from a variety of countries and had different language backgrounds: Russian (code Ru, n = 11); Spanish (Sp, n = 7); Chinese (Ch, n = 4); Filipino/English (Fi, n = 4); Nepalese (Ne, n = 2); Armenian (Ar), Bulgarian (Bg), Hindi (Hi), Hungarian (Hu), Thai (Th) and Vietnamese (Vt) (n = 1 for each). They were recruited through in-service training programmes and seminars organised for internationally educated health professionals, and also through the FNCLP participant register in which some had recently identified applying for a license as the main reason for taking the test. In addition to data from these participants, some key observations from an earlier data set of the project are also presented at the beginning of the section entitled 'Professional language as a resource'; these data include the FNCLP test performances of another 36 internationally educated health care professionals, 24 of whom were nurses recruited from the Philippines. This data set had already been analysed while creating the professional language assessment module, and for its participants simple pseudonyms (Axel, Peter) are used instead of codes.

First, the 34 key participants of the study took the intermediate level FNCLP test, followed by the professional language assessment module. Finally, they each participated in a post-test interview, which offered an insider view on the test performances. As Figure 6.1 below shows, the skill profiles obtained in the intermediate-level FNCLP test varied between a score of 3 = B1 and 4 = B2 for all but two participants (the whole assessment scale for FNCLP is 1–6); only two participants, NFi1 and NSp4 scored lower than 3 = B1 and thus did not meet the official language requirements for professional practice rights yet.

The research participants' performances in the professional language assessment module were assessed on a 1–5 scale according to the criteria created and pre-tested, and were analysed both qualitatively and quantitatively. The following three key criteria were applied in the assessment and will be present in our data analysis too: (1) task fulfilment and knowledge of the genre/discourse model; (2) knowledge of register and use of vocabulary and phraseology; and (3) targeting and indirectness. Comprehension of source materials was taken into account as part of the two first criteria. As mentioned above, all the tasks were integrated and thus covered more than only one sub-skill. The modality in which the outcomes were performed was taken as the basis for grouping the task performances into two categories, 'oral' or 'written'.

The test performances of all participants in both the FNLCP (scale 1–6) and professional language assessment module (scale 1–5) are presented in parallel in Figure 6.1. The FNCLP pillar shows the average level of general Finnish language skills, and the two PROF pillars together give

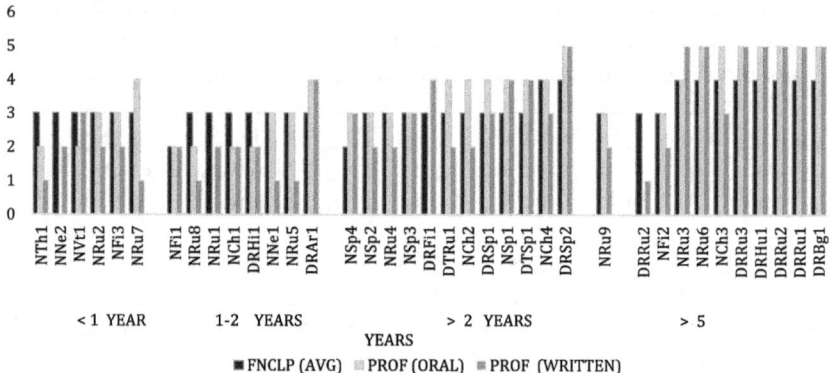

Figure 6.1 Test performance in the FNCLP and professional language assessment module. Scale of FNCLP: 1–6; scale of the professional language assessment module (PROF): 1–5.

an overview of the professional language skills (oral/written performance) of each participant. Some research participants did not succeed in recoding their oral performances on the computer, so one of the pillars is missing in that case. In this figure, the participants are arranged according to the duration of their health care work experience in Finland.

As Figure 6.1 shows, those participants who had less than 1 year of work experience in Finland typically had level 2–3 professional language skills, particularly in tasks relying on oral performance, while many of those with 1–2 years of work experience had already reached level 4, at least in orally performed tasks. Almost all participants with professional language skills of level 5 had worked in Finland for 5 years or more. The only exception was medical doctor DRSp2, who had much less work experience (c. 2 years) but had taken part in an intensive education programme for internationally educated medical doctors, focusing on field-specific language and the Finnish health care system. Also, doctor DRAr1, who attended the same programme as DRSp2, outperformed others in her group of participants with less than 2 years of work experience. The exceptionally low performance of doctor DRRu2, in turn, is explained by the fact that, mainly working as a researcher, she had used English instead of Finnish at work.

It has been observed in a longitudinal study on labour migration in health care (Suni, 2017) that some kind of 'click' is experienced by health professionals during their second year at work in Finland: fluency in both reception and production increases; communication feels easier; and the stress due to an earlier lack of Finnish language skills is finally relieved. Quantitative analysis of our data confirms this, showing the difference between those with less and more than 1 year of work experience in Finland, respectively. The participants with 0–1 year of work experience in Finnish health care institutions had obvious difficulties in the professional language assessment module: their grades were low. According to their interviews (n = 15), participants also found the FNCLP easier. The explanation frequently given was that they had no access or very limited access to health care language in Finland. We will return to this point in the discussion.

Figure 6.1 also shows that the development of general language proficiency, as assessed in the FNCLP, takes time. Only two participants with 1–2 years of work experience had reached level 4 (B2). This observation has implications for the suggested health care language policy changes; namely, that level 4 be required for those attending the licensure process (MEC, 2014). On the basis of these findings, such a requirement would cause a marked delay in getting through the process. It would hinder internationally educated professionals' access to authentic work environments – where field-specific language is most effectively learned – particularly if applied in the early stages of the process.

The next section presents a qualitative analysis of participants' test performance, focusing on the linguistic features central to expressing work-related content: field-specific vocabulary; chunks; constructions needed in polite interaction (e.g. reassuring, indirectness); targeting the addressee (e.g. patient, colleague, relatives); and choice of suitable register (e.g. professional, colloquial) (see e.g. Kela & Komppa, 2011). A functional and construction-based approach to language use was adapted in the linguistic analysis (see e.g. Ellis, 2003; Goldberg, 2006; Luodonpää-Manni & Ojutkangas, 2020). Illustrative examples are analysed to exemplify the main tendencies in the data set.

The feedback interviews, in turn, were analysed by applying thematic content analysis methods (Guest et al., 2012). It is to be noted that the interviews were only 15–20 minutes and were conducted in Finnish rather than in the participants' native languages (and were subsequently translated by the authors); thus, they remained at a rather general level. Nevertheless, the interview data provided insights into the authenticity (Elder, 2016; McNamara, 2009) and fairness and justice aspects (Hamp-Lyons, 1991; McNamara et al., 2019; McNamara & Ryan, 2011) of the professional language assessment module. This analysis will follow the linguistic analysis presented below.

Key Findings

Professional language as a resource

As mentioned before, much of professional language learning takes place in the workplace (e.g. Macqueen et al., 2016; Seilonen & Suni, 2016; Suni, 2011), and many of the participants in this study were more familiar with the professional language used at work than with so-called general language (see also Discussion). The following text (1) – a sample response to a prompt asking the test-taker to write a complaint letter about a restaurant – is a writing sub-test performance in the FNCLP. The text shows how professional language resources such as field-specific terms or elliptical expressions are sometimes used in the non-professional test context, and how health care expertise is thus evident in general language use too. Professional terminology is **bolded**, and elliptical use of compound verbs is <u>underlined</u> in Examples 1 and 2.

1) Terve! Minulla on iso ongelma. Viimeisenä lauantaina olen kiinalaisessa ravintolassa. Olen syönyt lihaa, perunoita ja sammakoita. Seuravana paivänä minulla oli **kuumotusta, närästystä, oksentelua** ja vatsa kipeytynyt koko päivä. Lääkket eivät auttaneet. <u>Hakeutunut ensiavuun.</u> Siellä oli tutkimuksia, labrakokeet ja sitten <u>hoitanut kirurgisen osastolla</u>. Siellä <u>saanut lääkeitä</u> **suonensisäisesti ja suun kautta**. Olin sairaalassa 5 päivän ajan. Mielestäni, liha ei ollut tosi hyvin paistettu. Haluaisin, että minun raha tulee takaisin ja kaikki lääkkeet te maksatte. - - Terveisin Axel

Hi! I have a big problem. Last Saturday I am in a Chinese restaurant. I've eaten meat, potatoes and frogs. Next day I had **a hot feeling, heartburn, vomiting** and stomach sore all day. The medicines didn't help. <u>Sought emergency care.</u> There were examinations, lab tests and then <u>treated on the</u>

surgical ward. There got medicines **intravenously and orally.** I was in the hospital for 5 days. In my opinion, meat wasn't really well done. I'd like that my money comes back and you pay all the medicine. - - Best regards Axel

After introducing background issues connected to a suspicion of food poisoning, the writer moves to describe the symptoms caused by the condition and the treatment received, whereby his expertise is highlighted at the textual level. The subject matter connected to illnesses and health care apparently leads him to utilise expressions that are typical of epicrises in Finnish and also common in the medical record entry programmes used by nurses (see Virtanen, 2013). In this type of text style, inherent to health care, one of the aims is concise expression, briefness of text and distancing the matter. For this reason, dictation can often be curt (*Lääkket eivät auttaneet. Hakeutunut ensiavuun.*) [*Medicines did not help. Sought emergency care.*] and prone to listing (*Seuravana paivänä minulla oli kuumotusta, närästystä, oksentelua ja vatsa kipeytynyt koko päivä.*) [*Next day had a hot feeling, heartburn, vomiting and a sore stomach all day.*]. It entails the elliptical use of compound verbs, with the omission of the modal verb (*Siellä saanut lääkeitä suonensisäisesti ja suun kautta.*) [*There got medicines intravenously and orally.*]. Furthermore, some of the wordings deviate from the everyday register (e.g. *vatsa kipeytynyt pro maha kipeä*, 'sore stomach') and represent a clearly professional, field-specific expression. The research participant thus relies on the health care genre and field-specific terminology even when formulating a complaint letter on such a general theme.

Health care professionals' identities were quite often enacted through their FNCLP performance (Seilonen & Suni, 2016), even though the writing task itself did not demand or encourage this. The following private message (2) includes a kind of self-made epicrisis. Actually, according to the task instructions, the test-taker was to write a message to a friend explaining that he has become ill, and moreover he needs to ask for help. Instead, the writer talks about symptoms and illness, using the professional code. As in the previous text (1), in this informal letter there are parallels with conventional health care text genres, their formulas and vocabulary.

2) Hei Sofia!
Olen sairastunut. Tänään en käynyt työssä vielä, olen sairauslomalla viime tiistaista lähtien. Kaksi viikkoa sitten minulla on ollut flunssa ja nyt minun korvani on kipeää, lisäksi **oireina on nenävuotaa ja poskissa on paineen tunnetta. Kuumetta ei ole ollut eikä kurkkukipuakaan.** Talven tullen aloitan hiihdon ulkona, joka on hyvää urheilua. Kuntosalin harjoitteen rinnalla se vaikuttaa tasapainoon myös. Mutta vielä minulla ei ole ollut **välikorvatulehdusta** koskaan. Ulkona on tosi kylmää...
Terveisin Peter

Hi Sofia!
I've gotten ill. Today I didn't go to work yet, I am on sick leave since last Tuesday. Two weeks ago I have had flu and now I have earache and additionally **symptoms are nose-running and there is a sensation of pressure**

in the cheeks. Have had neither fever nor sore throat. With winter approaching I will start skiing outside, which is good sport. Together with gym exercise it influences the balance too. But as yet I haven't had a **middle ear infection** ever. It is really cold outside...
Best wishes Peter

The use of specific health care terminology and conventionalised expressions of the field can also lead to the writer's register deviating from the expected. In the text above, the writer demonstrates a wide knowledge of field-specific terminology but may not be familiar with alternative, more colloquial ways of expressing similar matters. This limited knowledge of everyday vocabulary may prevent the writer from making the appropriate lexical decisions required in informal registers. Therefore, the writer may not be able to discuss illness in an informal manner, as the examples above demonstrate. On the other hand, this writer may not wish to do so since the context is a test situation, intended to bring out the strengths in test-takers' language proficiency and to demonstrate their ability to pass the test.

The effect of using field-specific terminology is potentially two-sided: on the one hand, it can show their knowledge; on the other hand, the use of professional terms in an inappropriate context can indicate weak language skills. This is often the case if a health care worker sticks to the professional code and does not succeed in interpreting the professional content to a patient. Many of the medical terms with Latin origin have their Finnish variants in colloquial language (e.g. *hematoma/hematoma* vs. *mustelma/ bruise*): for a doctor or a nurse, it is necessary to know and master both variants in order to be able to cope in different communicative situations (see also Bennink, 2015). In the following examples (3, 4), derived from our professional language assessment data, a health care worker summarises the medical report of an elderly patient to the patient's relatives.

In Example 3, the speaker NSp3 uses Latin-based professional concepts such as *hematoma, anticoagulant and saturation,* which probably remain incomprehensible for a non-professional listener who would expect more common, originally Finnish words to be used. The grounds for such usage are often a lack of sufficient language skills, which in this case does not enable flexible movement between registers.

3) kaatui, ja hänellä, oli lonkka murtuma, ja. **iso hematooma oli**, meni leikkaukseen, ja,− − nut annetan hänele, piikki vatsassa koska **ei saa antaa Marevan hänele. se on antikoagulaatio, aine,**− − tällä hetkellä ei tarvitse, happilisä, koska, **saturaatio** on ihan normaali ja, hengitä, normaalisti, ja, − − [NSp3]

fell, and she had hip fracture, and. **a big hematoma was,** went to surgery, and, - - now is given her an injection under skin, because **one may not give Marevan to her. it is an anticoagulant, agent.** - - at the moment doesn't need extra oxygen, because, **saturation** is all normal and, breathes, normally, and, - - [NSp3]

The speaker must confine herself to copying the expressions of the Latin-based medical ground text given in the test assignment. Due to her limited work experience in Finland (about 1 year), she has had little access to linguistic models. Shifting between general and professional registers is one of the key field-specific literacy skills to be assessed in the professional language assessment. Example 3 illustrates that the most challenging aspect of vocabulary is not the knowledge and use of the (often international) medical terminology, but how to explain it to laypersons and replace it with more informal and colloquial equivalents. Using the Latin-based terms is a rather common sign of a lack of resources in Finnish.

The use of paraphrases instead of Latin terms shows better language skills and the ability to change registers according to task requirements. In the following example (4), NSp1 explicates the concept of saturation and the need for special medication, using paraphrases understandable to the client's relatives. In Finland, clients of health care and other public services have a right to receive information in a comprehensible and accessible form, so foreign terminology, for example, should be avoided when possible and replaced by Finnish terminology (Administration Law 434/2003: §9; Virtanen, 2017).

4) - - ei nyt tarvitse lisähappe **siis hän saturoituu elikkä hän hengittää hyvin ilman, lisähappee,** -- **Klexane se on semmonen lääke että, se hoitaa että ei oo, ei oo. (veren verin), varten parantaa hänen veren- verenkierto.** [NSp1]

now doesn't need extra oxygen, **so she is saturated that is she breathes quite well without extra oxygen.** - - **Klexane is such a medicine that cures that, it is not, for promoting her blood circulation.** [NSp1]

This kind of smooth accommodation of the (assumed) listener is indicative of higher levels of professional language proficiency. In spite of her short work experience in Finland, NSp1 manages well with this aspect of second-language use. This may reflect her extensive Finnish language use in informal communication outside the work context and her conscious investment in language learning reported in the feedback interview. Her performance reminds us of the fact that professional language does not consist of medical language only, but also the ability to communicate on work-related themes with laypersons in a register familiar to them (see Kela & Komppa, 2011; Piikki 2010).

Providing information and giving instructions

In one of the tasks of the professional language assessment module, the participants had to write a short description on diagnosing a milk allergy in infants, to be delivered to parents at children's health clinics. The source material included in the assignment was a detailed video presentation in which a medical expert describes the principles and practices of this particular diagnosis. The presentation is directed at health care professionals, and it contains a great deal of professional terminology and special information in the form of medical speech combined with text and statistical charts. The conciseness of the information makes it challenging for test-takers to rephrase the information by choosing relevant, adequate facts and presenting the whole in a comprehensible form. In the next example, a fully comprehensible written performance by nurse NSp3 illustrates the difficulty of such a task for those at lower proficiency levels:

> 5) Maito allergia aiheuttaa paljon oireita kuten iho oireet ja suoli oireet. Laitetaan sitten ruokavalion ilman maitoa eli maito eliminaatio. Annetaan soija jos lapsi on yli puoli vuotta. Tarpeeksi on perusterveydenhuolto ja tarvittaessa sunnitellaan jatkohoito ja lapsi pitäisi mennä erikoislääkäriin. [NSp3]
>
> Milk allergy causes plenty of symptoms like skin symptoms and intestinal symptoms. Then is prepared a diet without milk or milk elimination. Soy is given if a child is over half a year old. Enough is primary health care and when needed further treatment is planned. [NSp3]

Participant NSp3 has written a brief description of symptoms, listed a few guidelines, and mentioned the level of the medical organisation at which the treatment should take place. All this information is correct, but the announcement is plain text that resembles notes more than how-to instructions for parents. The writer has succeeded in choosing and simplifying the most essential points of the rich material: key symptoms and the course of treatment are described, and the concept of the elimination of milk is explained clearly. However, a great deal of more detailed information, necessary for parents in everyday life, is left out. Here again, the still-limited linguistic repertoire hinders more versatile self-expression in the work environment. It can be inferred that the nurse in question copes well with many kinds of work tasks, but still needs some support in more demanding textual work for which advanced L2 skills are expected.

These observations are important from the point of view of conveying information, but also from the point of view of trust. In a study by Calnan and Rowe (2008), patients were asked to identify the most important dimensions of trust. For most of them, trust was created through their experience of care and the doctor's technical competence, communication skills, and personal manner. A doctor's personal manner involved tailoring advice to meet the patients' preferences and needs. In the previous example, such attempts are evident, but the limited linguistic repertoire limits the performance. Before returning to the question of trust (see section 'Establishing trust and reassuring'), we focus on the challenges of advising or urging action.

Indirect personal reference and indirect urging of action

Institutional relationships between health care professionals (experts) and their patients are hierarchical by nature (Haakana & Raevaara, 1999; Paananen, 2015). For treatment to be successful, the patients must adhere to the experts' instructions and must consent to procedures performed by them. In these situations, the expert has the power, and the patient is the recipient of the action. It is important for the nurse or doctor to know how to give instructions and handle sensitive issues indirectly without threatening the patient's face, creating a well-functioning care relationship by minimising the power relationship (see De La Croix & Skelton, 2009); indirect expressions are thus commonly favoured. Linguistic indirectness, expressed in Finnish by use of the passive voice or the zero-person construction, is utilised as a politeness strategy (Seilonen, 2013) to take the recipient into consideration or diminish the influence of the speaker. Indirectness is used, on the one hand, to dissipate the real or imaginary power of the speaker in relation to the listener (e.g. Candlin & Roger, 2013) and, on the other, to minimise the speaker's role as an active agent. Indirect expressions diffuse the commanding and demanding nature of requests for action (i.e. the allocation of overly direct requests). When a prompt for action is not targeted directly at the recipients, they are at least provided imaginary leeway in their interpretation (Brown & Levinson, 1987; Candlin & Roger, 2013).

In the following example (6), NSp3 must provide oral instructions to the patient in preparation for a specific medication procedure; the task is to adapt the lengthy and linguistically complex written instructions into a clear and understandable form for an elderly patient. NSp3 succeeds well in the selection, clarification and allocation of the information. She uses zero person (translated as *one* below) skilfully to express that the instructions are general and, therefore, apply not only to the recipient but also to any patient in a similar treatment situation; the positive and negative zero person forms are bolded in the example.

6) — — puhdas tukka ja kuiva tukka, **ei saa laittaa** mitään. **ei saa käyttää** esimerkiksi shampoo. ei, no tutkimuspäivä **saa syödä ja juoda**. ja annetaan varmasti esilääke. ja. pitäs, antaa meille. lääke sinun oma lääketiedot. sitten, no, tutkimuksessa, laitetaan elek-, tro- elektrodit, päässä, ja **pitää olla rentona** ja, silmät, kiini. [NSp3]

Clean hair and dry hair, **one may not put** anything. **One is not allowed to use** e.g. shampoo. Not, well test day **one may eat and drink**. Certainly pre-medicine is given. And you should give us. medicine your own medicine information. Then, well, in the test, elec, tro, electrodes, are put on the head, and **one must be relaxed**, and eyes closed. [NSp3]

By using person references like *pitäs antaa meille [should give us]* and *sinun oma lääketiedot [your own medication information]*, NSp3 further clarifies the allocation and explicates that the instruction applies specifically to the other party of the situation, i.e. the listener. It can thus be said that NSp3 already has good command of indirect and direct variation and is able to approach the elderly patient in a manner appropriate for the situation. Her expressions are not target-like Finnish, but this does not threaten the comprehensibility of her instructions. In the general language-proficiency FNCLP test, the participant NSp3 managed well (degree 3, the target level, B1) in all receptive and productive sub-tests; in the professional language assessment module, she similarly showed good language skills (degree 3).

Indirectness can also be used to refer to the speakers themselves or to another specific person, whereby their significance as the agent is not emphasised; instead, the focus is on the action (VISK, 2008: § 1254). This can be seen in Example 7: when talking about the patient's care procedures, NSp3 uses the passive forms *laitettiin, annetaan, laitetaan [were put, will be given, are put]*, by which she sets aside the agent – the health care staff – in the description of the action. In the task, NSp3 explains to the patient's family on the telephone how the patient has been treated recently, on the basis of the patient information text she has read. In spite of a lack of grammatical accuracy, she is able to use the passive constructions typical for such process descriptions in health care in a conventional manner. This implies that the construction has been picked up in the authentic work environment.

> 7) **laitetiin** myös, verta tippuman koska hemoglobiini oli mattala. verenpaine on, on tällä hetkelä, normaali, ja. nut **annetan** hänele, piikki vatsassa koska, **ei saa antaa** Marevan hänele. [NSp3]
>
> Also blood **was put dripping** because hemoglobin was low. Blood pressure is, is normal at the moment, and. Now **is given** him, an injection in abdomen, because **one may not give** Marevan to him. [NSp3]

The nature of Finnish passive voice also includes implicit reference to the plural agent (VISK, 2008: § 1256), which in this instance gives the impression that the patient is being cared for by a multi-member team of health care experts. The passive voice can also be used to generalise (VISK, 2008: § 1331), which would make the actions appear as regular routine procedures that are performed without the person being mentioned. The interpretation of generalisation here is supported by the fact that the zero person *ei saa antaa [one may not give]* refers to an unspecified actor, whereas the use of the passive *ei saada antaa [may not be given]* would in this context imply a reference to the speaker (see also Seilonen, 2013). However, the impersonal way of expression and indirectness are not optimal linguistic choices in all communication situations in health care. For instance, a more personal approach is recommended when handling issues difficult for the listener and when there is a wish to ensure confidentiality. The examples in the next subsection are connected to such situations.

Establishing trust and reassuring

Health care situations in which it is essential to inspire trust in the patient or their family are common (Candlin & Roger, 2013). Behaviours most strongly associated with patient trust and satisfaction include caring and comforting, technical competence and communication (Grant et al., 2000). Trust comprises a variety of dimensions, including competence, confidentiality, acting in the other's interests and personal manner. In a number of studies investigating patients' health care experiences, trust emerged spontaneously as a quality indicator, with patients suggesting that high-quality doctor–patient interactions are characterised by high levels of trust (Calnan & Rowe, 2008; Safran et al., 1998). For example, the doctor needs to convince the subject of the procedure that it is safe and that the patient is in capable hands (e.g. Northouse & Northouse, 1998). It is also important to be able to reassure a fearful or worried patient or their relatives when needed.

One of the tasks in the professional language assessment module was to inform an elderly patient's family member about her condition and treatment. The source text was a medical record, and the patient's situation was worrisome. Health information is a critical resource derived from successful health communication (Kreps, 1988, 2003); therefore, the selection and effective, sensitive verbalisation of relevant information between professionals, patients and relatives were included among the crucial skills to be demonstrated in the integrated tasks. In the following examples, some successful means employed by the research participants are shown.

In Example 8, the speaker (NSp1) individualises and personifies the patient through use of the second-person singular pronoun in the expression *sinun äiti [your mother]* instead of referring to the patient only with the *hän [she]* pronoun. The personification of the patient introduces a tone of empathy to the speech, which is one way to inspire confidence and trust in the relationship between the expert and the patient or their family (see Candlin & Roger, 2013). The establishment of individualisation and trust in this situation is further reinforced through the listener's direct and familiar addressing and highlighting of shared knowledge: *sä tiedät [you know]*.

> 8) joo kyllä, sinun, täällä, täällä osastolla on hoidossa, **sinun äiti**, joo, hetki pieni mä tarkistan vielä koneella hänen tiedot, joo. nii hän tullu tänään päivällä, ja, hän tullut Savon Sav- Savo Savosta sairaalasta, ja **me ni meillä on, me ole-, me olemme vuodeosasto**, ja hän tullut täällä varten jatkohoito, -- sitten, joo **me hoidetaan** hän on nyt, hänellä on nyt hyvä vointia paitsi on vuoteessa, (hän) voi kävellä nyt, **sä tiedät** että hän kaatuu hän kaatunu kotona, joo, kohta kolme viikkoa sitten, ja, vaikka ei oo mitään lonkkamurtumaa, kun se on, vanhuus ja ei se, ei se parantaa kun joku haava. [NSp1]

yes, your, here, here in the ward, is **your mother**, yes, just a moment I'll check her particulars on the computer, yes, so she arrived today, and, she has come from Savo hospital **we are the ward**, and she has come here for a further care -- then, **we take care of her now**, she has a good condition in spite of being is in bed, (she) can walk now, **you know** that she fell at home, soon three weeks ago, and although there is no hip fracture, because it is old age, and it doesn't cure like a wound. [NSp1]

The sense of security is also created and fortified by personal references (Example 8). By using first-person plural references such as *me olemme vuodeosasto* and *me hoidetaan [we are the ward; we take care of]*, the nurse instils trust specifically in the patient's relative. The agents are identified and, at the same time, their position of responsibility for the action is also expressed: *hoidosta vastaamme me [we are in charge of the care]*.

In addition to using personal references (*teidän äidillä; me hoidetaan, me annetaan [your mother, we will take care, we give]*), participant DRBg (Example 9) reassures the relative by highlighting positive points (*ei ollut murtumaa onneksi [luckily there was no fracture], vointi on tällä hetkellä hyvä ja jalka on jo aika hyvässä kunnossa [her condition is good and her leg is in rather good condition]*), explaining the procedures (*me hoidetaan tuo tromboosiriski [we will take care of that thrombosis risk]*), and describing the medication (*kleksaani on semmoinen lääke mikä me annetaan ihon alle [klexan is such a medicine we give under the skin]*).

9) on ollut, epäily että hänellä olisi, lonkka murtunut mutta onneksi ei oo semmoista ollut kyseessä vaan, on aika iso, iso mustelma on ollut reitissä mutta lonkka on kuitenkin, ihan ehjä ei ollut murtumaa onneksi - - teidän äiti on ollut tiputuksessa - - koska teidän äidillä on ollut tämä, sydämmen ongelma pitkä aikaa - - mutta me hoidetaan tuo, tuo antikoagulan-, tai, riski, tromboosiriski kleksaanilla eli kleksaani on semmonen lääke mikä me annetaan, ihon alle, kaksi kertaa, yks kerta vuorokaudessa. nyt teidän äiti jää meille seurannassa terveyskeskus vuodenosastolla vointi on tällä hetkellä hyvä ja, ja hänen jalka jo on aika hyvässä kunnossa että hän pysty liikkumaan, jos on vielä lisää kysyttävää totta kai te voitte ol- olla yhteydessä ja, ja kysyä voitte vierailuajoissa tulla, äidin luokse [DRBg]

It has been suspected that she had a hip fracture, but luckily it's not anything like that in question, but there is, a rather large bruise has been on the thigh but hip is alright, was no fracture luckily - - your mother has had a a drip - - because your mother has had this heart problem for a long time - - but we will take care of that anticoagulan-, or risk, thrombose risk with Klexan so Klexan is such a medicine we give under skin, twice, once a day. Now your mother stays for follow-up by us at the health centre ward and her condition is good at the moment and her leg is in a rather good condition so that she can move, and if there is more you can of course be in contact and, and ask you can come to see mother during visiting hours. [DRBg]

Calnan and Rowe (2008) note that communication is valued by the patients not only because it displays a professional's competence but also because it offers reassurance. This speaker has versatile linguistic means of reassuring and comforting, and she gives the impression of being a fluent speaker who can adjust her expressions according to the listener. She is generally more advanced than the other research participants, and thus provides an example of a realistic target level for those aiming to reach a position as a 'good fit' in Finnish health care organisations; quite obviously she could have also passed an advanced level FNCLP test, but she took the intermediate level test only. She has about 10 years' work history in Finland, first as a medical researcher for 1.5 years (work language English), and then as a doctor in clinical work for 8 years. The other research participants whose test performances have been analysed in more detail in this section are following the same trajectory. In spite of their more limited linguistic repertoires and partially inaccurate or unconventional performances, they all succeeded in completing the demanding work-related professional language test assignments with grade 3 or higher.

Participants' experiences

In the post-test interviews, the research participants expressed their views on the relevance of the task types, as reflected against their actual work tasks and their experiences of language use at work. Those with no or very limited (less than 1 year) work experience in Finland responded in a unified way to the question of difficulty of different parts of the assessment: for them, the general language test (FNCLP) was easier than the professional language assessment module. As participant NFi3 (recently arrived from the Philippines) put it in Finnish: *yki helpompi koska arkipäivä* – 'FNCLP easier because daily life'. Those with more work experience, in turn, commonly shared the view that the professional language assessment module was easier than the FNCLP; they were more familiar with the professional language used at work than with so-called general language.

10) tätä harjoittelee joka päivä (- -) pystyi paremmin näyttää mitä osaa, helpompi [NSp3]

this (one is) training every day (- -) could better show what one can, easier. [NSp3]

11) koska minä tuntuu, lähellä minun töissä lähellä minun, päiväpäivä [NSp2]

easier because at my work, close to my everyday life. [NSp2]

It is noteworthy here that the abstraction level of the tasks in the professional language assessment module was much higher than in the FNCLP, and the integrated tasks also combined several sub-skills at once, including the need to shift register according to the audience. As the interview excerpts above illustrate, these participants found the tasks easier because they resembled their daily work. This is a sign of authenticity, which was set as one of the key goals when designing the professional language assessment module.

Some participants also expressed that in the professional language assessment module they were able to demonstrate the strengths of their language proficiency:

> 12) mä en tiedä mä varmasti en pärjäisi jos mä en koskaan olis sairaalassa, työssä. [DRRu1]
>
> I could certainly not cope with the test without having worked in a hospital. [DRRu1]
>
> 13) niin mun mielestä ammattikieli kehittyy niinkun vain töissä, täs tää ei saa, ei pääse niinkun oppimaan, kurssilla. [DRSp2]
>
> I think professional language develops like at work only, this cannot, one cannot learn in a language course. [DRSp2]
>
> 14) että kuin pitkään, ihminen oli tai henkilö oli lääkärin työssä et se vaikuttaa, työkokemus, mä en usko et mä selvisin jos mä just olisin, aloittamassa, se olisi vaikeaa. [DrRu1]
>
> So how long a person was in medical work, it has an influence, work experience. I don't think I managed if I was just starting, it would be difficult. [DrRu1]

On the basis of the test performances, perceived familiarity, and authenticity reported in the interviews, it can be inferred that the professional assessment module was just and fair for the participants with longer than 1 year's work experience in their own field in Finland, but not for those with less experience. The participants also shared the view that the skills needed to accomplish the tasks of the professional module could only be developed in authentic work situations, and not in language courses.

Participant views are thus in line with Hamp-Lyons (1991), in that a field-specific approach is fair for test-takers who already have local work experience, because they – and only they – can actually show their real skills in a second language better than in a general language test. Professional language can well be the strongest aspect of one's language proficiency (see also Schleicher & Suni, 2021).

As some of the research participants noted, they experienced more language problems outside of health care institutions than when surrounded by familiar themes and expressions in their work community:

> 15) jos menen ulos työ minä joskus en ymmärtää. [NSp1]
>
> If I go out from my workplace I sometimes don't understand. [NSp1]

Such observations have not been commonly reported, but they are highly relevant for understanding the truncated nature of multilingual repertoires (Blommaert, 2010) and the social context of second-language development. If working life is the main domain for second-language use, it is most probably a central domain for second language learning as well; an uneven language skills profile in which professional language dominates is a natural outcome of this. At the same time, it is evident that many work tasks are linguistically complex and challenging. One of the medical doctors reflects on his earlier experiences with Finnish at work when having to explain medical terminology in Finnish:

> 16) ja sitten mä voin sanoo että oma kokemuksesta ensimmäinen kerta mul oli, todella shokki kun mun puhelimessa pitänyt sanoo mitä on kysta, se oli, mä olin just, mä olis ajatellut että voi kenelle voi selittää et mit- vaikee voi olla ulkomaalaiselle lääkärille, kun kieli, tai just, ne rajoitukset miten paljon. [DrRu1]
>
> Then I can say from my own experience that it was a real shock when I for the first time should have said what is 'kysta'. I was just thinking that whom can I explain how difficult it is for a foreign doctor when there are those limitations with language. [DrRu1]

The same doctor pointed out in the feedback interview that giving advice is particularly demanding for him in Finnish. This was one of the aspects taken into account in the test design and assessment criteria. Some participants also noted that, in order to figure out how people work and communicate in the Finnish workplace, one has to get access to these workplaces. The roles and practices may differ from those in one's country of origin, and language use is intertwined with this.

Two Nepalese nurses who were attending an in-service training tailored for internationally educated nurses also reflected on the contents of the professional language assessment module in relation to their current studies and future work:

> 17) en vielä tiedä ammattikieli. minusta se oli kinnostava lukea testia joka myöhemmin tule työelämässäni. [NNe1]
>
> I don't know professional language yet. It was interesting to read texts that come later at my work. [NNe1]
>
> 18) ne tuntui vaikea koska, koska en tiedä, nimi suomeksi (- -) kurssilla on vain kielioppi. [NNe2]
>
> Those [professional concepts] felt difficult because I don't know them in Finnish (- -) at the language course there is only grammar. [NNe2]

These comments can be interpreted as an indirect critique of form-focused language instruction, which does not provide sufficient access to field-specific vocabulary and text types. Similar critiques have been reported elsewhere (e.g. Suni, 2011). Developing and adopting a true work life-oriented language pedagogy takes time, but valuable progress has already been reported, and good practices shared (e.g. Combi project, 2019; Komppa *et al.*, 2014; Lehtimaja *et al.*, 2021).

Discussion

Mobility among health care professionals, which has increased in intensity in recent decades, is in part regulated by the language and migration policies applied in the receiving countries. The EU-level decision (2014) to limit the free mobility of the workforce in the health sector was an exceptional move, which highlighted the special value of language proficiency in work tasks in this field. In addition to regulations set by official language policies, mobile health care professionals may also face informal language policies and other socially demanding expectations when starting to work in a new language and new work environment.

All of these factors may have an impact on their careers and professional identities. Those health care professionals who start learning Finnish language as adults in order to be employed in Finland are in a much more demanding situation compared to those who have learnt English or German for many years before even starting their higher education, and who at some point apply for jobs in English- or German-speaking countries. Those migrating to Finland have to accept the necessity of extensive investment in language learning (Schleicher & Suni, 2021); in the beginning of their new career, they will need substantial support from their work community. The fear or experience of losing one's professional identity in their new environment (see e.g. Suni, 2017) is evident in many cases; the gap between one's linguistic and other skills is quite wide in the beginning.

Analyses of such contexts of less commonly taught L2s are highly relevant locally, but they may also broaden the view on the very nature of work-related L2 needs and skills in general. In these cases, the languages and sociolinguistic environments as such may be quite different from English-speaking contexts, which still largely dominate the research field of language for work. Learning a new L2 – useless outside the borders of the country in question – which, in the case of Finnish, has a particularly complex morphology, original (e.g. non-Latin-based) vocabulary, and its own sociolinguistic variation patterns (see e.g. Lesonen, 2020), also highlights the fact that not only employability and professional identity but also language awareness and aptitude are put to the test.

The starting point of the project and its language assessment experiment, from which came the data excerpts discussed earlier, was that professional language is much more than vocabulary. From a lay perspective, it may seem to be just field-specific terminology, but for language teachers and learners the reality looks quite different (Lehtimaja *et al.*, 2021).

Mastering the frequent shifts between oral and written modalities is a key aspect of successful professional language use, as is addressing different age groups in a socially acceptable manner; conveying field-specific information in a suitable linguistic style and register; managing directness when giving advice; or comforting and reassuring fearful patients and communicating with their relatives. Our findings indicate that practical experience received in an authentic work environment is necessary for coping with these linguistically complex aspects of health care interaction.

In integrated tasks in which authentic source materials are used for testing various skills, from comprehension to oral or written production, a feeling of 'real life' was to some extent achieved, even though the communication partner was a computer. What was missing, however, was the presence and real-time feedback from the other interlocutor. Furthermore, these tasks lacked multilingual practices typical of increasingly diverse work communities (Kurhila et al., 2021). Although Finnish or Swedish are to be used with patients, health professionals may rely on their other language resources (e.g. English, different L1s, Latin terminology) between themselves in real work environments (Paananen, 2019; Virtanen, 2017).

Our aim has been to investigate how second-language assessment and pedagogy in the health sector can be developed. The findings reported in previous sections show the kinds of language skills the research participants were able to demonstrate in the assessment as a whole and in the tailor-made professional language assessment module in particular. The examples also showed the participants' perceptions of the integrated tasks; how their work experience was reflected in their test performances and in their post-test interviews; and their views on and experiences with different parts of the assessment experiment. The piloted professional language module complemented the FNCLP test in a meaningful way, particularly by providing a place to show the pragmatic aspects of professional language use. The feedback interviews confirmed that the genres and functions covered by the module were similar to everyday texts and tasks at work. The integrative nature of the tasks also brought authenticity, because that is how real work life functions: written information gets conveyed in oral form and vice versa, and formal and colloquial varieties alternate in the flow of work tasks where technologies are also constantly present. This reflects the key idea of multiliteracies (e.g. Holloway & Gouthro, 2020): different modalities, genres and semiotic systems intersect at work, which should be considered as relevant for both field-specific language education and assessment. Furthermore, the level of abstraction in the professional language module was high – much higher than in the FNCLP – but that was obviously compensated for by familiarity with the topics and tasks.

The participants' views support Hamp-Lyons' (1991) argument: by providing tasks representing the disciplinary area with which the test-taker is familiar, a discipline-based approach is more just and fair to the participants than a general language test. The participants will perform in closer alignment with their real ability if their skills are assessed using tasks related to those that they typically encounter in their daily work.

The main pedagogical inference based on our findings is that professional language can be learnt early on, and thus in parallel with general language as opposed to afterwards, as has been more common. The prerequisites for this are high motivation and scaffolding received from others at work. Some participants also called for tailor-made language instruction: a shift from a grammar-based approach to a more functional approach was preferred, according to some feedback interviews. We also found promising evidence indicating that intensive field-specific training programmes may promote development quite well (see Seilonen *et al.*, 2016). National models for such programmes have also been developed for both doctors and nurses, but only short-term, project-based funding has been provided for running these programmes so far. It is necessary to establish more permanent models for training, including field-specific language education and flexible mentoring practices that grant the availability of grass-roots level peer support for those entering a new work community as L2 speakers.

The following questions arose: if participants with 1–2 years' health care work experience in their own field in Finland cope well in field-specific language use, is it worth launching a separate national assessment system to demonstrate these skills, as has been suggested? And if only few of them have reached level 4 (CEFR B2) in FNCLP by then, is it just and realistic to set the official language requirements at that level as a part of the licensure process, as has similarly been suggested (see MEC, 2014) and recently also has been done in certain settings (Toikkanen, 2021)? Our findings imply that this is not necessarily the case, particularly if such policies were applied at the early stages of the licensure process. Our findings imply that this is not necessarily the case. Instead, smooth access to work life should be ensured for those health care workers having an L2 proficiency of level 3 in FNCLP (CEFR B1). Experiences of language mentoring in the health sector have been particularly positive (e.g. workplace coaching and language advocate programmes; see Berg & Sjösvärd, 2021; Kuparinen 2017), and such practices should thus be introduced widely across health sectors and included in field-specific education models. If professional language skills are to be assessed, this should merely be integrated into such national education models and not used to create yet another barrier for employment. Sufficient time and tailored educational support should also be provided in order to reach a higher level in general language skills; this is a longer process than is commonly understood. Finally, the lived experiences and self-assessments of internationally educated health professionals themselves and the observations made by their employers should be carefully attended to when updating the language policies concerning this target group.

References

Bennink, A. (2015) Searching for understanding in the medical consultation. Accommodation and the use of dialect variants among Latino patients. In M. Zabielska, E. Wąsikiewicz-Firlej and A. Szczepaniak-Kozak (eds) *Discourses in Co(n)text: the Many Faces of Specialised Discourse* (pp. 60–88). Newcastle upon Tyne: Cambridge Scholars Publishing.

Blommaert, J. (2010) *The Sociolinguistics of Globalization*. Cambridge: Cambridge University Press.

Brown, P. and Levinson, S.C. (1987) *Politeness: Some Universals in Language Usage*. Cambridge: Cambridge University Press.

Calnan, M. and Rowe, R. (2008) *Trust Matters in Healthcare*. New York: McGraw-Hill.

Candlin, S. and Rogers P. (2013) *Communication and Professional Relationships in Healthcare Practice*. Sheffield: Equinox.

Combi Project (2019) Teacher's toolkit. https://combiproject.eu/wp-content/uploads/combi-teacher-training-toolkit.pdf (accessed 6 April 2020).

De La Croix, A. and Skelton, J. (2009) The reality of role-play: Interruptions and amount of talk in simulated consultations. *Medical Education* 43 (7), 695–703.

Elder, C. (2016) Exploring the limits of authenticity in LSP testing: The case of a specific purpose language test for health professionals. *Language Testing* 33 (2), 147–152.

Elder, C. and McNamara, T. (2016) The hunt for "indigenous criteria" in assessing communication in the physiotherapy workplace. *Language Testing* 33 (2), 153–174.

Elder, C., Pill, J., Woodward-Kron, R., McNamara, T., Manias, E., Webb, G. and McColl, G. (2012) Health professionals' views of communication: Implications for assessing performance on a health-specific English language test. *TESOL Quarterly* 46 (2), 409–419.

Ellis, N.C. (2003) Constructions, chunking, and connectionism: The emergence of second language structure. In C.J. Doughty and M.H. Long (eds) *The Handbook of Second Language Acquisition* (pp. 63–103). Malden, MA: Blackwell.

Esmaeili, H. (2002) Integrated reading and writing tasks and ESL Students' reading and writing performance in an English language test. *Canadian Modern Language Review* 58 (4), 599–622.

Goldberg, A.E. (2006) *Constructions at Work: The Nature of Generalization in Language*. Oxford: Oxford University Press.

Grant, C.H., Cissna, K.N. and Rosenfeld, L.B. (2000) Patients' perceptions of physicians' communication and outcomes of the accrual to trial process. *Health Communication* 12, 1–27.

Haakana, M. and Raevaara, L. (1999) Divertikkeleitä vai pussukoita? Lääketieteen kieli vuorovaikutuksessa. *Kielikello* 3, 9–14.

Hamp-Lyons, L. (1991) Pre-text: Task-related influences on the writer. In L. Hamp-Lyons (ed.) *Assessing Second Language Writing in Academic Contexts* (pp. 127–151). Norwood, NJ: Ablex.

Holloway, S.M. and Gouthro, P.A. (2020) Using a multiliteracies approach to foster critical and creative pedagogies for adult learners. *Journal of Adult and Continuing Education* 26 (2), 203–220.

Kela, M. and Komppa, J. (2011) Sairaanhoitajan työkieli – yleiskieltä vai ammattikieltä? [Nurse's language needs – Standard language or professional language? Functional approach to professional second language learning; abstract in English]. *Puhe ja kieli – Speech and Language* 131 (4), 173–192.

Komppa, J., Jäppinen, T., Herva, M. and Hämäläinen, T. (2014) Korkeakoulun ammatilliset suomi toisena kielenä -viitekehykset. *Metropolia Ammattikorkeakoulun julkaisusarja Aatos-artikkelit* 16.

Kreps, G.L. (1988) The pervasive role of information in health and health care: Implications for health communication policy. In J. Anderson (ed.) *Communication Yearbook* 11 (pp. 238–276). Thousand Oaks, CA: Sage.

Kreps, G.L. (2003) Impact of communication on cancer risk, incidence, morbidity, and quality of life. *Health Communication* 15, 161–169.
Kuparinen, K. (2017) Keeping up with the nurses – On-the-job language coaching of the health care professionals of immigrant background. *Proceedings of ICERI2017 Conference 16th–18th November, Seville, Spain* (pp. 477–480). Valencia: IATED.
Kurhila, S., Kotilainen, L. and Lehtimaja, I. (2021) Orienting to the language learner role in multilingual workplace meetings. *Applied Linguistics Review* 25.
Lado, R. (1961) *Language Testing: The Construction and Use of Foreign Language Tests: A Teacher's Book.* Bristol: Longmans, Green and Company.
Lehtimaja, I., Virtanen, A. and Suni, M. (2021) Finnish L2 proficiency for working life: Towards research-based language education and supervision practices. *Nordand: Nordisk tidksrift for andrespråksforskning* 16 (1), 57–76.
Lesonen, S. (2020) Valuing variability: Dynamic usage-based principles in the L2 development of four Finnish language learners. Dissertation, University of Groningen.
Luodonpää-Manni, M. and Ojutkangas, K. (2020) Laadullinen aineistopohjainen kielentutkimus. In M. Luodonpää-Manni, M. Hamunen, R. Konstenius, M. Miestamo, U. Nikanne and K. Sinnemäki (eds) *Kielentutkimuksen menetelmiä I-IV* (pp. 412–441). Helsinki: Suomalaisen Kirjallisuuden seura.
Macqueen S., Pill, J. and Knoch U. (2016) Language test as a boundary object: Perspectives from test users in the healthcare domain. *Language Testing* 33 (2), 271–288.
Marcus, K., Quimson, G. and Short, S.D. (2014) Source country perceptions, experiences, and recommendations regarding health workforce migration: A case study from the Philippines. *Human Resources for Health* 12, 62.
McNamara, T. (2009) Principles of testing and assessment. In K. Knapp, B. Seidlhofer, and H.G. Widdowson (eds) *Handbook of Foreign Language Communication and Learning* (pp. 607–628). New York: Mouton de Gruyter.
McNamara, T. and Ryan, K. (2011) Fairness vs justice in language testing: The place of English literacy in the Australian Citizenship Test. *Language Assessment Quarterly* 8 (2), 161–178.
McNamara, T., Knoch, U. and Fan, J. (2019) *Fairness, Justice, and Language Assessment. The Role of Measurement.* Oxford: Oxford University Press.
MEC (2014) Kielitaidon määrittäminen sekä kielitaidon ja EU/ETA-alueen ulkopuolella hankitun koulutuksen täydentäminen terveysalalla [Evaluating language proficiency and complementing language proficiency and qualifications obtained in a non-EU/EEA country in the health care sector; summary in English]. *Reports of the Ministry of Education and Culture, Finland* 2014:5. Helsinki: Ministry of Education and Culture.
Mikkonen, M. (2021) Lääkärin puutteellinen kielitaito vaarantaa potilasturvallisuuden. https://www.valvira.fi/-/laakarin-puutteellinen-kielitaito-vaarantaa-potilasturvallisuuden (accessed 22 October 2021).
Moore, T., Morton, J., Hall, D. and Wallis, C. (2015) Literacy practices in the professional workplace: Implications for the IELTS reading and writing tests. *IELTS Research Reports Online Series* 1/2015.
NIHW [National Institute for Health and Welfare] (2021) *Statistical Yearbook on Social Welfare and Health Care 2021.* Helsinki: National Institute for Health and Welfare.
Northouse, L.L. and Northouse, P.G. (1998) *Health Communication. Strategies for Health Professionals* (3rd edn). Stamford, CT: Appleton & Lange.
Paananen, J. (2015) Kuinka eleet helpottavat yhteisymmärrystä? Ikoniset ja deiktiset eleet monikulttuurisilla lääkärin vastaanotoilla [How does gesturing facilitate mutual understanding? Iconic and deictic gestures in multicultural general practice consultations; abstract in English]. *Puhe ja kieli – Speech and Communication* 35 (2), 73–95.
Paananen, J. (2019) *Yhteisymmärryksen rakentaminen monikulttuurisilla lääkärin vastaanotoilla* ['Constructing Mutual Understanding in Multicultural Primary Care Consultations; summary in English]. Turku: University of Turku.
Piikki, A. (2010) Terveydenhoitoalalla riittävä suomen taito – Mitä se on? *Sutina* 1, 30–33.

Raunio, P. (2013) Työhön Suomeen? Tutkimus työperusteiseen maahanmuuttoon liittyvistä koulutusprosesseista [Moving to Finland for work? Dissertation of the processes concerning pre-departure training and labor; summary in English]. *Acta Electronica Universitatis Tamperensis* 1331.

Roberts, C. (2021) *Linguistic Penalties and the Job Interview – Studies in Communication in Organisations and Professions.* Sheffield: Equinox.

Safran, D.G., Taira, D.A., Rogers, W.H., Kosinski, M., Ware, J.E. and Tarlov, A.R. (1998) Linking primary care performance to outcomes of care. *Journal of Family Practice* 47 (3), 213–220.

Schleicher, N. and Suni, M. (2021) Healthcare professionals on the move: Investing in the learning a new language for work. *Lähivõrdlusi – Lähivertailuja* 31, 191–228.

Seilonen, M. (2013) Epäsuora henkilöön viittaaminen oppijansuomessa. [Indirect references in Finnish learner language]. Dissertation, University of Jyväskylä.

Seilonen, M. (2014) "Tuntuuko, jos tästä painaa?" Epäsuoruus, toimintaan kehottaminen ja asiantuntijuus terveydenhuollon ammattilaisten teksteissä ["Does it hurt, if one presses here?" – Indirectness, urging action and professionality in the texts of health care professionals; abstract in English]. *Lähivõrdlusi – Lähivertailuja* 27, 221–243.

Seilonen, M. and Suni, M. (2016) Ohjeita, tietoa ja turvaa kielen keinoin. Ulkomailta palkatut sairaanhoitajat ammatillista suomen kielen taitoaan osoittamassa [Advice, information, and safety by means of language: Internationally recruited nurses demonstrating their professional Finnish language skills; abstract in English]. *Lähivõrdlusi – Lähivertailuja* 26, 450–480.

Seilonen, M., Suni, M., Härmälä, M. and Neittaanmäki, R. (2016) Ammatillisen kielitaidon arviointikokeilu terveydenhuollon alalla. [Performance based professional language assessment experiment in health care] In R. Hilden and A. Huhta (eds) *Kielitaidon arviointitutkimus 2000-luvun Suomessa* (pp. 110–141). Jyväskylä: AFinLA.

Suni, M. (2011) Missä ja miten maahanmuuttajat kehittävät ammatillista kielitaitoaan? [Where and how do immigrants develop their work-related language skills? Abstract in English] *Ammattikasvatuksen aikakauskirja* 13 (2), 8–22.

Suni, M. (2017) Working and learning in a new niche: Ecological interpretations of work-related immigration. In J. Angouri, M. Marra and J. Holmes (eds) *Negotiating Boundaries at Work. Talking and Transitions* (pp. 195–215). Edinburgh: Edinburgh University Press.

Tervola, M. (2019) Maahanmuuttajalääkärien suomen kielen taito ja kielitaitotarpeet: Erityisalan kielitaidon näkökulma lääkärin työhön [Immigrant physicians' Finnish language skills and language needs: The physician's work from the perspective of language skills for specific purposes; summary in English]. Dissertation, University of Tampere.

Tervola, M., Pajunen, A., Vainio S., Honko, M. and Mattila, K. (2015) Maahanmuuttajataustaisten lääkärien suomen kielen taito laillistamiskuulustelussa [Writing texts, being evaluated: Cultural and disciplinary norms in academic writing; summary in English]. *Duodecim* 131 (4), 339–346.

Toikkanen, U. (2021) Eta-alueen ulkopuolella koulutettujen lääkärien kielitaitovaatimus kiristyy. *Lääkärilehti* 76 (42), 2373.

Valvira [National Supervisory Authority for Welfare and Health] (2021) Professional practice rights. https://www.valvira.fi/web/en/healthcare/professional_practice_rights (accessed 15 January 2023).

Virtanen. A. (2017) The multivoicedness of written documentation: An international nursing student documenting in a second language. *European Journal of Applied Linguistics* 5 (1), 115–140.

VISK [Hakulinen, A., Vilkuna, M., Korhonen, R., Koivisto, V., Heinonen, T.R. and Alho, I.] (2008) Iso suomen kielioppi [Big Finnish grammar]. http://scripta.kotus.fi/visk/.

7 The Role of Soft Skills in Vocational ESL: Their Potential to (Dis)Empower Migrant Employment Seekers

Julie Kerekes and Jeanne Sinclair

Introduction

In recent decades, pragmatic competence has been recognised as a critical component of language proficiency, despite being more difficult to identify and teach than many structural aspects of language such as grammar, vocabulary and pronunciation (Kasper, 1997; Monwoorian *et al.*, 2016; Rose, 2005; Takahashi, 2010). The ability to convey a message effectively means that, beyond its literal and transactional meanings, the message must produce a desirable response and the intended impression (Kerekes, 2018). The message conveyed is determined not only by what is said, but also by who says it, to whom, for what purpose, and in what context. In Kasper's (1997: 2) words, pragmatic competence refers to 'knowledge of communicative action and how to carry it out', as well as 'the ability to use language appropriately according to context'. This includes an understanding of the relative (in)directness required of certain speech acts in certain contexts (Kasper, 1997), the ability to convey one's intended meaning, and the ability to understand a speaker's intentions (Bialystok, 1993), in order to communicate effectively.

In places of employment, migrant language learners' needs to communicate effectively with their superiors and co-workers have been recognised as vital to their success in obtaining and keeping jobs in their new countries of residence (see also Chapters 5, 6 and 8 in this volume). How successful communication is identified and taught, however, is less clear. In this chapter, we explore how language instructors in a Canadian vocational training programme for newcomers understand these competencies and apply this understanding to their practice, as well as the implications for their migrant students seeking employment in Canada.

Pragmatic Competence by Many Names

While language classes address pragmatic competence, in workplaces around the globe such localised concepts as *horizontal skills* (Greece), *Finnishness* (Finland), *kemahiran insaniah* or skills in *being human* (Malaysia), and *social competencies* or *human skills* (Hungary) refer to traits considered essential for effective workplace communication. The term *soft skills* has become ubiquitous in China (literally translated as 软技能 or ruǎn jì néng), New Zealand, the United Kingdom, North America, and around the globe in human resources settings as well as among laypeople discussing work. Many popular career-related reports and websites[1] emphasise the critical importance of soft skills for job-seeking success.

Although vaguely defined, soft skills generally include one's abilities to adapt, problem-solve, collaborate, resolve conflicts, empathise, negotiate and persuade, in both written and spoken modes of communication (Bancino & Zevalkink, 2007; Casner-Lotto & Barrington, 2006; Holmes *et al.*, 2014; Mitchell *et al.*, 2010; US Department of Labour, 2009). Academic descriptions of soft skills in the workplace vary, from specific aspects of cultural intelligence (Del Vitto, 2008), personality traits (Heckman & Kautz, 2012), emotional intelligence (Wheeler, 2016), and mindset (Tsey *et al.*, 2018), to vaster concepts of 'pervasive skills' (Viviers *et al.*, 2016) and 'human qualities' (Yan *et al.*, 2019). According to Louw *et al.* (2010), soft skills comprise knowing, and being able to say, what is culturally appropriate in a given context. Although the demarcation between hard and soft skills is not always clear (Angouri, 2018), the nebulous attributes and abilities associated with soft skills stand in contrast to hard skills or technical skills, which are often more easily measurable and describable, such as a nurse's ability to check vital signs, or a software engineer's coding skills.

A common motif across academic fields is the framing of soft skills as an unchanging quality or set of skills, regardless of one's work environment. Yan *et al.* (2019: 244) state, for example, that '[s]oft skills are cross-disciplinary, independent of job or industry'. Similarly, Cinque (2016: 14) describes soft skills as 'competences transferable from job to job, from company to company, from one economic sector to another'; while Tsey *et al.* (2018: 3) note that the 'relevance of such skills extends beyond the workplace to improve individual competencies and capabilities in most areas of one's life – families, friends, other organizations, and the community'. Indeed, the broad applicability of soft skills could be considered their defining feature, according to this body of research. Yet, a common perception of employers is that, for internationally educated professionals, recognising and using *culturally specific* communication skills may help them to bridge the gap between how their technical expertise was perceived in their country of origin and how it is perceived in the host country (their new home) (Allan, 2016; Caggiano *et al.*, 2020; Fernández-Sanz *et al.*, 2017). As perceived soft skills are needed for both obtaining and maintaining employment, adopting locally appropriate skills is a high-stakes issue for immigrant jobseekers in gatekeeping encounters (Kerekes, 2006) such as job interviews, merit reviews and workplace advancement (see also Chapter 5 in this volume).

Two other common terms in the varied definitions of soft skills are 'communication skills' and 'interpersonal skills' (e.g. Andrews & Higson, 2008; Stevens & Norman, 2016). Ahmed *et al.* (2012) surveyed 500 job postings for software engineers in five global regions, for example, finding that the nature of soft skills varies somewhat according to region, but all regions demonstrate a high demand for communication and interpersonal skills and a moderate demand for analytical skills. Jones *et al.* (2017) similarly found in their survey of large American companies that communication and interpersonal skills are in the top third of sought-after soft skills, along with positivity, respect, trustworthiness and initiative.

The link between soft skills and business success is made explicit in some of these works. For example, a study of soft skills expected by New Zealand–based technology firms (Stevens & Norman, 2016: 7–8) links soft skills with entrepreneurial acumen:

> Every interviewee was emphatic that soft skills bring commercial benefits.... [S]oft skills enable faster staff integration and happier, more productive teams. [S]oft skills are vital in creating relationships, building customer trust and generating repeat business.... Teaching entrepreneurial skills covers many soft skills and may result in new business start-ups and graduates with a better understanding of business drivers; [sic] creating wins for both the university and industry.

Of the literature reviewed here, only Stevens and Norman (2016: 9) address the ethics around workplace-based soft-skills training. In their interviews with hiring directors, they found that:

> [i]ndustry is split on whether soft skills can be taught or if it is moral to even try.... A number hold the view that soft skills are fixed, cannot be taught in the work environment and it may be immoral to even try. Consequently industry tends to recruit for existing soft skills that facilitate team work, rapid learning of new technical skills and customer empathy.

Thus, we see a hint at the problematisation of soft skills, what they are, who has them, who can acquire them, and who (if anyone) can teach them.

Objective

By examining perceptions of soft skills in a Canadian vocational training setting, from the perspectives of language instructors, we attempt to understand a set of ideologies behind the use and application of this term, and its effect on employment seekers (their students). Through our analysis, ideologies relating 'soft skills' to 'cultural fit' are revealed and discussed in the context of their significance for newcomers seeking employment in Canada.

The Canadian Context

Canada's population has for a decade included the largest proportion of immigrants among the G8 nations (Statistics Canada, 2013), which according to the 2016 census is 21.9% (Statistics Canada, 2017a). Between 2011 and 2016, Canada became home to approximately 1.2 million new permanent residents (Statistics Canada, 2017a). Seventy-three percent of Canada's immigrants reported having a mother tongue[2] that is neither English nor French, Canada's two official languages (Statistics Canada, 2017b). Language skills, but not soft skills *per se*, have received tremendous attention by immigration services. Citizenship and Immigration Canada (CIC) has stated, for example, that '[l]anguage constitutes the most serious barrier newcomers face to furthering their education or training and is among the most serious barriers to finding employment' (CIC, 2010: v). Thus, in recent decades, Canada's federally funded adult English as a Second/Additional Language (ESL/EAL) programmes have heightened their focus on work-related language training (Fleming, 2007). This initiative spans a wide range of ways to address newcomers' language needs, from Language Instruction for Newcomers to Canada (LINC), a programme designed for learners with varied levels of English proficiency, to Enhanced Language Training (ELT), a sector-specific language course for students with advanced English proficiency. Many settlement organisations offer Occupation-Specific Language Training (OSLT), a bridging programme for immigrants who are skilled in a specific professional field but who are perceived to lack adequate job-related English language competencies (Bartel, 2013).

Certainly, the efficacy of these language programmes is critically important to immigrants' long-term quality of life, and government-sponsored evaluations have determined LINC and ELT programmes to be 'successful' and 'appropriate' (CIC, 2008, 2010). However, despite Canada's reputation for integrating immigrants into a cultural mosaic rather than forcing them to assimilate into a melting pot, recent scholarship suggests that adult ESL programming in Canada may not adequately honour immigrants' cultures, histories and languages, and indeed it may act to assimilate them into an idealised Canadian workplace culture that is assumed to be homogeneously White and monolingually English (Guo, 2013). Thomson and Derwing (2004: 30) concur, suggesting that 'one of the implicit cultural values that immigrants learn outside the classroom is that in Canada we do not value the education and skills that newcomers bring'. Fleming (2010), Haque and Cray (2007) and Maitra (2015) have similarly found Canada's language programmes to be part of a troubling neoliberal trend in Canadian immigration policy that promotes economic values over other qualities of life.

A website for new immigrants to Canada (www.settlement.org), which is federally and provincially funded in Ontario, illustrates this point. It sets out a list of soft skills that immigrant jobseekers in Canada need: 'communication, problem solving, positive attitudes and behaviours, adaptability [and] working with others' (Ontario Council of Agencies, 2015). Soft skills, delineated here, clearly encompass language skills, as language is the primary tool used to achieve these communicative goals. Soft skills also fall within the purview of 'culture', if we use the definition of culture offered by the Centre for Advanced Research on Language Acquisition (2019: para 1) as 'shared patterns of behaviors and interactions, cognitive constructs, and affective understanding'. Thus, while questions of soft skills and organisational 'fit' may appear innocuous, they actually comprise a complex issue involving the conscious decision to modify one's culture to adapt to a purported dominant norm, i.e. to exhibit 'Canadianness' (Kerekes *et al.*, 2013: 275) in order to succeed in Canadian industry.

While often taught as a component of language training, soft skills encompass identity, culture and economic prospects. Market-based rhetoric about soft skills and organisational 'fit' can often present as a socially acceptable form of bias against members of non-dominant linguistic and cultural groups. The purported need for newcomers to adopt 'Canadian' soft skills lies implicitly at the core of linguistic and cultural assimilation and the maintenance of, or convergence with, a perceived mainstream cultural identity (Guo, 2013). Haque (2017: 107) posits that an assimilationist mentality underlies Canadian ESL soft skills instruction, which, she argues, teaches 'amorphous behavioural competencies . . . to remediate and augment a purported lack . . . [and] perceived deficit . . . in newcomer'. As an example, Haque (2017: 107) reported on a soft skills consultant whose objective was to teach Canadian newcomers to be able to demonstrate that they:

> 'are not really that foreign' . . . because his finding was that 'employers don't want to experience this sense of foreignness'. He concluded that the goal of teaching immigrants soft skills was 'to wash out this foreignness – not the "visibles" but the verbal and non-verbal . . . because employers don't want to experience this sense of foreignness'.

Cultural Identity as a Site of Regulation

Foucault (1991) wrote of 'governmentality', a modern technique of power that focuses on the 'conduct of conduct'. Rather than overtly punish people for eschewing cultural and linguistic norms, governmentality is a 'soft power' that both enables and limits the scope of people's possible actions in the social and political world. Though less overtly punitive than technologies of power prevalent in previous centuries, governmentality guides agents toward an end goal (here employment), by presenting seemingly self-evident choices, often in the form of a dichotomy. For example, an immigrant may be forced to make a choice to anglicise their name to assuage management and ensure a smooth hiring process, versus retain their given name and send a message, however inadvertently, that their culture and identity are more important than market pressures. Immigrants, in turn, may yield to this pressure to 'wash out the foreignness', but they can also resist it, drawing on what Foucault (1982: 790) calls the 'recalcitrance of the will and the intransigence of freedom'.

Haque's (2011) Foucauldian framework in her research on Canadian language policies and educational practices underscores how 'official' discourse on language policy does not 'identify' a language problem to remedy; rather, it constitutes such problems through a discourse anchored in a power imbalance, and then directs resources toward fixing these problems. While much of Haque's work is relevant to the current study, her 2017 study on the rising neoliberal 'mentality of rule' in ESL classes for immigrants to Canada is the most pertinent. In this text, Haque argues that the nation's perceived need for skilled immigrant labour has made adult immigrant ESL programmes 'a site of increasing concern and regulation for the Canadian Government' (2017: 97). Further, she argues that these programmes enact language policies to 'organise and regulate newcomers' (2017: 97) toward an outcome of becoming a self-regulating, entrepreneurial immigrant. This process makes invisible those structural barriers, such as institutional discrimination, which impede immigrants' access to work appropriate for their skill level. Instead, the onus is on immigrant work applicants to adapt and navigate; the assumption is that loss of cultural uniqueness is merely collateral damage in a trade-off for secure and adequate employment. This aligns with Foucault's (2008: 226) concept of *homo economicus*, the neoliberal vision of the individual as 'an entrepreneur of himself'. Under the neoliberal paradigm, *homo economicus* is not simply a trading partner who contributes to the health of the economy. Rather, *homo economicus* becomes the market, and the market existence becomes life, superseding all other aspects of being – including honouring one's cultural and linguistic identity.

Haque (2017) argues that the ideology underpinning Canada's adult immigrant ESL programmes conceives of immigrants' linguistic and cultural identities as an economic liability. Specifically, it is a liability that immigrants themselves must ameliorate in order to participate fully in the market. This ideology has been operationalised by the works of Lionel Laroche, one of Canada's 'leading experts on how immigrant professionals find jobs in Canada' (MosaicBC, n.d.). Laroche and Yang's (2014) book, *Danger and Opportunity: Bridging Cultural Diversity for Competitive Advantage*, reports that US-based employers commonly choose not to hire technically qualified internationally trained job candidates because they are 'not a good fit', while in Canada similar outcomes are reached because the candidates 'don't have Canadian experience'. Laroche and Yang argue that these statements do not necessarily mean what their face value conveys. Rather, these statements refer to immigrant candidates' soft skills:

> When a candidate calls to ask why he or she is not going forward in the process, in the US, they often hear 'you are not a good fit,' whereas in Canada they often hear 'you don't have Canadian experience'. We spoke with a number of HR professionals and hiring managers, asking them to define 'fit' and 'Canadian experience. . . . People mentioned words such as *attitude, initiative, enthusiasm, getting along with coworkers* – in other words, soft skills'. . . . Through such conversations, the people we spoke to came to realise that Canadian experience is not the same as having worked in Canada, just as fit does not mean having worked in the US. (Laroche & Yang, 2014: 126, emphasis in the original)

Laroche and Yang (2014) describe this conundrum but do not critique it; indeed, much of their writing recommends strategies immigrants can adopt in order to fit into the Canadian workplace. They neglect to consider the 'involuntary diminution of social capital' (Ricento, 2014: 146), or the sacrifice of professional and personal status, which immigrants often undergo upon arrival to Canada. Involuntary diminution aligns with Bourdieu's (1989) concept of symbolic capital, which is the capacity – held largely by the dominant class – to determine what behaviours, experiences and languages are right, legitimate and 'normal'. Laroche and Yang (2014) ascribe normalcy to assimilative behaviours, and also perpetuate the monocultural assumption that immigrants must take most of the responsibility for bridging the ostensible cultural divide:

> Most immigrants to Canada expect to make the bulk of the adaptation themselves because they chose to come to Canada. Coming from hierarchical cultures, where minorities are usually expected to adapt to the majority to a greater extent than in egalitarian countries, making more than 50 percent of the adaptation is obvious to them. In turn, the average Canadian is fine with making 20 percent of the adaptation – going some of the way is okay, but meeting halfway does not seem fair to most Canadians. (Laroche & Yang, 2014: 117)

Guo (2013: 36) problematises this perspective, which 'promotes a one-way process of integration . . . [and] conformity to a presentation of the "ideal Canadian employee"'. Further, Angouri (2018) notes that language use in professional environments is not generalised; interactions and practices are specific to each workplace and can be considered in flux; this contradicts the notion of homogeneity in workplace language and culture.

In *Danger and Opportunity,* Laroche and Yang (2014) ground their ideas in the work of Geert Hofstede, a Dutch social psychologist, whose controversial work claims to identify, via statistical analysis, five dimensions of culture that can be differentiated across nations: power distance, uncertainty avoidance, individualism, masculinity, and long-term orientation (Hofstede, 2001). Scholars critique Hofstede's model as a form of colonial discourse that constructs 'the world as characterized by a division between a "developed and modern" side and a "traditional and backward" side' (Fougère & Moulettes, 2007: 15). Kim (2007: 28) continues this line of critique, arguing that the very concept of 'pitting the individual against the group' reflects a 'Western individualistic worldview'.

Laroche and Yang (2014) expound upon one aspect of Hofstede's oeuvre that has now become 'institutionalized as legitimate knowledge' (Fougère & Moulettes, 2007: 15): the concept of 'hierarchized' versus 'egalitarian' cultures. For example, Laroche and Yang (2014: 32) offer this commentary on global culture: 'Most Asian, African, Eastern European, Latin American, or Middle Eastern countries are significantly more hierarchical than either the US or Canada'. Laroche and Rutherford's (2007: 183) book, *Recruiting, Retaining and Promoting Culturally Different Employees,* connects soft skills with this purported dichotomy, claiming that 'hierarchical people' tend to 'be obedient', 'ask their managers to make decisions', and 'prioritize tasks . . . based on the position and title of the delegating person'. They suggest 'egalitarian people' are more likely to 'be empowered', 'prioritize tasks . . . based on urgency and importance', and 'feel relatively comfortable disagreeing with their boss' (2007: 183). The field of sociolinguistics has been at the vanguard of critiquing such dichotomisation, by emphasising that social worlds are not static but instead constantly evolving – 'becoming' – through language (Angouri, 2018; Gee, 2015).

The attribution of soft skills to Canada's purported Western, non-hierarchical workplace culture is echoed in the Ontario Society of Professional Engineers (2014) research report on internationally trained engineers (ITEs):

> ITEs have challenges fitting into a Canadian workplace culture . . . . [T]here appears to be a perception [that] many ITEs may have acquired their experience in more traditional, hierarchical workplaces. Consequently, they may not have the 'soft' skills needed for working in a team . . . . Many Canadian employers seem to require clarity around how non-Canadian experience (which they explicitly or implicitly equate with traditional hierarchies) produces the right fit for a Canadian organization that uses a team model for engineering work. (Ontario Society of Professional Engineers, 2014: 6)

This statement suggests that internationally trained professionals may lack a capacity for teamwork, and, importantly, that such a purported lack is sufficient grounds to deny employment. Kerekes *et al.* (2013) corroborate this notion in their analysis of the difficulties internationally trained engineers encounter when seeking employment in their field in Canada. Immigrant research participants in Kerekes *et al.*'s (2013: 276) study concluded that the primary reason they were not successful in securing employment was that they 'were not Canadian and, therefore, they were neither trusted nor the right "fit"'. Kerekes *et al.*'s (2013: 277) participants recognised and critiqued this situation, associating their difficulties with their divergence from 'the dominant Discourse'. Indeed, immigrants who are new to the host country may not recognise an expectation to communicate two potentially contrasting messages: a sense of loyalty and deference to the work team as well as an entrepreneurial drive that makes clear their ability to contribute personally in a meaningful way (Reissner-Roubicek, 2017).

Background to the Project

This study began as a collaborative project between Laura, the manager of Mesa Centre,[3] and Julie, a professor of applied linguistics (and co-author of this chapter). Mesa Centre (or, simply, 'Mesa') has, for many decades, provided a wide range of social services in urban areas of Ontario, including affordable housing, senior wellness and childcare. One of its main programmes is Immigrant Settlement, which provides, among other services, English language instruction, counselling and mentoring, settlement workshops, and employment bridging programmes for internationally educated professionals. Mesa offers Language Instruction for Newcomers to Canada (LINC), a federal programme designed to meet the needs of learners ranging from beginner to advanced English users. It also offers advanced, sector-specific language instruction through its Enhanced Language Training (ELT) programme, targeting speakers of EAL from health care, information technology, office administration, and finance/accounting sectors, with the aim of helping them to find jobs in their professional fields.

Laura had approached Julie before this project began, in order to explore how *soft skills* could be taught more effectively to the newcomers in Mesa Centre's ESL courses. She wanted to identify areas for growth in Mesa's curriculum, in order to better meet students' needs and market demands. For Julie, the collaboration offered an opportunity to create a curriculum which would enable her Master of Education (M.Ed.) graduate students to obtain hands-on experience in empirical research, as well as a way to apply her research to immigrant services. The collaborative project, therefore, sought insights about both Mesa Centre's teaching practices and the learning experiences of M.Ed. students enrolled in

Julie's graduate course, Intercultural Workplace Communication (IWC). The IWC course description states, 'We will use sociolinguistic tools to ... investigate what makes for successful multicultural/intercultural workplace interactions. We will analyse authentic examples of written and spoken language in a variety of workplace settings'. Julie and Laura set up an apprenticeship-collaboration (described as a *twinning*[4] project in Kerekes, 2022) to support Mesa's soft skills instruction, through which graduate students in Julie's course became contributing student researchers.

Project Design and Procedure

Students from Julie's class interested in participating in the twinning project submitted written statements describing their interests and professional/educational backgrounds. Julie and Laura reviewed them together, interviewed each of the students, and then placed them in teams of two to three students according to their qualifications and interests. The student-research teams were then matched with Mesa Centre language courses and their respective instructors; these became their sites of data collection. After receiving training in data collection and analysis in their IWC course, Julie's students, in their research teams, designed their respective mini-studies and collected a variety of data addressing soft skills: they observed Mesa Centre classroom practices, interviewed Mesa's language instructors and English language students, led focus groups with the staff and administrators at Mesa, and examined the documented curriculum used by Mesa's instructors, according to each team's particular research questions.[5] The student-researcher teams collected over 14 hours of data at Mesa Centre, resulting in almost 200 pages of transcription. Each team subsequently analysed their respective sets of data and wrote them up as research papers for their term projects in the IWC course. Their findings, as well as a summary report by Julie, were shared with Laura, the manager of Mesa Centre, and utilised by Mesa's staff in their subsequent design of an online curriculum for teaching soft skills.

Subsequent Data Analysis

The collaboration between Julie's IWC class and Mesa Centre's staff and students resulted in a rich set of classroom observation and interview data. Julie and her then-graduate assistant, Jeanne (co-author of this chapter), created a plan to examine the IWC students' analyses in order to better understand the role of soft skills instruction in the ideologies of immigrant success conveyed by Mesa Centre to its clientele. The original data collected by the graduate student teams were reviewed, and their transcriptions were completed and refined, according to Gee's (2011) recommendation for transcription granularity. These included transcriptions from classroom observations, focus group discussions with Mesa instructors and administrators (led by graduate student researchers), and interviews conducted by the graduate student researchers with the ESL students and instructors they had observed.

We (Julie and Jeanne) coded the data into emergent themes (Given, 2008). Through an iterative and collaborative process, we used an inductive analytic strategy that was both grounded in the data and conceptually connected to extant literature on the topic of normative instructional practices in ESL settings. We sought to understand emic (local) definitions, usages, applications and rationales for the importance attributed to soft skills instruction at Mesa.

Research Question

Our work investigated the roles, perceptions and implications of soft skills instruction in ESL courses at Mesa Centre. As the largest and most linguistically diverse province in Canada, and as the province that receives the greatest number of new immigrants each year, Ontario was an appropriate setting in which to seek evidence or counter-evidence in relation to Guo's (2013: 37) claim that Canada's adult ESL programmes are vehicles 'for assimilating immigrants into the norms of the dominant culture'. Furthermore, we investigated whether the data substantiated Haque's (2017: 110) idea that Canadian adult ESL classes encourage learners to take responsibility for 'moulding themselves through language and "soft skills" . . . into desirable workers for Canadian employers'. We used a critical lens to examine how adult ESL courses in the Canadian context conceptualise and teach vocational language skills to recent immigrants. Specifically, *how are soft skills, customer service skills, and the idea of fitting into the Canadian workplace conceptualised and addressed at Mesa Centre?*

Findings

What are soft skills?

Our resulting analysis responded to the student-researchers' data analyses, which concluded that, while some effective soft skills instruction was occurring at Mesa, there was also room for improvement. An emic definition of 'soft skills' should be derived from the local use and application of the term. Yet the interview and focus group data suggested that Mesa staff were not fully aligned in their articulations of what soft skills are (and are not). They did agree in their view of soft skills as a component of English language competence which can and should be addressed across all levels of ESL instruction. Laura, who managed Mesa Centre's Enhanced Language Training (ELT) programme (and whose specific objective was to update the curricula of their ELT and LINC courses by improving how they teach soft skills), illustrated this point by presenting examples of soft skills that can be addressed in beginning ESL courses: '[W]hat is okay to ask in certain situations, body language, eye contact . . . what is considered to be polite in Canada . . . showing initiative. Now that can be broken down to a very, very basic level'. Laura valued students' willingness to express their opinions and make suggestions, which she saw as aspects of pragmatic competence in the workplace. Furthermore, she referred to documented policies – The Canadian Charter of Rights and Freedoms (1982) – regarding the values to which she ascribes:

> You don't have to just follow the teacher, you can suggest. We appreciate your opinion. Respect the Canadian Charter of Rights . . . . [I]t's the culture. The unspoken culture is what to some extent I assume can be incorporated into a lower level already.

In a quest for a formula for defining and utilising soft skills for employment, Laura expressed her preference for a small number of discrete competencies which can be taught in the classroom and specifically addressed in the documented curricula:

> I would like to identify a certain set of soft skills . . . five core soft skills without which we would all agree it is difficult to function in this cultural environment, this new country, Canada . . . . These are the core five, for the sake of argument, core five soft skills . . . and we give examples as to how they can be taught with real examples, not just vague descriptives. Then hopefully all our instructors would be able to better incorporate it into our curriculum.

In the same interview, paradoxically, Laura described how soft skills are intertwined with personality, thus challenging her own notion of teaching 'five core soft skills':

> [Y]ou can't just say that from one to five these are the soft skills. The more you go into it, the more personality traits you will come across. Be positive. Now [laughs] you know, you're new, you're nervous in the country, be positive.

Roma, one of Mesa's ESL instructors, corroborated Laura's attribution of soft skills to cultural fit, and also pointed out discrepancies in definitions of soft skills:

> I have a problem with soft skills because everybody defines it differently. . . . My Bible for teaching ELT is Lionel Laroche, and he defines soft skills as 'cultural fit'. That's the way I see it . . . and I think that no one can teach ELT without reading his book . . . . He gives a very clear definition -- what is it exactly that students don't know? They don't know what they don't know, especially culturally how they define it. So what I teach . . . I call it 'culturally-fitting skills', not 'soft skills'.

In essence, soft skills were equated (by Laura and some of her staff) with the ability to do things the 'Canadian' way, as demonstrated in her description of the pedagogical approach of Ron, one of Mesa's teachers:

> He basically told me he weaves soft skills into most of what he teaches. So any opportunity that arises, he's going to show his students how to do it *the Canadian way*. [emphasis added]

Whether distinguishing between cultural fit and soft skills, or equating the two concepts, the instructors converged in their perspectives that it was their responsibility to assist their students in understanding 'Canadian culture' in order to be able to communicate effectively. Marjorie, one of the student researchers in Julie's IWC course, corroborated this point of view: without considering that 'Canadian culture' may have numerous varieties, she presented a monocultural view of Canadian culture, and stated, simply, 'you have to be aware of what the culture is here'.

Fundamentally, a clear definition of 'soft skills' was lacking, although staff firmly express the need to teach such skills. One message conveyed here is that the culture of Canada cultivates a willingness to express one's opinion and 'be yourself', while another, ironically, is that this disposition of offering one's thoughts and suggestions *must* be adopted, even if it does not come naturally.

Workplace manners and small talk

In the focus group data, much of the teachers' discussions of soft skills centred on getting along with others in the workplace while, at the same time, speaking one's mind – to a certain degree. Roxanna, an ELT instructor at Mesa, suggested that 'agreeing, making a suggestion, [and] responding politely' comprise soft skills, as well as knowing how to interact with others: 'how do you say "no", how do you be assertive, how do you give and respond to criticism?' Marjorie, the graduate student researcher who facilitated this focus group, stated that '[i]n Canada you are expected to sell an idea', and this entails convincing one's team to 'buy in'. Roxanna concurred, pointing out that '[s]oft skills are how to initiate [as well as] how to be a team player'. This concept is corroborated by the LINC Classroom Activities for Level 2, which were developed by Algonquin College and funded by Citizenship and Immigration Canada. The LINC curricular material emphasises the need for employees to share their personal characteristics and skills, such as being friendly:

> At work employees like to be friendly. They go on coffee breaks and lunch together. They talk to each other about things that are unimportant or don't cause bad feelings. This friendly conversation is called small talk. (Algonquin College, 2009)

The ability to make appropriate small talk was identified by the instructors as a crucial component of soft skills. The classroom observation data indicate that appropriate small talk topics in Mesa ESL classes included greetings, the weather, clothing, food, pets, sports, what one did or will do on the weekend, one's children and, in general, 'shared interests'. In a LINC Level 2–3 classroom, responding to prompts, the students identified topics *not* appropriate for Canadian small talk: marriage, politics, religion, one's salary, one's weight and 'personal questions'. They did not, however, consider the complications of topics which may be 'shared interests' and still inappropriate. Furthermore, small talk appropriateness was considered strictly in terms of topic choice. The instructor, Sofia, used a handout in her class that focused on appropriate topics for small talk, but it did not address such intricacies as appropriate *ways* to talk about the various suggested topics, or the possibilities that the context, as well as who one's interlocutor is, would be influential in determining the appropriateness of a given topic. The implicit message of these lessons on workplace manners is that normative expectations of small talk differ substantially between the students' home countries and Canada, but the Canadian expectations alone are self-evident and natural.

'Fitting in': A monocultural model

A fundamental issue related to soft skills and addressed by virtually all the Mesa staff is that of 'fitting in' to Canadian cultural norms. Aligned with Laroche's ideas, Laura characterised the inability to fit into a Canadian workplace culture as the main reason internationally educated professionals have difficulty finding jobs in their fields. She concurred with Laroche in her dispute of the widely held belief that a lack of Canadian work experience is the most prominent obstacle to obtaining suitable employment:

> Really I think Canadian experience is a mix of . . . . Canadian cultural values, expectations, uh, if an employer sees that a person will easily integrate into their team and has the hard skills, then no employer will say, 'Whoa, whoa, but you don't have any experience in Canada'.

What is lacking in the instructors' responses, however, is a critical examination of what it means to 'easily integrate'. Laura shared her perspective, while again expressing the belief that soft skills are inseparable from personality traits: she encouraged language students to create for themselves a new 'persona' in their new country of residence, setting aside their former identity and replacing it with one that fits into the new (Canadian) setting. In fact, she described this process as her 'most successful moment' mentoring internationally trained professionals:

> . . . I realised that I have to build, we have to build a persona. A Canadian persona . . . . [An] internationally trained engineer who spoke English

very well... came from a very different culture. And it was very difficult to understand him and also to get his nonverbal communication skills anywhere close to a Canadian-ish, resembling anything that would be successful in an interview here. And [then] I told him that uh he really needs to think of himself as... as *who he is, but who he is in Canada*. So... not a complete... not a different person, but the Canadian version of himself. And... he started working on it, and we got to incredible results just after a few classes because he realised that it goes deep down to identity. That he really has to somehow figure out a Canadian identity for himself.

Laura described the assignment she gave this student: he was to search for a celebrity that he would like to emulate, so that he 'could build a Canadian identity based on that kind of a role model'. Thus, she stated, 'it was their homework to figure out who they were, in this new culture. *So it wasn't me prescribing anything.* It was a bit of a journey. And it was interesting. The results were good' (emphasis added). Laura's student was expected to take responsibility for adapting his very identity to assimilate to Canadian society.

The teaching staff at Mesa appeared to operate under a binary hierarchical/egalitarian paradigm for understanding cultural differences, echoing the work of Laroche described above, as one Mesa instructor noted:

I would say to students, how would you describe a meeting in your previous work, in your previous milieu.... And some of them were very much 'one person in authority, the chair of the meeting speaks, and everybody listens and makes notes and thanks the person who spoke,' and that's it. And that's not the Canadian version of a meeting.... We'd always talk a lot about team meetings.... You have to be able to speak up and give your opinion. And don't always look at the leader of the meeting. Don't always speak to the leader of the meeting. You have to look around and speak to everyone else. So we would practice things like that.

For this Mesa instructor, workplace communication as taught in this vocational ESL course could be dichotomised between a Canadian, non-hierarchical form, and a non-Canadian, hierarchical form, although the theoretical grounding for this distinction was not substantiated.

As for needing to be both a 'team player' and an initiator, few clues were given for determining the appropriateness of offering an opinion, or under what circumstances it may be appropriate to offer an opinion. Brandon, another ELT instructor at Mesa, suggested:

[I]t's a teaching point to say, you know, in Canada it's not acceptable... to say this or to... be making these sorts of statements. Even if we have these opinions we probably need to say it differently, but to be... blatant and frank and to make some statements that you might make in your own country is unacceptable here.

Thus, two distinct messages emerged: when in Canadian society at large, opinions are to be kept to oneself; yet in workplace meetings, employees are expected to voice their opinions. These messages are conveyed implicitly. The English language students were not invited to compare the appropriateness of expressing opinions in the different settings, nor were they invited to critique this duality. Mesa's staff appeared to want to shape their English language students' values to fit this idealised monocultural Canadian picture of employment culture, which includes speaking one's opinion in meetings, but holding one's opinions when in other workplace settings. An ideological divide was evident between the interview and focus group discussions with staff, on the one hand, and the graduate student researchers' classroom observations, on the other; we explore this in the next section. In contrast to the perspective offered by Laroche and Yang (2014) and echoed by Laura, that 'hierarchical' culture has no place in the Canadian workplace, we find that, quite to the contrary, immigrants preparing to enter the Canadian workforce should expect a highly hierarchical workplace in which they have little possibility for advancement.

Effecting buy-in

Some of the workplace soft skills lessons observed at Mesa appeared to be grooming the English learners for low status, low-paying jobs in Canada. Textbook materials and teacher-supplied examples of jobs included working in the fast food industry or becoming a telemarketer, landscaper, delivery person, hair-cutter, or childcare worker. In over seven hours of Mesa classroom recordings, the students were asked about their previous employment in only one instance. Strategies for maintaining employment conveyed an orientation to low-status jobs, such as what we see in the following lesson excerpt, in which students were learning tips on procuring a job at a fast food restaurant. The lesson materials included the LINC Classroom Activities for Level 2.

> Instructor: So we are going to listen now to a job interview, so there is a senior woman who wants to work as a night cook in Burger Heaven. In Burger Heaven. So what is Burger Heaven, Burger Heaven? (5) Burgers, burgers, they make burgers. (5). Ok, so first I want you to listen, then you will do the exercise. And I would like you to answer this question: what kind of food do they make in a restaurant called Burger Heaven. What kind . . . of food . . . do cooks make . . . in the restaurant called . . . Burger . . . Heaven . . . . Okay . . . . Ready to listen?
>
> *Audio Recording of Burger Queen:*
>
> Manager: How old are you, Mrs. Rudi?

Mrs. Rudi:	Oh, that's not important for the job. I'm not going to answer. The important thing is that I am the best burger maker ever. Everyone calls me 'The Burger Queen'. There is a good reason for it. They know my burgers are the best in the city. Here. I'm going to make you one of my burgers right now. Wait until you taste it. It's s-o-o delicious!
Manager:	Stop, Burger Queen! I mean Mrs. Rudi. You have the job. You're hired. Now, please can I have one of your burgers?

After a discussion of the audio-recording and some comprehension questions, the instructor engaged her students in this dialogue:

Instructor:	So she makes . . . a delicious . . . burger. Okay and what is the way . . . how she present her [sic], how, the way she said that? So ( ) said she was happy, energetic. She was energetic. And I would say something else uh. That's not important for this job. Everyone calls me the Burger Queen. There is a good reason for it. My burgers are the best. I can make the right one right now.
Female student:	She make presentation
Instructor:	Yes she makes presentation, gives presentation. Is she self-confident? Self-confident? Anything else we can say? So she she shows that self-confidence.
Male student:	Self-confidence
Instructor:	Self-confidence. What is self-confidence? I am the best. She is the best. The best at making burgers. Okay, so she presented her [sic] with self-confidence. And energetic. You know my burger's the best in the city I'm going to make . . . . They know my burgers are the best. The way she is speaking, yeah, the manager became more interested in her, yeah, and so right away, I will hire you, you are hired, you are hired.

These data support Haque's (2017: 98) claim that Canada's immigrant language training policies emphasise the development of 'entrepreneurial . . . flexible, autonomised and responsibilised subjects' and 'desirable workers' (2017: 15). In this lesson, soft skills instruction was framed as a way to sell the self into a job. In other words, the successful job seeker needs to say she's the best to get the work. It's not enough to do a job well: she needs to embody the role of 'Burger Queen'. However, as Kerekes (2022) notes, such self-entrepreneurship may not be appropriate across cultures, and different cultures value self-entrepreneurship differently.

Girard and Bauer (2007) argue that Canadian job-seeking immigrants are regulated by an institutional cultural capital that prioritises certain qualities over others. Personality traits such as 'easy-going', 'motivated' and 'open-minded' differ greatly in their interpretations across cultures; within some cultures these qualities may not be prized. As can be seen in the next excerpt, taken from an instructor-facilitated discussion in a LINC Level 2–3 class, the importance of adopting these personality traits in one's work is emphasised:

Instructor:	You are going to match words with definitions. You can read the definition aloud, and the student who has the word that matches with the definition can say the word, can call out the word. Okay.
Male student:	Li – listens to other
Instructor:	Listens to others
Class:	Open-minded?
Instructor:	Open-minded. Yes
Class:	Open-minded
Instructor:	Listens to others. Open-minded. ( ) Again please?
Male student:	Always arrive on time.
Class:	( )
Instructor:	Listen listen
Male student:	Always arrive on time.
Instructor:	Always arrived on time.
Class:	( )
Instructor:	It's your word just say it. Punctual. Punctual punctual ( )
Female student:	You love and enjoy your work
Instructor:	You love and enjoy your work . . . . Motivated. Motivated. Ok good. Ok, now you read your definitions and these students will match with the definitions with your word. Ok so let's see ( ) so we can start.
Female student:	Understand ( )
Instructor:	Mmm hmmm. Understand and learn quickly. (4) Understand and learn quickly
Female student:	Fast learner
Instructor:	Fast learner. Yes, fast learner. Okay good. Uh ( ) you do yours.
Female student:	What uh do what do do what you premise

Instructor:	Do what you promise.
Female student:	What you promise.
Instructor:	Do what you promise. Do what you promise.
Male student:	re—
Instructor:	Responsible. Responsible. Responsible. Responsible. Good. Okay. Responsible
Male student:	Don't take long break ( )
Instructor:	Don't take, uh huh again?
Male student:	Don't take long breaks work overtime.
Instructor:	Don't take long breaks and work overtime.
Class:	Hard worker. Hard worker.
Instructor:	Hard worker. Hard worker. Good.
Female student:	Winking and smiling at everyone.
Instructor:	Winking and smiling at everyone. Winking and smiling at everyone.
Class:	Friendly.
Instructor:	Friendly, friendly.
Female student:	Who friendly?
Instructor:	Friendly, you have friendly?
Female student:	Yeah.
Instructor:	Easy-going. Relaxed.
Female student:	Relaxed.
Instructor:	Yeah. Relaxed. Easy-going. Relaxed.

Here the personality traits were named by the instructor and repeated by the students as a prescriptive lesson. Little attention was paid to the contextual appropriateness of, for example, 'winking and smiling at everyone'. These traits were presented as truths rather than as concepts that may help raise students' critical awareness, and there was no mention of how these traits may differ across the English language students' cultures. In this initiation-response-evaluation sequence, time is not allocated for the class to reflect on how the adoption of this prescribed range of traits may be alienating or perhaps even painful for some students.

As a subsequent activity, the instructor told the students:

> Imagine that you are having an interview and you need to talk to the employer. So what are you going to say about yourself? About your good qualities, about your personal qualities? *What is good about you?* Thinking about personal skills that are connected, related to the job, your work. [emphasis added]

To ask 'what is good about you?' in the context of the job search appeared to be an effort to equate the self as worker. While the concept of 'soft skills' usually incorporates communication skills and related competencies, here, the question 'What is good about you?' turned the focus away from a set of skills that are necessary for work, and toward a whole self that can be defined by a work-ready personality and traits.

Customer service

Mesa's soft skills instructions for customer service interactions resemble in many ways the instructions for job interview conduct: they emphasise self-entrepreneurship, appear to be grooming immigrants for low-salary jobs, and seem to be designed to encourage students' buy-in to this system. However, they are different in that the instructions are imbued with an emotional message: the marketplace is where immigrants, as members of the workforce, can experience emotional satisfaction and, in turn, supply that to the customers they serve. Creating an emotionally satisfying experience is critical for customer service, and the students should provide this service by giving all of themselves, at all times – regardless of salary!

Brandon's prompt illustrates this disposition in his Enhanced Language Training course specialising in Customer Service and Administration for CLB Levels 5–7. To introduce the lesson, he asked his students to imagine themselves as recipients of good customer service, and to provide descriptive words about that experience:

Brandon:	Descriptive words about the way you felt, when you received good customer service. OK? So you can come up with as many as you want . . . . When you were a customer, when you are a customer, and you received good customer service, how would that make you feel?
Student 1:	I would feel happy, maybe.
Student 2:	I happy, yeah, I always happy. Relaxed.
Brandon:	Relaxed, like all your problems have been solved. Oh that burden, all my worries are gone now.

In this exchange, Brandon attempted to elicit an emotional response from his students. He reacted to their responses that they would feel 'happy' and 'relaxed' by proclaiming that receiving good customer service would make students more than happy; they would feel that all of their 'problems have been solved'.

In the next exchange, Brandon indicated what he meant by 'excellent service':

What do we need to do . . . what do we need to do as an organisation, as a business, as whatever service provider to make sure our customer service is excellent? That we are going to get repeat business? That people are going to be leaving our business satisfied and not upset? Happy and not disappointed? *Comfortable that we came in and we got served and not processed?* [emphasis added]

Here, Brandon indicated that there is a difference between being 'served' and being 'processed'. The latter implies that the employee merely did their job, while the former emphasises the subservient nature of the employee. The lesson materials Brandon used supplied a list of negative emotion words to describe how customers feel when they receive poor customer service (negative, uncomfortable, embarrassed, let down, helpless, frustrated, disgruntled, angry, cheated, upset, disappointed and annoyed). After they discuss the negative adjectives, the students explored a list of positive emotions associated with good customer service (happy, blissful, special, valued, elated, fulfilled, motivated, encouraged, shocked and jovial). In a role-play activity that followed, Brandon stated, 'you're the customer and you're expressing a feeling', infusing the customer service pedagogy with a great deal of emotion.

Following the explorations of this emotional vocabulary, one student suggested that better customer service may be associated with better salaries. Brandon replied:

Brandon: OK. Let's take away the salary aspect of it. Think about all the people who work at places like . . . all the retail stores . . . McDonald's . . . where minimum wage is paid. Do you get . . . really horrible service because of that?

Student: Sometimes.

Brandon: Very rarely. Because these businesses, especially in the food industry, let's say McDonald's, Burger King, the fast food chains, customer service is important. Because the people serving the coffee, serving the sandwiches, and so on, even though their salary is small, the minimum wage is paid, they are trained, they have to have good customer service. Even if they have a horrible day, they have to, right? So sometimes salary, yes, is a big factor, and it makes us happy, because we want salary, and then sometimes people are generally, it doesn't matter what job they do, once their job is to provide a service, they give it their hundred percent. And that's what we as customer service people are supposed to do . . . . So let's look at customer service best practices. So the first thing any organization [does], they provide a service. *Service, service, with no excuse. No excuses. My job is to provide a service, so that is what I am supposed to do.* [emphasis added]

In this exchange, students were presented with certain societal norms as truth. English language students are expected to buy into the service model, regardless of salary. Brandon did not suggest that a subservient attitude would result in students moving into better-paying positions; rather, good customer service is a duty that employees must fulfil at all times, without exception. In the context of the language classroom, presentation of these norms was not accompanied by an opportunity for criticism; thus, language teaching has the potential to serve as an apparently benign cloak that masks the ideologically-driven norms being taught.

Mesa's English language students are expected to accept low-paying customer service positions, and to embrace them without concern for salary. Mesa's top-down pedagogy reflects the expectation that students should surrender their cultural/personal idiosyncrasies in order to fit into the purported White Canadian middle-class business milieu. Some English language students may resist this paradigm, but much of their classroom participation is passive. As Brandon's students learn to provide emotionally-driven services, they are also taught how to expect the same as customers. In this way they become 'empowered' to participate in Canadian capitalism as both producers and consumers of services, as 'homo economicus' who experience full personal and professional satisfaction as players in the market. The classroom data reveal a pedagogy that may indoctrinate students into advanced capitalism, a hierarchy in which they are expected to acquire capitalist work attitudes and to take a subservient role.

Conclusion

We have observed and described ideologies which convey power imbalances to English language students in vocational ESL programmes in metropolitan Canada. These ideologies, though nuanced, promulgate inequitable treatment of immigrants by affecting the attitudes of Canadian employers (through their institutions) and the immigrants/job seekers themselves. A prescriptionist, deficiency-oriented teaching philosophy appears to underpin some of the pedagogical methods utilised at Mesa for soft skills instruction. Students are expected to be passive recipients of cultural norms and to adapt their own identities to these norms, such that they will acquire a 'Canadian' persona, fit into a (monocultural) Canadian workplace, and buy into existing ideologies that maintain a status quo unfavourable to internationally educated professionals aspiring to climb the socioeconomic ladder within their professional fields.

Symptomatic of its deficiency orientation is Mesa's concept of 'fit' and assimilation, aligned with Laroche and Yang's (2014) suggestion that immigrants are largely responsible for adapting their communication style and even personality to ostensible Canadian cultural norms, not vice-versa. Further, it appears to be taken for granted at times that Mesa's students will be seeking employment in a monocultural workplace, presumably one in which the majority of co-workers are Canadian-born English-dominant speakers. Laura's (and her staff's) position on cultural adaptation is presented as truth, contextualised neither by Canada's history as a country built on successive waves of immigration, nor by the current demographics of its five largest metropolitan areas, in which immigrants make up 20–46% of the population (Statistics Canada, 2017a). Given the multicultural, multilingual reality of modern urban Canada, Laura's emphasis on developing a 'Canadian identity' has the markings of an ideologically loaded pedagogical approach that, on the surface, appears to be entirely self-evident – as indicated by her description of assigning her students to develop for themselves a Canadian persona: 'It wasn't me prescribing anything'.

Some limitations exist for this study. Since the data were collected using a variety of methods and by a number of different graduate students, they may not represent a comprehensive scope of pedagogical practices and beliefs at Mesa Centre. They do provide, however, illustrative examples that help bridge the conceptual concerns in the existing literature and can be used to make constructive suggestions for developing culturally sensitive language teaching approaches.

There may be more effective and sensitive methods for soft skills instruction in newcomer language classes than those discussed here. Thomson and Derwing (2004: 20), for example, recommend that 'culture should be *explored* rather than *taught*' (emphasis in original). They continue: 'Dominant values should be taught not for purposes of emulation', but they should be taught in a critical light so that newcomers can 'make their own choices' (Thomson & Derwing, 2004: 29). Newton and Kusmierczyk's (2011: 84) survey of research on second language teaching for the workplace shows us that the majority of studies recommend exploratory methods rather than the teaching of 'normative generic discourse patterns'. This approach, the authors argue, works to 'empower these people, rather than attempt to make them fit' (Newton & Kusmierczyk, 2011: 78). Dahm and Yates (2013: 4) concur that how much of the pragmatics instruction learners decide to actually use 'is ultimately a matter of personal choice'. Fleming (2003: 76) also agrees, suggesting that Canadian culture cannot be taught as a 'pristine set of immutable facts . . . . Presentations about hockey, for example, are one-sided if limited to mythic representations of frozen ponds and Canadian team sweaters'. While some scholarship still recommends the explicit teaching of pragmatics as self-evident truth without a critical or reflexive lens (e.g. de Bres, 2009; Laroche & Yang, 2014; Louw *et al.*, 2010; Wood, 2009), the time is ripe for a critical, reflexive praxis in the teaching and learning of soft skills to come to fruition in actual teaching methods and curricular materials.

Appendix: Transcription Conventions

( ): unintelligible speech
(number): pause in speech with number indicating time in seconds
...: Pause of less than a second
....: Pause of 1–2 seconds

Notes

(1) E.g. http://career-advice.monster.com/career-development/getting-promoted/six-soft-skills-everyone-needs-hot-jobs/article.aspx; http://searchcio.techtarget.com/definition/soft-skills.
(2) As stated in Statistics Canada (2019), 'Mother tongue *refers to the first language learned at home in childhood and still understood by the person at the time the data was collected*'.
(3) 'Mesa Centre' as well as all participants' names and other identifying information, other than the researcher-participant (Julie), are pseudonyms.
(4) A twinning project is a collaboration involving two teachers/leaders and their respective students/colleagues who create a project that is carried out collaboratively, with different learning objectives and outcomes for the two groups (Blanchet *et al.*, 2022).
(5) This project was approved by University of Toronto's Ethics Review Board. Names of the participants and any other identifying factors were changed, in order to maintain their anonymity. All participants signed consent forms to participate in this project and to allow for eventual publications out of the project.

References

Ahmed, F., Fernando Capretz, L., Bouktif, S. and Campbell, P. (2012) Soft skills requirements in software development jobs: A cross-cultural empirical study. *Journal of Systems and Information Technology* 14 (1), 58–81.
Algonquin College (2009) LINC Classroom activities: Language instruction for newcomers to Canada: LINC 2. http://www.moresettlement.org/LINC1-4/LINC4/LINC_2_Classroom_Activities.pdf (accessed 18 July 2021).
Allan, K. (2016) Going beyond language: Soft skill-ing cultural difference and immigrant integration in Toronto, Canada. *Multilingua* 35 (6), 617–647.
Andrews, J. and Higson, H. (2008) Graduate employability, 'soft skills' versus 'hard' business knowledge: A European study. *Higher Education in Europe* 33 (4), 411–422.
Angouri, J. (2018) *Culture, Discourse, and the Workplace*. London: Routledge.
Bancino, R. and Zevalkink, C. (2007) Soft skills: The new curriculum for hard-core technical professionals. *Techniques: Connecting Education and Careers (J1)* 82 (5), 20–22.
Bartel, J. (2013) Pragmatics in the post-TESL certificate course "Language Teaching for Employment". *TESL Canada Journal* 30 (7), 108–124.
Bialystok, E. (1993) Symbolic representation and attentional control in pragmatic competence. In G. Kasper and S. Blum-Kulka (eds) *Interlanguage Pragmatics* (pp. 43–57). Oxford: Oxford University Press.
Blanchet, J., Carignan, M., Deraîche, M. and Guillot, M. (eds) (2022) *Intercultural Twinnings: Commitment for a Pluralistic Society*. Leiden: Brill Publishers.
Bourdieu, P. (1989) Social space and symbolic power. *Sociological Theory* 7 (1), 14–25.
Caggiano, V., Schleutker, K., Petrone, L. and González-Bernal, J. (2020) Towards identifying the soft skills needed in curricula: Finnish and Italian students' self-evaluations indicate differences between groups. *Sustainability* 12, 4031.
Canadian Charter of Rights and Freedoms (1982) Part 1 of the Constitution Act, 1982, being Schedule B to the Canada Act 1982 (UK), c 11.

Casner-Lotto, J. and Barrington, L. (2006) *Are They Really Ready to Work? Employers' Perspectives on the Basic Knowledge and Applied Skills of New Entrants to the 21st Century US Workforce*. Washington, DC: Partnership for 21st Century Skills.

Centre for Advanced Research on Language Acquisition (2019) What is culture? http://www.carla.umn.edu/culture/definitions.html (accessed 16 January 2023).

Cinque, M. (2016) "Lost in translation". Soft skills development in European countries. *Tuning Journal for Higher Education* 3 (2), 389–427.

Citizenship and Immigration Canada (2008) Enhanced language training initiative: Formative evaluation. http://www.cic.gc.ca/english/resources/evaluation/elt/index.asp (accessed 18 July 2021).

Citizenship and Immigration Canada (2010) Evaluation of the language instruction for newcomers to Canada (LINC) program. http://www.cic.gc.ca/english/resources/evaluation/linc/2010/linc-eval.pdf (accessed 18 July 2021).

Dahm, M.R. and Yates, L. (2013) English for the workplace: Doing patient-centred care in medical communication. *TESL Canada Journal* 30 (7), 21–44.

de Bres, J. (2009) Language in the workplace project and workplace communication for skilled migrants course at Victoria University of Wellington, New Zealand. *Language Teaching* 42 (04), 519–524.

Del Vitto, C. (2008) Cross-cultural "soft skills" and the global engineer: Corporate best practices and trainer methodologies. *Online Journal for Global Engineering Education* 3 (1), Article 1.

Fernández-Sanz, L., Villaba, M.T., Medina, J.A. and Misra, S. (2017 A study on the key soft skills for successful participation of students in multinational engineering education. *International Journal of Engineering Education* 33 (6), 2061–2070.

Fleming, D. (2003) Building personal and nation-state identities: Research and practice. *TESL Canada Journal* 20 (2), 65–79.

Fleming, D. (2007) Adult immigrant ESL programs in Canada. In J. Cummins and C. Davison (eds) *International Handbook of English Language Teaching* (pp. 185–198). Boston, MA: Springer.

Fleming, D. (2010) Becoming citizens: Racialized conceptions of ESL learners and the Canadian language benchmarks. *Canadian Journal of Education* 33 (3), 588–616.

Foucault, M. (1982) The subject and power. *Critical Inquiry* 8 (4), 777–795.

Foucault, M. (1991) Governmentality. In G. Burchell, C. Gordon and P. Miller (eds) *The Foucault Effect: Studies in Governmentality* (pp. 87–104). Chicago, IL: University of Chicago Press.

Foucault, M. (2008) *The Birth of Biopolitics: Lectures at the College de France, 1978–1979* (ed. M. Senellart). Basingstoke: Palgrave MacMillan.

Fougère, M. and Moulettes, A. (2007) The construction of the modern West and the backward rest: Studying the discourse of Hofstede's *Culture's Consequences*. *Journal of Multicultural Discourses* 2 (1), 1–19.

Gee, J.P. (2011) *An Introduction to Discourse Analysis: Theory and Method* (3rd edn). London: Routledge.

Gee, J.P. (2015) *Social Linguistics and Literacies: Ideology in Discourses*. London: Routledge.

Girard, E.R. and Bauder, H. (2007) Assimilation and exclusion of foreign trained engineers in Canada: Inside a professional regulatory organization. *Antipode* 39 (1), 35–53.

Given, L.M. (ed.) (2008) *The Sage Encyclopedia of Qualitative Research Methods*. Thousand Oaks: Sage.

Guo, Y. (2013) Language policies and programs for adult immigrants in Canada: A critical analysis. *Canadian Ethnic Studies* 45 (1), 23–41.

Haque, E. (2011) A Foucauldian approach to language policy: The case of Canada. *OLBI Working Papers* 3, 95–107.

Haque, E. (2017) Neoliberal governmentality and Canadian migrant language training policies. *Globalisation, Societies and Education* 15 (1), 96–113.

Haque, E. and Cray, E. (2007) Constraining teachers: Adult ESL settlement language training policy and implementation. *TESOL Quarterly* 41 (3), 634–642.

Heckman, J.J. and Kautz, T. (2012) Hard evidence on soft skills. *Labour Economics* 19 (4), 451–464.

Hofstede, G.H. (2001) *Culture's Consequences: Comparing Values, Behaviors, Institutions and Organizations across Nations*. Thousand Oaks: Sage.

Holmes, A., Hjartarson, J. and McGuire, N. (2014) *Think Fast: Ontario Employer Perspectives on Immigration Reform and the Expression of Interest System*. Ontario: Ontario Chamber of Commerce. https://hireimmigrants.ca/wp-content/uploads/2018/06/ThinkFast_immigration_OCC.pdf (accessed 18 July 2021).

Jones, M., Baldi, C., Phillips, C. and Waikar, A. (2017) The hard truth about soft skills: What recruiters look for in business graduates. *College Student Journal* 3 (Fall), 422–428. https://www.ingentaconnect.com/content/prin/csj/2017/00000050/00000003/art00014.

Kasper, G. (1997) *Can Pragmatic Competence be Taught?* Honolulu: University of Hawai'i. http://www.nflrc.hawaii.edu/NetWorks/NW06/ (accessed 18 July 2021).

Kerekes, J. (2006) Winning an interviewer's trust in a gatekeeping encounter. *Language in Society* 35 (1), 27–57.

Kerekes, J. (2018) Language preparation for internationally educated professionals. In B. Vine (ed.) *The Routledge Handbook of Language in the Workplace* (pp. 413–424). New York: Routledge.

Kerekes, J. (2022) Training for settlement organizations, ESL students, and graduate education: A collaborative approach. In J. Blanchet, N. Carignan, M. Deraîche and M.-C. Guillot (eds) *Intercultural Twinnings: Commitment for a Pluralistic Society*. Leiden: Brill Publishers.

Kerekes, J., Chow, J., Lemak, A. and Perhan, Z. (2013) Trust or betrayal: Immigrant engineers' employment-seeking experiences in Canada. In C. Candlin and J. Crichton (eds) *Discourses of Trust* (pp. 269–285). Basingstoke: Palgrave Macmillan.

Kim, M. (2007) Our culture, their culture and beyond: Further thoughts on ethnocentrism in Hofstede's discourse. *Journal of Multicultural Discourses* 2 (1), 26–31.

Laroche, L. and Rutherford, D. (2007) *Recruiting, Retaining and Promoting Culturally Different Employees*. London: Routledge.

Laroche, L. and Yang, C. (2014) *Danger and Opportunity: Bridging Cultural Diversity for Competitive Advantage*. New York: Routledge.

Louw, K.J., Derwing, T.M. and Abbott, M.L. (2010) Teaching pragmatics to L2 learners for the workplace: The job interview. *Canadian Modern Language Review/La Revue canadienne des langues vivantes* 66 (5), 739–758.

Maitra, S. (2015) Between conformity and contestation: South Asian immigrant women negotiating soft skill training in Canada. *Canadian Journal for the Study of Adult Education* 27 (2 SE), 65–78.

Mitchell, G.W., Skinner, L.B. and White, B.J. (2010) Essential soft skills for success in the twenty-first century workforce as perceived by business educators. *The Journal of Research in Business Education* 52 (1), 43–53.

Monwoorian, S.M.A., Homayoun, M.R. and Nasab, A.J. (2016) Is pragmatics teachable? *International Academic Journal of Social Sciences* 3 (1), 144–151.

MosaicBC (n.d.) Lionel Laroche talks to immigrants. https://www.mosaicbc.org/news/keynote-address-immigrants-professional-conference-provides-emphasizes-importance-soft-skills/ (accessed 18 July 2021).

Newton, J. and Kusmierczyk, E. (2011) Teaching second languages for the workplace. *Annual Review of Applied Linguistics* 31, 74–92.

Ontario Council of Agencies (2015) What do Canadian employers want? http://settlement.org/ontario/employment/working-in-canada/workplace-culture/what-do-canadian-employers-want (accessed 18 July 2021).

Ontario Society of Professional Engineers (2014) *From the World to the Workforce: Hiring and Recruitment Perceptions of Engineering Employers and Internationally*

Trained Engineers in Ontario. Ontario: OSPE. https://ospe.on.ca/public/documents/advocacy/2014-world-to-workforce.pdf.

Reissner-Roubicek, S. (2017) Teamwork and the 'global graduate': Negotiating core skills and competencies with employers in recruitment interviews. In J. Angouri (ed.) *Negotiating Boundaries at Work: Talking and Transitions* (pp. 66–86). Edinburgh University Press.

Ricento, T. (2014) On the loss of social capital. In B. Spolsky, O. Inbar-Lourie and M. Tannenbaum (eds) *Challenges for Language Education and Policy: Making Space for People.* New York: Routledge.

Rose, K. (2005) On the effects of instruction in second language pragmatics. *System* 33 (3), 385–399.

Statistics Canada (2013) *Immigration and Ethnocultural Diversity in Canada: National Household Survey,* 2011. Ottawa, ON: Statistics Canada for Minister of Industry. http://www12.statcan.gc.ca/nhs-enm/2011/as-sa/99-010-x/99-010-x2011001-eng.pdf.

Statistics Canada (2017a) Immigration and ethnocultural diversity: Key results from the 2016 Census. *The Daily,* 25 October. https://www150.statcan.gc.ca/n1/daily-quotidien/171025/dq171025b-eng.htm (accessed 5 November 2021).

Statistics Canada (2017b) Linguistic integration of immigrants and official language populations in Canada: Census in Brief. https://www12.statcan.gc.ca/census-recensement/2016/as-sa/98-200-x/2016017/98-200-x2016017-eng.cfm (accessed 22 July 2022).

Statistics Canada (2019) Dictionary, census of population, 2016: Mother tongue. https://www12.statcan.gc.ca/census-recensement/2016/ref/dict/pop095-eng.cfm.

Stevens, M. and Norman, R. (2016) Industry expectations of soft skills in IT graduates: A regional survey. *Proceedings of the Australasian Computer Science Week Multiconference,* 1–9.

Takahashi, S. (2010) The effect of pragmatic instruction on speech act performance. In A. Martínez-Flor and E. Usó-Juan (eds) *Speech Act Performance: Theoretical, Empirical and Methodological Issues* (pp. 127–140). Amsterdam: John Benjamins.

Thomson, R.I. and Derwing, T.M. (2004) Presenting Canadian values in LINC: The roles of textbooks and teachers. *TESL Canada Journal* 21 (2), 17–33.

Tsey, K., Lui, S.M. (Carrie), Heyeres, M., Pryce, J., Yan, L. and Bauld, S. (2018) Developing soft skills: Exploring the feasibility of an Australian well-being program for health managers and leaders in Timor-Leste. *SAGE Open* 8 (4). https://doi.org/10.1177/2158244018811404.

US Department of Labour, Office of Disability Employment Policy (2009) Soft skills: The competitive edge. http://www.dol.gov/odep/pubs/fact/softskills.htm (accessed 18 July 2021).

Viviers, H.A., Fouché, J.P. and Reitsma, G.M. (2016) Developing soft skills (also known as pervasive skills): Usefulness of an educational game. *Meditari Accountancy Research* 24 (3), 368–389.

Wheeler, R. (2016) Soft skills—The importance of cultivating emotional intelligence. AALL *Spectrum* 20 (3), 28–34.

Wood, D. (2009) Preparing ESP Learners for workplace placement. *ELT Journal* 63 (4), 323–331.

Yan, L., Yinghong, Y., Lui, S.M. (Carrie), Whiteside, M. and Tsey, K. (2019) Teaching "soft skills" to university students in China: The feasibility of an Australian approach. *Educational Studies* 45 (2), 242–258.

8 Impression Management Games: Language and Mobility among Southern European Migrants in a London Call Centre

Johanna Tovar

Introduction

Goffman (1956: 8) first theorised the term 'impression management' to refer to someone 'trying to control the impression' others form of them. Research (e.g. Ashforth & Humphrey, 1993; McFarland *et al.*, 2023; Raghuram, 2013) suggests that service sector employees and others rely on impression management to orchestrate and flatten relationships with customers. Several studies of Indian call centres (Mirchandani, 2004, 2012; Pal & Buzzanell, 2008; Raghuram, 2013) confirm that call centre agents commonly employ impression management tactics. In Indian call centre studies, tactics used when talking to Americans, Australians and Britons were found to include adopting an alias, evoking a different accent and phone voice as well as using scripts to smooth interaction (Mirchandani, 2004, 2012; Pal & Buzzanell, 2008; Raghuram, 2013). Call agents often did so to counter xenophobia they supposed call recipients might harbour against them and enact in rudeness. So far, the relevance of impression management has only been explored in Indian call centres. Given that call centres worldwide are employment generators, and that agents working in call centres often take and make calls in second or third languages, the question emerges whether impression management is also relevant in these contexts.

This chapter explores impression management in just such a context. I operationalise Goffman's definition by seeking strategies that agents declare they use in presenting themselves to others to make a favourable impression. Agents receive tailored calling scripts outlining expected conversation and pointers for what to say at each moment. Agent calls are monitored to ensure they follow the structure of the script. Yet, following Giddens (1984: 14), I argue that these agents are also able to 'act otherwise' (see also Woydack & Rampton, 2016), empowering themselves in the phone interactions.

I find that impression management tactics are a key transferable skill in which all agents at CallTown, a call centre based in London, UK, are trained and which they master over time. Skills such as strategic speaking increase agents' job mobility in a competitive market, especially for agents whose first language is not English. The immediate context of this research is 2008-2014 London, prior to the outbreak of the Covid-19 pandemic in 2020 and before the United Kingdom exited the EU ('Brexit') in January 2020 ending a long period of visa-free migration from other EU countries. I focus here on newly arrived EU migrants from Southern Europe who work as agents at CallTown, as their case highlights the utility of impression management tactics, how they empower users and their transferability in the workplace, in ways still relevant today. Although the research is situated in the decade prior to Brexit and the Covid-19 pandemic, its importance and that of call centres have only increased due to a rising demand for remote accessibility worldwide since Covid-19 (cf. impact of Covid-19 on call centres: Nielsen, 2022; Tovar, 2022a).

My research is based on interviews with and observations of 30 highly educated migrant informants from Southern Europe who worked at CallTown as agents. Like their call centre colleagues, who were either British or of other nationalities, they were successful in finding well-paid jobs outside the call centre industry after working at CallTown for a year or less. These agents mentioned in interviews that impression management skills were a key factor in this success. I suggest that impression management training and skill adoption at CallTown are effective because managing the cross-cultural contexts of calling customers who reside outside one's homeland, often in a second or third language, is more challenging in terms of developing communicative competence than in many other service sector jobs. In addition, on the phone, an agent and call recipient do not see each other, creating a range of opportunities that require a caller to pay significant attention to aural cues and voice.

It is common for agents who have foreign accents to encounter rudeness and xenophobic reactions on the phone. Impression management training eases the handling of cross-cultural divides, even in the face of verbal abuse or harassment, by developing skills that carry forward beyond the call centre. While call centres have often been criticised for providing an overly standardised, pressurised work environment precluding agency, agents performing impression work demonstrate flexibility, agency and some linguistic power during scripted telephone conversations and training sessions, thereby increasing their linguistic facility. Nonetheless, this research does not aim to romanticise call centres but builds on my work published using my maiden name, Woydack (2019a) and Woydack and Rampton (2016), in which we develop nuanced accounts of call centres as workplaces that hold advantages for agents. Agents' imaginative presentations of themselves in their phone personas are creative, unforced and extend even beyond Giddens's (1984: 14) notion of agency as the ability to 'act otherwise'.

A more complex notion of agency and a multidimensional notion of linguistic power is central to two frameworks on which I build in this chapter. First, I adapt Raghuram's (2013) framework on impression management[1] in Indian call centres for my project. I have modified her framework to fit this study's context. Second, I employ Hall's (1995) work in which she attends to a multi-dimensional definition of power evidenced in the telephone calls of sex line operators. I also argue that the lack of a visual link in phone calls can lead to an imaginative presentation of self, neither oppressive nor demeaning.

Call Centres, EU Migration and CallTown

It is established that call centres employ migrants; moreover, as research has shown, call centres are a popular port of call for newly arrived migrants in countries such as New Zealand and Canada (see e.g. Brophy, 2017) but also in EU countries (Brophy, 2017; Woydack, 2019; Woydack & Lockwood, 2020). In the EU, Ireland stands out as an example where multinational corporations operating multilingual call centres led to a boom in internal EU migration for employment (see Brophy, 2017). As already mentioned, many of CallTown's agents in London were EU migrants at the time of my research. CallTown recruited them as the organisation relied on foreign language speakers to conduct their IT campaigns. While agents at CallTown were from a variety of places, such as Britain, the US, Australia, Nigeria, Switzerland, Norway and Turkey among others, during my fieldwork at least half of the agents came from Southern European countries, such as Italy, Spain and Portugal. Prior to Great Britain leaving the EU on 31 January 2020, thereby ending visa-free migration within the EU, and prior to the outbreak of the Covid-19 pandemic, agents moved to London seeking and finding employment in order to improve their English.

The high number of Southern European migrants working at CallTown is in line with studies that have documented the mass migration of young people from Southern European countries, such as Italy, Spain, Portugal and Greece up to 2019 (Bartolini *et al.*, 2017; Moyer, 2018; Pratsinakis *et al.*, 2020; Scotto, 2015). The studies suggest that this exodus intensifies during times of economic crisis and austerity programs, and involves emigration to big economic hubs in Northern Europe, such as London. I could not find recent information on current numbers of Spanish, Portuguese or Greeks migrating to London post-Brexit and post-Covid. However, young Italians, the most populous group of the Southern European countries are still flocking in large numbers to the British capital despite Brexit and Covid, making them the most common nationality in the capital (Kantor, 2023) and their numbers have doubled as opposed to a decade ago (Kantor, 2023).

My fieldwork at CallTown began during the global financial crisis in 2008/2009, shortly after the initiation of the economic crisis of those years, and lasted until 2014, when an economic downturn was still current in some of the Southern European countries. Among the reasons for the exodus of these often highly educated individuals was high underemployment of youth (Eurostat, 2018, 2021) and the European Union's freedom of movement policy among member states which facilitated migration (Bartolini *et al.*, 2017; Moyer, 2018; Scotto, 2015). This meant that individuals from EU member states did not require a work permit or visa to work in United Kingdom which was an EU member state at the time.

In spite of the current ease of moving within EU member states, migrating to another country often involves challenges, such as when one needs to learn or work in a different language and culture. In fact, one's mastery of a new language as well as managing cultural and professional divides can affect one's professional standing and career (Kramsch & Whiteside, 2008; O'Neill, 2013). Previous studies (Favell, 2008) have explored the mobility of highly educated successful Europeans working in prestigious jobs: so-called 'Eurostars'. However, there is less research on EU migrants who do not succeed in finding a job immediately upon having moved to another country. Little is known of their experience of (im)mobility abroad. Indeed, their immigration trajectories may begin with low-skilled jobs and a need to improve language competency for anticipated future employment.

Overall, I find two studies particularly useful. Both were researched and written in a pre-Brexit and pre-Covid context, yet the observations made are still valid. The first is by Scotto (2015) on young Italians in London. The second is by Moyer (2018) on young Spaniards in London. Italians and Spanish were the largest migrant populations in this South to North flow and the most representative groups at CallTown.

Scotto (2015) observes that most of the Italian migrants in London hold advanced degrees. They do not like to be referred to as 'migrants' as this carries a stigma from the low-skilled migration to the UK from Italy in the 1970s (Scotto, 2015: 158). They prefer to be called 'mobile workers'. As my informants also consider themselves mobile workers, this is the term I use in this chapter to refer to all Southern European migrants working at CallTown.

When it comes to the work the Italian mobile workers perform, Scotto (2015: 155) cites a report published by the Italian Embassy in London noting that not only do young Italians work as engineers, teachers, researchers, doctors, and in finance but:

> (…) many young people live in the country, sometimes for long periods, to improve their knowledge of the English language and [a] significant part of them settle[s] for several years, finding jobs in the services sector.

Scotto (2015) focuses more on the high achiever, but among the Italians mentioned in the Embassy report, several also work in multilingual call centres while not only improving their English but also aspiring to careers outside the call centre industry.

In her study of Spanish immigration to London, Moyer (2018: 424) found many young Spaniards purposefully moving to London to learn or improve their English, hoping to become more qualified and skilled workers. Moyer (2018: 424) argues that part of neoliberal ideology 'naturalizes the use of English as a language needed to obtain employment and to participate in the global economy', with London being considered an authentic place for learning English. Yet, as Moyer (2018) points out, migration to London is not always in line with the migrants' imagined or intended goals. A highly competitive job market might mean that mobile workers end up taking low-skilled service jobs, including working in a call centre, instead of the high-profile jobs they first envisioned. My informants refer to the aforementioned process as 'London socialisation' (Woydack, 2017a). Moreover, as Moyer (2018) found, London's cosmopolitan fabric and ethnic diversity make it hard for migrants to meet and engage with locals to practise their English grammar, vocabulary and pronunciation. Frequently, recent migrants find themselves in ethnically diverse residential settings with others who may not speak English fluently. Scotto (2015) found the same: Italians found it hard to become friends with the English. They became friends with either Italians or others of different nationalities (see also Favell, 2008; Woydack & Lockwood, 2017, 2020). These accounts show that new migrants use call centres for language learning purposes, as the environment is linguistically and pedagogically helpful.

To summarise, newly arrived migrants from Southern Europe in the UK, such as those that work at CallTown, may struggle with language issues such as vocabulary, pronunciation and grammar when they arrive, as well as with communicative conventions. Their struggles can expose them to rudeness on the phone as the people they interact with may attribute their poor language skills to a limited intelligence and low level of education. While I was doing fieldwork at CallTown, I observed new agents frequently losing face on the phone and being visibly upset. As a result, team leaders offer coaching on what I refer to here as impression management.

The Literature on Impression Management and Call Centres

The concept of impression management has been widely applied to online contexts (e.g. Nessi & Bailey, 2014) but is less studied in relation to call centres worldwide. One of the reasons may be a lack of access for researchers who wish to conduct long-term studies or detailed interviews. Existing ethnographic studies of Western call centres suggest that agents feel their work is devalued by outsiders, as it is thought to require little or no skill (Matos, 2012; Tovar, 2020, 2022b; Woydack, 2017b). They also note a generally negative impression of call centres and offshoring, making call centre managers reluctant to open their workspaces and employees to researchers.

Offshoring, which is the practice of setting up call centres outside a company's national home, is controversial among Westerners. As a result, agents in call centres outside the West may experience negative comments, abuse and xenophobic remarks if identified by call recipients as 'foreign' (Kahlin & Tykesson, 2016; Mirchandani, 2012). The most telling research focuses on Indian centres and Raghuram (2013: 1472) notes that India's colonial history shapes perceived relations of power between caller and recipient if the nationality of callers from India is identified by Western call recipients. Initially, in the early 2000s when offshoring started, Indian agents, especially, were encouraged to mask their locations by pretending to be in the countries to which they directed calls (Das *et al.*, 2008; Krishnamurthy, 2004; Nath, 2011; Poster, 2007). According to Mirchandani (2012) and others, over time this approach was recognised as counterproductive. Call centre agents more recently are typically not pushed to conceal where they are from or from where they are calling. For example, pseudonyms, once commonly used to depict a caller as a person from a particular society, are no longer compulsory in scripts that regulate the presentation of agents. However, as Raghuram (2013) points out impression management of various kinds may still be encouraged and that agents may also voluntarily choose strategies including the use of pseudonyms to avoid xenophobic interactions and create a protective psychological barrier. She further argues that impression management on the telephone is more complex than in face-to-face settings, since phone or email restrict the possibility of conveying information visually. Instead, agents adapt verbal aspects of impression management and associated qualities of voice, volume, pitch and tempo to match their own speaking with that of their customers and their expectations (cf. also Raghuram, 2013: 1475).

As Goffman (1956) observed, the performance of self is contextually sensitive, and audience expectations for role enactment likewise vary with context. Applying this to the call centre context, we can draw two conclusions. First, agents working the lines perform continuous management of their impressions in response to various customers' demands. Second, agents are required to be spontaneous on the phone and maintain their performance of their 'phone persona' as they interpret cues the call recipients provide. In this respect, Raghuram (2013: 1475) argues that accommodation theory (Giles & Ogay, 2006) facilitates analysis of verbal aspects of impression management strategies. She emphasises that convergence, a set of accommodative strategies that agents may employ to decrease imagined social distance between them and the other person on the phone, has a positive impact on conversation. Other studies have suggested that several factors lead to a successful and respectful interaction and a positive response from call recipients. These range from agents' skilful individualised use of voice quality, pitch, volume and the rhythm of pauses (Purdy *et al.*, 2000), to careful choice of wording and phrases scaffolded by scripting (Woydack & Lockwood, 2017). Call centre agents in both India and London share these strategies in cross-cultural contexts. In each case, they need to learn about accents, pauses, speech rates and vocabulary to be well received by call recipients and to be successful. This is especially true of mobile workers from Southern Europe in London.

Like Raghuram, in earlier work Hall (1995) points out the agentive side of standardised telephone work, but is more detailed in suggesting how some tactics might help agents. Although Hall (1995) does not explicitly use the term 'impression management' in her study of telephone sex operators, what her informants describe can be read from an impression management angle. Her informants consciously use 'sweet talk' that has many features traditionally associated in linguistics with submissive speech, which is more typical of 'the speech patterns of women than men' in America's heterosexual environments (1995: 184). As Hall (1995: 184) notes, the sweet talk of her sex line operators 'is precisely what has been defined by language and gender theorists since Lakoff as "powerless"'. Similarly, in the call centre case, linguists have suggested that scripts render call centre agents powerless and take away their agency. However, I argue that, as in Hall's study, the call centre agents skilfully use linguistic structures, jargon and stereotypical expectations of performance to achieve their interactional goals.

For Hall's informants, the combination of analysis of callers' speech to discern anticipated stereotypes and performance of alternative personas allows them to distance themselves from their phone identities. These skills are evidenced with regard to impression management in Indian call centres too. But despite the many insights from the literature on impression management use and tactics in Indian call centres, reports remain abstract when it comes to concrete details and analysis. For instance, although Mirchandani (2012) and Poster (2007) write that scripts play a role, they give few details on how scripts are integrated into practice. Similarly, Raghuram (2013) mentions that agents rehearse possible interactions to express values associated with a social group that they wish to appear to be part of (Ashforth & Humphrey, 1993; cf. also Raghuram, 2013: 1474), but no examples are presented. Therefore, this chapter provides and examines concrete examples of impression management drawing on Goffman (1956), Hall (1995) and Raghuram (2013) to frame an approach. I foreground agents' use of conversational cues from paralinguistic and linguistic features of call recipients' remarks to set their own parameters for self-presentation. I further explore how agents adapt their scripts, for example, by adapting pseudonyms, playing on stereotypes, and adjusting their speech, which I understand as demonstrations of agency.

Field Site and Methodology

The research in CallTown reported here was a part of a larger project: an ethnography of a call centre (Woydack, 2019a). The research was approved by the King's College London Ethics Committee. I conducted participant observation and worked first as a paid agent and later as a team leader (an individual who rises from the position of agent to take on leadership responsibilities on the call centre floor). Training in impression management was one of my duties. Management approved my research, and my fellow employees were aware that I was a researcher. I attended meetings, briefings, training sessions (first as an incoming agent then as team leader) and listened to agents make calls. My research role was discussed in detail with all participants.

The company has on average 60 seats with agents collectively using at any one time about 20 languages as primary tongues for calling. Agents come from a range of different countries across the world. There were also British agents from London and other parts of the UK. Turnover was high with typically about 20 new agents starting every week. I conducted over 120 interviews with agents, managers and team leaders. Out of these, about 30 were with Southern Europeans (Italians, Spanish and Portuguese). The majority of agents during my tenure with the company were in their twenties or early thirties and were recent university graduates. Some of them also had post-graduate qualifications. Interview questions were semi-structured and focused on how each agent had joined the call centre, what their background was, what their plan was for the future, and what their language learning and mobility experience had been like. I also interviewed agents after they had left the call centre to see how they were getting along, whether they had found new jobs, and if so, what kinds of jobs and to ask them to reflect back on their experience at the call centre. Interviews took place outside the call centre.

The agents, as other studies have suggested, were highly educated. Lacking sufficient opportunities in the fields of their interests (including law, medicine and other professional domains) in their native countries, they had come to London searching for new opportunities. Their professional aspirations meant they were using a call centre position to bootstrap their way into their preferred professional world. The mobile workers reported that it took time for their qualifications to be validated in the UK. Management at CallTown was supportive of agents finding better jobs, with managers often recommending agents for permanent, better-paid jobs outside the call centre industry.

Since CallTown agents work in more than 20 languages, there is a good chance that agents from a particular linguistic community can call in their first language as well as in English. However, many explicitly stated that they joined the call centre to improve and practise their English by interacting with a wide range of individuals in the UK and across other English-speaking countries. Accordingly, new agents were most likely assigned at least some calls in English and were given a seat next to an experienced caller who mentored them (Woydack & Lockwood, 2017, 2020). This structure has been described in the literature as legitimate and peripheral participation (LPP) (cf. Lave & Wenger, 1991). The novice agents also received guidance from team leaders and peer novice callers when they sat together, creating a collaborative learning environment (cf. Woydack & Lockwood, 2020, for discussion of call centres as learning environments). In the following paragraphs, a short description of the CallTown context is provided to help the reader situate the examples.

Scripts are one important tool that management uses for helping novice agents (cf. Woydack, 2019a; Woydack & Lockwood, 2017, 2020). Scripts at CallTown are meant to help new agents get comfortable with the structure for calls. The process of preparing for making calls leaves room for agents to develop their voice (Woydack, 2019a, 2019b). As I have argued elsewhere (e.g. Woydack & Lockwood, 2017, 2020), scripts are an example of verbal scaffolding. As implemented on the floor, they provide room for novice callers to reformulate sentences within a framework, and create a tactful and smoothly flowing conversation of their own. Scripts are considered important for call centres like CallTown, as many of the campaigns the call centre runs entail outbound cold calls structured not only for commercial but also for legal purposes. These calls are only to businesses, never to private households. As the calls are unsolicited, a contacted IT professional might be in the middle of something else when a call is received. Hence, interruption may generate frustration. Although agents in this context do not sell anything and their job is to get IT professionals to agree to receive emails with reports, people might still believe they are sales personnel and be rude to them for that reason. Call recipients may also guess that agents are calling from a call centre and potential customers may be abusive for that reason. I overheard call recipients addressing agents rudely and making sexually explicit remarks, or asking an agent whether they or their parents are not embarrassed that they are working in a call centre. With these insights into agents' (especially migrant agents') vulnerabilities, and managerial encouragement of socialisation for agents and enhancement of their linguistic expertise, I examine how the workers talk about impression management on the phone and their experiences at CallTown.

I coded my field notes and the interviews from my informants using NViVo. In some instances, I drew on some of Raghuram's (2013) categories for impression management. Several of her categories did not apply to this case study, as the cultural differences and power imbalances between Indians and Britons and Americans are far greater than the cultural distinctions and power differentials between Southern Europeans and Britons. These gaps make the two cases difficult to compare at times. In the end, derived from the literature and my own observations and interviews, I developed the following categories for coding and analysis:

(1) Preparing for impression management.
(2) Tactics migrant agents use for impression management:
    (i) use of a pseudonym and creating an alter ego;
    (ii) trying out different accents and voices;
    (iii) rehearsal;
    (iv) listening for clues;
    (v) adapting scripts;
    (vi) playing with stereotypes and potential stereotypes;
    (vii) feedback from call recipients.
(3) Impact of impression management on agents:
    (i) self-esteem and segmentation of phone identity from non-phone identity;
    (ii) learning about differences between one's 'own' culture and a new culture.
(4) Call centre impression management in hindsight from the perspectives of mobile workers.

Findings

The data analysis shows the multiple demands that agents face for impression management as they interact with others on the phone. Exploring their careers at CallTown and the tactics they use, I present findings in a chronological narrative of how mobile agents first learn about impression management, realise its importance, and make it their own. I later address how they evaluate impression management in hindsight once they have left the call centre.

Preparing for impression management

On their first day, before mobile agents make their first phone calls, they receive half a day of training by team leaders. As part of this training, they perform in role-plays with other new agents and receive tips from the team leaders as to how they can positively influence the people they speak with on their calls. Some of these tips are summarised in handouts, which are organised depending on the language and country agents will call. Agents are encouraged to adapt the scripts they are given so that the conversations represent their personality. I explore some of these tactics in the next section in more detail.

As previous agent callers, team leaders have lived experience of impression management. This includes listening to others on the phone for cues, putting themselves in a call recipient's shoes, and speaking to try to ensure that those they call have a good impression of them. For example, Hugh, a British team leader, said the following in Excerpt 1 illustrating the core findings from my interviews.

Excerpt 1:
[…] I don't mean just listening to what they're saying. […] you don't have time to sit there and get to know them, [or concentrate on] what they're saying but [we focus on] how they're saying it. That's all we have. […] I think the best callers are the callers that can understand very, very quickly what this guy wants in this conversation in terms of how he wants you to deliver it, what he wants from you. They tend to be the people that I, for me, make the best callers, an awareness, a social awareness [social intelligence] which I think is important when you're cold calling people. (Hugh, team leader) (Source: Woydack, 2019a: 119)

He continues that he likes to use the pronoun 'we' and avoids saying 'I'm calling on behalf of' as it would suggest that he works in a call centre:

Excerpt 2:
[…] I say […] 'Yeah, we've just put this together', [as opposed to 'I'm calling on behalf of' written in the script] but I do it very casually so it sounds… […] then sounds like I'm part of [the company]… they can't picture me, say, in a call center calling them. (Hugh, team leader) (Source: Woydack, 2019a: 116)

Yet Hugh is also aware that agents at first do not realise the importance of impression management, and that it takes some time for them to experiment and play with it until they understand its power and discover how it can help them be in control of a conversation. I now look further into what these tactics entail.

Southern European agents' tactics for impression management
Use of a pseudonym and creating an alter ego

Using a pseudonym is a common strategy for managing one's impression, something that was also confirmed by previous studies on Indian call centre agents (Mirchandani, 2004; Pal & Buzzanell, 2008; Raghuram, 2013; Taylor & Bain, 2005). In my interviews, about 10 migrant agents said they use a pseudonym. This is represented in the Excerpt 3.

Excerpt 3:
'Hi, good afternoon, this is Claudia calling…' actually I used to change my name. Many people in call centre[s] change their names. For one thing

I think [it] makes you... there is an alter ego, you know, [it] creates an alter ego and, is... I don't know why, it makes you faster, it makes you more creative maybe. At the end of the day it's an act, you know. And, at the end of the day, you know, no one sees you. (Alessia, agent) (Source: Woydack, 2017b: 11)

These pseudonyms are often meant to signify a different nationality, in this case British, and to avoid dissonance with a call recipient and potential xenophobia and awkwardness. As one Portuguese agent told me when calling the UK, the British appreciate authenticity, and talking to someone with a British-sounding name helps the call recipient to extend trust. The likelihood of a call being successful is perceived by agents to be greater with the use of pseudonyms because of what they perceive to be common xenophobia among the general British population.

Excerpt 4:
You [the call recipients] want [...] authenticity. [...] If you're receiving a phone call from a British number you want the caller to sound British. [...] There is a bit of racism involved in this [...] and nostalgia. (Fred, agent) (Source: Woydack, 2017a: 233)

For some, the pseudonym is part of the process of creating an alter ego, e.g. one agent chose the name Kate Hudson 'to make people think of the white blond attractive Hollywood star'. She further talked with a high-pitched voice since her audience, as she told me, are '99% men'. Choosing the name of a global superstar encouraged people to associate her phone person with attractiveness, stardom and nativeness. The agents mention linguistic strategies which echo Lakoff's (1973) women's language. This includes extreme politeness and hedges. However, as the conversations on the phone revolved around IT and were rather technical (see Figure 8.1 on p. 164 for an example of the typical script content), agents were more limited in their creative use of words than, for example, Hall's (1995) informants were. For instance, they cannot suddenly use what Lakoff (1973) termed 'empty adjectives' as Hall's informants did.

At the same time, most female agents mentioned that they used other strategies including 'laughing', which they perceived as making them more attractive to their primary male audience. This is echoed by the male agents, e.g. Pedro, a Spanish agent, said 'female agents have an advantage as the audience for the calls is usually males'. But he tried to learn from his female peers and adapt their strategies as 'society values the female way of speaking'. Overall, it is this combination of analysing the social situation, being aware of the clichés their audience holds, and naming an alter ego that compares to the initial steps of what Hall describes for her informants. The process implies that agents have a deep understanding of the stereotypes, demands and expectations which they believe their audience holds.

Other agents commented that adopting a different name helped to separate their work and off-work personalities. If others are rude, they are rude to the phone persona, but not to them. This helped create a barrier to protect the self. In addition, imagining how a call recipient might feel by 'putting yourself into their minds' allowed the agents to perform conversationally and politely as someone else. They can remind themselves that this performance, this interaction on my part, 'is just an act'.

> *Excerpt 5:*
> You're always going to face people who are going to tell you to, 'Oh, just go away, I don't want to talk to you', and you'll feel bad, but don't let it affect you because you have to make the next call. [...] People can be very rude on the phone [...] But I try to put myself into their shoes and also remember that it's not me that they are angry with. [...] I create a phone persona to separate it [that persona] from me and remain polite and gentle, not to let it get to me. (Isabelle, agent)

Adopting different names leads to modifying voices and accents to suit the pseudonymous character and takes us to the next point: trying out different accents and voices.

Trying out different accents and voices

About 10 agents talked about adopting a posh British accent, believing that this would make the other person think that they are educated and hide the fact that they work in a call centre.

> *Excerpt 6:*
> When I made calls, I tried to speak with a British upper-class accent [...] trying to lose my strong Italian accent as much as possible. I don't know if I ever managed. (Sara, agent)

And an equally significant pattern was noted by those who were attempting to imitate a Standard American accent that would go along with their Hollywood phone persona.

> *Excerpt 7:*
> I will never sound [pass as] English to English ears. So I think it's better to go for a different accent. [...] An American accent is more widely understood. In many places, e.g. the Emirates, they like an American accent. It is a clearer and more powerful accent. At least that's my impression [...]. (Caterina, agent)

Accents were not the only aspect of their performance that agents changed. Female agents reported trying to use both a higher and lower voice to achieve success. The higher voice was used to sound more feminine and more attractive when talking to male IT personnel. They also wanted to sound friendly and non-threatening so that their counterpart on the phone would judge that they were talking to someone they could trust, like a friend. This strategy reduced the social distance between them and removed the awkwardness that cold calling bestows. Conversely, a deeper masculine voice was attempted when talking to women in the IT department, especially with gatekeepers, who are usually women, in order to be taken more seriously and not perceived as being a young inexperienced girl. Thus, when talking to women, female agents tried to pass as mature professional women.

Excerpt 8:
Gatekeepers are so rude. I don't know why they are so rude to us. If I manage to make my voice sound very deep and masculine, sometimes then they put me through. It is a lot of work though. [...] I try to imagine what the gatekeepers may want to hear and how they are screening calls. It helps that I have worked as a secretary, too, some time ago in Italy (Alessia, agent).

The strategies used in Hall's (1995) study in relation to gender, passing and linguistic stereotypes overlap with those of CallTown's operators. First, as mentioned before, Hall's informants repeatedly remark on using consciously (exaggerated) feminine language to pass as feminine and satisfy their audiences' perceived desire for this. It is like Hugh, the agent cited earlier said, 'the best callers are the callers that can understand very, very quickly what this guy wants in this conversation in terms of how he wants you to deliver it, what he wants from you'. In Hall's study, phone sex operators examine language to identify what linguistic images and stereotypes their audience desires and expects. How skilful they are at this emerges with the fact that she mentions a male bi-sexual caller easily passing as female in various fantasies he performs. At CallTown, I also often observed male agents choosing to deliberately perform as female without management requiring or suggesting that they to do so (cf. Tovar, 2020, for a discussion of the LGBT culture at CallTown). Yet despite an agent aiming to deliver what 'the person on the phone wants to hear' and 'letting them [the call recipient] dictate the tone and terms they want to talk to you on', call centre agents at CallTown were adamant that they were in control of the conversations and the narrative they tell. As Hugh told me:

Excerpt 9:
[....] You should always dictate where it [the conversation] is going [....] (Hugh, team leader) (Source: Woydack, 2019a: 119)

One important way for agents to learn how to be in control of the conversation besides using scripts are rehearsals.

Rehearsal

Agents rehearsed roles off the phone with colleagues, but also with gatekeepers before actually talking to a desired person in the IT department. An agent from Italy described this process in the following way to me: 'It's like playing a game, you practice till you get good at it [...] As they say, practice makes perfect'. Or as Eduardo from Spain said to me using the following metaphor: 'It's like learning how to ride a bike, it takes time'. The first step in this rehearsal process is often to adapt the standardised calling script and rewrite it by hand using their own language in order to develop the voice they wish to use. The roleplay in Figure 8.1 provides an example of such a process. Once agents adapt their scripts, they may make a few calls to see how the audience reacted to various versions of their scripts (see Woydack, 2019). Then they may rehearse with colleagues to perfect their script, to improve their performance, or for a different reason.

Overall, agents' success may depend on how well they perceive a gatekeeper's stereotypes and whether they can pass as a caller other than a call centre agent. If agents always use the same voice, name and script, their delivery can drone on, and this can make a gatekeeper suspicious. Thus, agents have to be creative and agentive to do their job convincingly and to engage their clients. Rehearsals engender familiarity with a script or topic that also allows for spontaneity in discussions. In the words of one agent, 'if we sound like voice recordings or monotonous, we have already lost'. This brings us to the next tactic agents may pursue to maintain their persona, which is playing with stereotypes.

Playing with stereotypes and potential stereotypes

Some agents realised that their accents were too strong to hide their national or cultural identities. In those cases, they claim they tried to make the most out of these characteristics by exaggerating them or playing with stereotypes to make themselves more likable to the call recipient. An agent from Italy suggests:

Excerpt 10:
You're more selling yourself than the product. [...] The guy with the Italian accent, Andrea, half the time I don't understand a thing he says but he talks to the managers for ages. They are interested in talking to him [...] he is so funny. [...] they like it because it's a change. [...] He sounds like he is from a mafia movie [...] but he makes his heavy Italian accent work for himself. (Emanuele, agent) (Source: Woydack, 2019a: 160)

Listening for clues

Agents reported listening to the tone of voice of their call recipients and to background noises so they might discern whether the call recipient was in a meeting or outside, or sitting quietly at their desk. They also worked from the information they received from the gatekeeper to know how to approach a target recipient and break the ice. These steps further helped them to 'think on their feet'. As I heard from over 15 informants, 'listening is so important' (see Woydack, 2019a).

Adapting scripts

Agents reported consciously using language that they believed made them sound less as if they were calling from a call centre. Some of these tactics are included in the handout they receive (Woydack & Lockwood, 2020). For instance, they try to use technical language, even jargon, to

	THE SIB MASTER SCRIPT PITCH	ESTELLE'S SIB MASTER SCRIPT PITCH
S.0	Good morning. My name is X. I'm calling you on behalf of SIB.	Hello, Sir, good morning. My name is Estelle. I'm calling **you** on behalf of SIB.
S.1	The reason for my call today is that SIB has put together a complimentary report on SIB (Safe Browsing Policy.)	*This is not a sales call, it's a quick call to send you a report. We are sending it to different IT managers across the UK.*
S.2	The SBP is the bedrock of any organisation's management of employee use of corporate IT systems.	It is a complimentary report about SBP that **we**'re sending.
S.3	This whitepaper is written by an external company that looks at the legal implications of making sure your SBP is solid.	It talks about how to manage <u>internally with emails</u> and it has a lot of tips, really useful information.
S.4	By reading this whitepaper you will learn about: • Common mistakes and myths when creating a SBP • What should be in a SBP • Provide practical tips to maximise compliance and minimise risks • Explain how to create and enforce a SBP effectively	There are no strings attached and you will not receive any further emails from us.
S.5	Other IT Personal have received it and found it to be very useful.	Ø
S.6	Can I send you the whitepaper it is completely complimentary?	If **you** like **I** could send this information **for you**.

Key:
Ø = omission from original text Other font = deviant from the original script <u>words underlined</u> = grammatical errors **bold** = added pronouns.

Figure 8.1 The master script pitch and Estelle's personalisation

impress call recipients with their insider knowledge. They integrate the fact that they are calling from London, a high-status place, and use personal pronouns such as 'we' to sound as if they work directly for the company rather than being that one step removed in a call centre (see also Woydack, 2019a, for more detail). They often speak to create convergence aiming to match their language of professionalism with the professional expertise of the call recipient. The following (Figure 8.1) is an example of how agents changed scripts using the strategies discussed here. The text is reported verbatim and hence includes grammatical errors. This excerpt stems from an interview roleplay in which agents showed me how they would adapt a script.

In the example, Estelle, an agent from Spain, uses the strategy of making the text more colloquial so it sounds as though she is speaking on her own with deep familiarity of the company and its goals. Yet she is doing so in an informal way (allowing the inference that the caller is knowledgeable) to tie herself (hopefully) to the experts receiving the call.

Agents reported that the structure and phrases from scripts allowed *them* to decide where a conversation was going and to be in control instead of letting the script take away their agency. This has also been confirmed by other studies (e.g. Leidner, 1993; Woydack & Lockwood, 2017).

Feedback from call recipients

Interview data and observations suggest that customer reactions were considered important for the assessment of an agent's impression management success(es). In this case, migrant agents believe a positive reaction means that their strategies are working, while a negative reaction means that their strategies are not successful and new ones need to be tried out. It is not unheard of that agents are shouted at by call recipients on the phone. This is confirmed by Eduardo.

> *Excerpt 11:*
> You are not always a master of your emotion, you know, you try that. Sometimes you've had a lot of hard calls, you know, few feedback or hard feedback from the calls, people are rude and may shout at you, and eventually you start to feel less enthusiastic, so your inflection changes [and your numbers go down]. Then I rewrite my script. (Eduardo, agent)

Sometimes agents manage to help each other by sharing strategies that make one seem non-threatening and perhaps even create some status in the eyes of the call recipients (Woydack, 2019a; Woydack & Lockwood, 2017). However, applying these strategies can be exhausting, and may remind them of the brutal nature of cold calling and working in a call centre as a migrant during times of crises in their native countries.

Nevertheless, studies (e.g. Hochschild, 2012) show that as agents gain more experience with showing emotions that are not in line with their feelings, e.g. when dealing with rude call recipients, this takes them less effort and emotionally exhausts them less.

Impact of impression management on mobile agents
Self-esteem

The majority of the migrant agents reported that following the experience of working at CallTown they have become more confident on and off the phone.

> *Excerpt 12:*
> After working at CallTown, I feel that I can handle many difficult situations on the phone and off the phone. They can throw anything at me and I keep my cool. (Leo, agent)

Two tactics especially have made agents more confident. First, relying on a script in case one encounters rudeness because of a foreign accent or mispronunciation can increase an agent's confidence. Second, agents may find that the segmentation of their phone identity from their non-phone identity further improves confidence. We saw from Isabelle's comment earlier (Excerpt 5) that agents realise that they are not targeted personally, and her phone persona (alter ego) helped her to deal with this.

Learning about differences between their culture and a new culture

Southern European migrant agents reported that talking to others on the phone in Britain as well as using phone scripts and tips has made them aware of the specificities of their new host culture, such as the value placed on indirectness and negative politeness, and differences between lingua/cultural contexts. Alexandra thought that Brits are very polite in comparison to Italians:

> *Excerpt 13:*
> British people are so much more polite than Italians. It's so different. There are so many subtle differences and you don't learn them at class. (Alexandra, agent)

All in all, the agents seem to become acutely aware that they need to tailor their impression management not only to the context of a situation, which may differ depending on whom they are talking to (e.g. gender or class), or regional and cultural differences. Since a few of the team leaders at CallTown were British, agents could practise their impression management with their team leaders off the phone to see whether their team leaders appreciated the way they put themselves 'into other people's shoes'.

Call Centre Impression Management in Hindsight: Learning to Put Oneself into Other People's Shoes

This chapter started by pointing out that highly educated Southern European migrants immigrated to the UK because of the crises in their home countries. These mobile workers hoped that CallTown would add to their mobility in the highly competitive job market that they encountered in London. In the interviews, agents could agree on two things. First, that in their calling responsibilities they learned a lot about social awareness and how to build on that knowledge to present themselves to call recipients (and potential employers) in a favourable light. Second, they felt that they learned how to cope with stress, rudeness and xenophobia. However, they also generally agreed that they did not wish to work at a call centre again once they achieved the confidence and presentation of self that they desired, as well as local certifications that would allow their 'proper' professional appointment.

Despite this, migrant agents state that if it were not for their experience at CallTown practising impression management, they would not have the success they found or hoped to find elsewhere. All of the mobile agents interviewed found highly-paid jobs outside the call centre industry after having worked on average 6–12 months at CallTown (Woydack, 2019a; Woydack & Lockwood, 2020). The underlying assumption of working at CallTown is that one learns about cultural differences, but also one learns what works with different groups in their new culture. Agents learned to detach and abstract themselves from their previous culture and developed social awareness for a new society. They learned to 'act otherwise' (Giddens, 1984), agentively building a repertoire of social styles for their phone interactions that provided them with some form of linguistic power.

Insights from the present study

The theoretical framework used in this chapter – a combination of modified frameworks of Raghuram (2013), Hall (1995) and Goffman (1956) adapted to the context of mobile workers in a London call centre – allows us to work with a multi-dimensional understanding of power, underpinned by long-term ethnography. Despite the many advantages of Raghuram's (2013) framework, she did not develop a complex notion of power. In the same vein, Hall's (1995) sophisticated analysis of sex-line workers does not draw on impression management, although she alludes to it. Combining the three frameworks thus allows us to explore interactional dynamics in phone conversations in a new multi-dimensional way.

This new framework highlights not only the human potential for agency and power, even in highly constrained settings such as call centres, but also the subtle nature of agentive moves to garner power and control in non-visual environments. These insights can only be made apparent through long-term ethnography. Equally, the framework enabled us to see how scripts, rather than being oppressive and confining structures, turn out to scaffold learning and communicative competence, especially when agents have the freedom to adapt impression management techniques.

Although agents do not use the term impression management, I argue that what agents describe comes close to what Goffman (1956) theorised under this term. The CallTown agents learned to analyse the speech of their interlocutors on the phone and create a narrative flow that approached these others' expectations. This strategy relies on the imaginative license a phone call permits and creates a two-way power dynamic between agent and call recipient. The case for CallTown is made based upon agents' own suggestions that mastering impression management contributed to their upward mobility. This chapter has further shown that Goffman's impression management tactics, although initially documented for visual contexts, are relevant to all cross-cultural contexts for business-oriented phone conversations including call centres. Moreover, communication and conversational flow in cross-cultural contexts improve for business phone conversations without visual enhancement when impression management tactics are used.

In closing, some of these ideas have already been applied to intercultural training of expatriates (e.g. Giacalone & Beard, 1994). However, the training could be enriched in contexts in which agents are not from privileged backgrounds to address more broadly how impression management contributes to (im)mobility. This study has shown the range of strategies agents use and are aware of as promoting success in their work and beyond. To that effect, call centre agents will continue to develop impression management strategies. Further research can investigate their form and function in more detail and in other settings.

Note

(1) Although it has been suggested that emotional labour is a form of impression management, in this chapter, emotional labour and emotion work are understood to be separate from impression management. Unlike emotional labour, impression management is not conceptualised as a managerial tool forced upon the agent in the call centre (see Ashforth & Humphrey, 1993).

References

Ashforth, B.E. and Humphrey, R.H. (1993) Emotional labor in service roles: The influence of identity. *The Academy of Management Review* 18 (1), 88.
Bartolini, L., Gropas, R. and Triandafyllidou, A. (2017) Drivers of highly skilled mobility from Southern Europe: Escaping the crisis and emancipating oneself. *Journal of Ethnic and Migration Studies* 43 (4), 652–673.
Brophy, E. (2017) *Language Put to Work: The Making of the Global Call Centre Workforce*. Cham: Springer.

Das, D., Dharwadkar, R. and Brandes, P. (2008) The importance of being 'Indian': Identity centrality and work outcomes in an off-shored call center in India. *Human Relations* 61 (11), 1499–1530.
Eurostat (2018) EU unemployment statistics. https://ec.europa.eu/eurostat/statistics-explained/index.php?title=Unemployment_statistics#Recent_developments (accessed 6 January 2023).
Eurostat (2021) EU unemployment statistics. https://ec.europa.eu/eurostat/web/products-eurostat-news/-/ddn-20221017-1 (accessed 17 January 2023).
Favell, A. (2008) *Eurostars and Eurocities: Free Movement and Mobility in an Integrating Europe*. Malden, MA: Blackwell Pub.
Giacalone, R.A. and Beard, J.W. (1994) Impression management, diversity, and international management. *American Behavioral Scientist* 37 (5), 621–636.
Giddens, A. (1984) *The Constitution of Society: Outline of the Theory of Structuration*. Oxford: Polity Press.
Giles, H. and Ogay, T. (2006) Communication accommodation theory. In B. Whaley and W. Samter (eds) *Explaining Communication: Contemporary Theories and Exemplars* (pp. 293–310). Hillsdale, NJ: Lawrence Elrbaum Associates.
Goffman, E. (1956) *The Presentation of Self in Everyday Life*. Edinburgh: University of Edinburgh Press.
Hall, K. (1995) Lip service on the fantasy lines. In K. Hall and M. Bucholtz (eds) *Gender Articulated: Language and the Socially Constructed Self* (pp. 183–216). New York: Routledge.
Hochschild, A.R. (2012) *The Managed Heart: Commercialization of Human Feeling* (updated with new Preface). Berkeley, CA: University of California Press.
Kahlin, L. and Tykesson, I. (2016) Identity attribution and resistance among Swedish-speaking call centre workers in Moldova. *Discourse Studies* 18 (1), 87–105.
Kantor, A. (2023) Italians flock to London despite Brexit. *Bloomberg*, 10 January. https://www.bloomberg.com/news/articles/2023-01-10/moving-to-london-italians-defy-brexit-to-seize-uk-job-opportunities?leadSource=uverify%20wall (accessed 17 January 2023).
Kramsch, C. and Whiteside, A. (2008) Language ecology in multilingual settings. Towards a theory of symbolic competence. *Applied Linguistics* 29 (4), 645–671.
Krishnamurthy, M. (2004) Resources and rebels: A study of identity management in Indian call centers. *Anthropology of Work Review* 25 (3–4), 9–18.
Lakoff, R. (1973) Language and woman's place. *Language in Society* 2 (1), 45–79.
Lave, J. and Wenger, E. (1991) *Situated Learning: Legitimate Peripheral Participation. Learning in Doing*. Cambridge: Cambridge University Press.
Leidner, R. (1993) *Fast Food, Fast Talk: Service Work and the Routinization of Everyday Life*. Berkeley: University of California Press.
Lockwood, J. (2017) Learning for the workplace. In A. Burns and J. Richard (eds) *The Cambridge Guide to Learning English as a Second Language* (pp. 146–155). Cambridge: Cambridge University Press.
Matos, P. (2012) Call center labor and the injured precariat: Shame, stigma, and downward social mobility in contemporary Portugal. *Dialectical Anthropology* 36 (3–4), 217–243.
McFarland, L.A., Hendricks, J.L. and Ward, W.B. (2023) A contextual framework for understanding impression management. *Human Resource Management Review* 33 (1), 100912.
Mirchandani, K. (2004) Practices of global capital: Gaps, cracks and ironies in transnational call centres in India. *Global Networks* 4 (4), 355–373.
Mirchandani, K. (2012) *Phone Clones: Authenticity Work in the Transnational Service Economy*. Ithaca: ILR Press.
Moyer, M. (2018) English in times of crisis. Mobility and work among young Spaniards in London. *Language and Intercultural Communication* 18 (4), 424–435.

Nath, V. (2011) Aesthetic and emotional labour through stigma: National identity management and racial abuse in offshored Indian call centres. *Work, Employment and Society* 25 (4), 709–725.

Nessi, L. and Bailey, O.G. (2014) Privileged Mexican migrants in Europe: Distinctions and cosmopolitanism on social networking sites. *Crossings: Journal of Migration and Culture* 5 (1), 121–137.

Nielsen, K. (2022) Call center timespace and working from home: Enregistering global professionals during the Covid-19 pandemic in India. *Sociolinguistic Studies* 16 (1), 19–38.

O'Neill, F. (2013) Making sense of being between languages and cultures: A performance narrative inquiry approach. *Language and Intercultural Communication* 13 (4), 386–399.

Pal, M. and Buzzanell, P. (2008) The Indian call center experience: A case study in changing discourses of identity, identification, and career in a global context. *Journal of Business Communication* 45 (1), 31–60.

Pratsinakis, M., King, R., Himmelstine, C.L. and Mazzilli, C. (2020) A crisis-driven migration? Aspirations and experiences of the post-2008 South European migrants in London. *International Migration* 58 (1), 15–30.

Poster, W.R. (2007) Who's on the line? Indian call center agents pose as Americans for U.S.-outsourced firms. *Industrial Relations* 46 (2), 271–304.

Purdy, J.M., Nye, P. and Balakrishnan, P.V. (Sundar) (2000) The impact of communication media on negotiation outcomes. *International Journal of Conflict Management* 11 (2), 162–187.

Raghuram, S. (2013) Identities on call: Impact of impression management on Indian call center agents. *Human Relations* 66 (11), 1471–1496.

Roberts, L.M. (2005) Changing faces: Professional image construction in diverse organizational settings. *Academy of Management Review* 30 (4), 685–711.

Scotto, G. (2015) From 'Emigrants' to 'Italians': What is new in Italian migration to London? *Modern Italy* 20 (02), 153–165.

Taylor, P. and Bain, P. (2005) 'India calling to the far away towns': The call centre labour process and globalization. *Work, Employment and Society* 19 (2), 261–282.

Tovar, J. (2020) Call center agents' skills: Invisible, illegible, and misunderstood. *Journal of Sociolinguistic Studies* 14 (4), 437–458.

Tovar, J. (2022a) Current trends and the way forward on call center research in a post-covid world: An introduction. *Sociolinguistic Studies* 16 (1), 7–17.

Tovar, J. (2022b) Rethinking call centers: From stigma to productive experience. *Sociolinguistic Studies* 16 (1), 87–107.

Wenger, E. (2008) *Communities of Practice: Learning, Meaning, and Identity*. Cambridge: Cambridge University Press.

Woydack, J. (2017a) Superdiversity and a London multilingual call centre. In K. Arnaut, M.S. Karrebæk, M. Spotti and J. Blommaert (eds) *Engaging Superdiversity: Recombining Spaces, Times and Language Practices* (pp. 220–247). Bristol: Multilingual Matters.

Woydack, J. (2017b) Call center agents and the experience of stigma. *Working Papers in Urban Language Literacies* 215.

Woydack, J. (2019a) *Linguistic Ethnography of a Multilingual Call Center: London Calling*. Cham: Springer International Publishing.

Woydack, J. (2019b) Language management and language work in a multilingual call center: An ethnographic case study. *Revista Internacional De Organizaciones* 23, 79–105.

Woydack, J. and Rampton, B. (2016) Text trajectories in a multilingual call centre: The linguistic ethnography of a calling script. *Language in Society* 45 (5), 709–732.

Woydack, J. and Lockwood, J. (2017) 'Scripts are beautiful': Managers' and agents' views of script use in call centers. *International Journal of Business Communication* 58 (3), 333–357.

Woydack, J. and Lockwood, J. (2020) Affordances for language learning in a call centre. *Journal of English for Specific Purposes* 60, 159–178.

9 Understanding the Immigrant Actor through a Multilingual Lens

Art Babayants

Introduction

Research on emotions and performing in a second language (L2) is currently in its nascent stage. A number of years ago, Swain (2012) advocated the inclusion of emotion into the study of L2 acquisition, explaining this existing paucity of research on emotions by the overall dominance of cognitivism in L2 studies. In general, the cognitive tradition relies on the Descartian separation of *body* and *mind* and Socrates' division of *reason* and *emotion* (Swain, 2012). Due to this conceptual framework, emotions have been largely excluded from L2 research (see Dewaele & Li, 2020, for a comprehensive review on the subject). Aneta Pavlenko's (2006) *Emotions and Multilingualism*, was indeed the first comprehensive volume exploring the very nature of emotions and their expression in and through different languages. This seminal volume, similar to other calls for a holistic view of emotions (Imai, 2010), proposed a complex multi-level view of emotions as they pertain to multilingualism which informed the angle this chapter takes.

Pavlenko starts her *Emotions and Multilingualism* with a powerful first-hand account of a complex relationship a multilingual person can have with their languages and, by extension, their dialects and accents:

> The words of my native language, Russian, brim with intimacy and familiarity. They are permeated with memories of my childhood and youth, friendships and intimate relationships, happiness and disappointments. For me, Russian has no neutral words – each one channels voices, each one inspires feelings. Yet it is also a language that attempted to constrain and obliterate me as a Jew, to tie me down as a woman, to render me voiceless, a mute slave to a hated regime. To abandon Russian means to embrace freedom. I can talk and write without hearing echoes of things I should not be saying. I can be me. English is a language that offered me that freedom, and yet it is also my second language, whose words – in the unforgettable terms of another fellow bilingual, Julia Kristeva – make us strangers to ourselves. (Pavlenko, 2006: 22)

This inseparable and yet complicated connection between emotions and languages is at the centre of my research. Specifically, in this chapter, I focus on two immigrant/first generation Canadian actors (based in Toronto, Ontario, Canada) in order to see how they experienced acting in various languages while they were co-devising a multilingual production with me, the director, and 10 other performers, both multilingual and monolingual. By looking at the phenomenological experience of two immigrant actors performing in various languages, I first discuss the idea of the language-body-emotion disconnect experienced by the performers in their L2. Second, I illustrate how the immigrant performers oriented themselves toward that disconnect through practice. Finally, I link the performers' phenomenological experience to the current research on emotions and multilingualism, specifically, to the concept of *affective linguistic conditioning,* or rather the possible lack of it when it comes to performing in one's L2.

Methodology: Artistic Practice as Research

My research project followed the artistic research methodology developed at the Central School for Speech and Drama in London, UK. Nelson (2013) called this artistic *practice as research* (PaR), which is different from both qualitative and quantitative research. Nelson argues that PaR's theoretical foundations are rooted in phenomenology, specifically in the phenomenological school of thought that focuses on perception and embodiment. Subsequently PaR aims to uncover or, in Nelson's (2013: 56–57) terms, 'evidence' embodied knowledge using artistic practice as the method of research, not a research object.

Typically, at the centre of PaR lies a broader research inquiry. Nelson (2013: 97) explains: 'I prefer the term "research inquiry" to "research question" since questions may imply answers and the kinds of work typically undertaken in the PaR PhD context, while they yield findings, do not typically produce solutions to problems in the mode of answers'.

With that approach in mind, I formulated my research inquiry as a combination of three co-dependent components or themes that focused on multilingual dramaturgy, multilingual actors and multilingual audiences; however, in this chapter I am focusing on only one of them. Specifically, this chapter discusses multilingual actors' processes of performing as well as learning to perform in more than one language within the framework of the devised multilingual performance.

This PaR project comprised six weeks of collective devising with professional, student and amateur performers, who eventually co-created a multilingual show based on the experiences they had brought to the table. I organised the devising process in two phases: during Phase One (the first three weeks) we were mostly focused on sharing stories of language learning and migrations as well as creating multilingual improvisations based on those stories. The second three-week phase was about crafting scenes out of the improvisations and putting together the show, which was eventually entitled *In Sundry Languages*, a nod to Hieronimo's line from Kyd's (1592/2007: 78) *Spanish Tragedy*: 'Each of us must act his part // In unknown languages, // That it may breed the more variety'.

In our PaR show, the twelve performers were encouraged to act in a minimum of three languages: one they spoke well (their dominant tongues be they L1 or L2), one they were less proficient in (non-dominant languages) and one that they have never spoken or studied before (an 'unknown' language). I, being the artist-researcher myself, was the organiser, co-deviser and the director of *In Sundry Languages*.

After each devising session, the participants were encouraged to write brief journals where they were to document their Lived Experience Description (LED). In the LEDs, which essentially represent a common tool of phenomenological reduction (Van Manen, 2014: 298), the participants described an embodied experience of improvising, rehearsing or performing in their dominant, non-dominant and unknown languages. As part of the LED collection, I invited the participants to submit their journals by formulating my request as follows:

> Describe a few moments (or scenes/improvs) when you had to perform in your non-dominant language. What challenges did you experience? What positive discoveries did you make? What did that different language do to your mind, voice and body? Remember to indicate which scene(s) or improvs you're talking about.

Some of the discoveries that were documented in the journals eventually found their reflection in the content and the genre of the show, which was eventually performed to a multilingual audience. After the public performances of *In Sundry Languages* were completed, I also conducted post-performance non-structured interview-conversations with each of the participants in order to better understand their process of performing in the languages of the production as well as how performing in various languages had affected their identity. In the analysis below, I use the actors' journals in full as well as select quotes from their post-performance interviews – specifically those that expand on what the actors identified in the journals. Those quotes can be read as representative of the participant's view on their phenomenology of performing in different languages.

Research Participants: Immigrant Actors

While the project had a total of 12 performer-participants, in this chapter, I will only analyse the LED's of two – both male, in their late 30s, with English as their second language but also dominant language along with their respective mother tongues. The reason I have selected these two performers is because they were the only two professionally trained and professionally working actors in Toronto, where they had emigrated from their respective countries. The other participants were either amateur or student performers for whom acting (at least at the time of my research) was more like a hobby rather than a job.

My first participant is Yury, who came to Toronto from Moscow, Russia – an ethnic Russian who grew up monolingual and learned English later in his life as part of his studies. He received his original actor training in one of Moscow's leading theatre schools, and after his immigration continued taking classes in various theatre and circus genres in Toronto. My second participant, Mario, originally from Portugal, grew up speaking Portuguese and went to Lisbon's preeminent theatre school where he trained as a dramatic actor. After immigrating to Canada, he studied the art of clowning – this time in English. At the time of my research, he was also starting to do his MA degree in psychology at the University of Toronto.[1]

Yury's LED: Body-Mind-Emotion Disconnect

In his LED, Yury documents his experience of the multilingual improvisations of Phase One while consistently throughout his writing also juxtaposing English – his L2, which he speaks fluently with Russian (his L1). This juxtaposition hints at how he conceptualises those languages and his own relationship to them – an essential piece of information indicating how Yury orientates himself towards the languages he performs in. He writes:

> Speaking in english,[2] my adopted language, requires an extra effort, as well as I can get tired speaking it after a certain amount of time. Both mentally and physically. The first several months after I moved to Canada from Moscow I felt a jaw pain when spoke only English for a long time. Although, back home I spoke English for 12 years on and off.

> I am never tired speaking Russian. Performing any text in English takes some extra time, not only I need more time to fully understand the text, but to adopt it and make it less foreign as to me an actor as well as make it believable these are my character's very own thoughts and words.

> When speaking in English in simple phrases i have no problems keeping an eye on grammar and the right use of words and their order, but when too exited to tell a story or overwhelmed with emotions I will loose control and most likely make mistakes. Never happens when I am speaking my mother tongue – Russian.

> When performing in English, my minds is preoccupied with words, and meanings and other linguistic nuances, and the acting is always secondary. Even when I have a good grip on English text, I might have a slip or two, deforming the proper English intonation to my Russian ways of expressiveness.

When you grow up using Russian for everyday life and for strong emotions (anger, surprise, jealousy) your body and gestures are naturally in sync with the words, for you have developed them at the same time. How do you sound when you are angry in English? What is your body doing when you are scared and talking at the same time. All those extreme emotions might be expressed and felt a bit plainer when speaking in non dominant language. (Yury's Journal)

It becomes clear that Yury associates effort with his L2 but not L1: English, in his view, is more taxing and time-consuming, which is not unusual when it comes to processing a L2 (see, for instance, Dong *et al.*, 2022). He even mentions physical pain associated with English. What is more important is that he identifies a disconnect between his L2 and his body, possibly complicated by emotion – when he gets emotional it gets harder to control his L2. He is also concerned about not quite knowing how to express a full range of emotion in L2: 'How do you sound when you are angry in English?'.

In his post-performance interview, he also provided more reflection on his LED, specifically on our very first group improvisation where everyone had to 'hush' each other by using interjections and gestures coming from an unfamiliar language. Yury got to work with a particular dialect of Arabic where the expression sounded like *Hosh!* (or *Hahsh!*) accompanied by a powerful raise of a hand:

Y: Yury
A: Art (Author)

Y: I remember that class [improvisation], yeah. It's almost like with the dance, when you tried something for the first time and it doesn't sit well with you and it doesn't and I don't even think about that. And there is so much more variations of how it can be done, sexy, it can be seductive, it can be harsh and punishing. And with that yeah, it's like I only have one pain (UNCLEAR), its pain hush hush like that's all I know, like there's no, no circumstances like there's no infrastructure around it. I can't play with it

A: Yeah no colour.

Y: Yeah there's only one tune, one note (sound)

A: Did you try to play with it?

Y: I don't remember... no.

A: You were like very mechanical?

Y: Yeah very like, what I do …but there was something else that I said about body was doing something Russian, or like something, I, because we all did that, and your body is doing it in Russian but like that's not Russian gesture. Some conflict there.

(Yury's Interview)

With regard to English, his second dominant language, Yury also consistently refers to the emotion-mind-body disconnect, especially when it comes to executing more control over his language processing, which makes English tiresome to speak and perform in. In contrast, Russian remains a language that is easy, comfortable and always enjoyable – 'I never get tired of speaking Russian' (Yury's journal). Overall, there seems to be some distancing and effort associated with English – in some way akin to Pavlenko's (2006) quote earlier; however, unlike Pavlenko, Yury does not see Russian as a language of cultural obliteration. In other words, there is no trauma associated with his L1 – rather, it is English that brings him 'pain' (sometimes literal pain in his jaw) and effort.

Mario's LED: A Foreign Mask

Here is how Mario constructs his phenomenological experience of performing in his L2 after an improv in which he had to perform a few prescribed lines in a completely unfamiliar accent:

> When I was improvising in a second language with the sentence 'Ladies and gentlemen the show is about to begin...' using a thick British accent, it felt like I was using a foreign 'mask'. This 'mask' (it felt) could be shaped in as many forms as I liked. For example, I could stretch and/or accentuate syllables in any part of the sentence without having my mind interrupting, as to tell me that I was not making intonations properly. It was as if there was permission to shape the language without feeling that I had stepped outside the 'proper'/ normative/ intelligible boundaries assigned to it. The same with body language, I could exaggerate gestures (lift my chest, bend backwards) without a self-evaluative 'noise' in my head. In this way, I experienced a sense of liberation in wearing this 'mask'. This may be because the 'mask' is devoid of personal history or conflict. It also felt more 'superficial' than when speaking in my mother-tongue. The same sentence in Portuguese (first language) invoked memories, and attached to these memories there were deeper feelings. I felt more serious, less playful, but also connected at a deeper personal level. An insight I gained was that when speaking in a second language I felt more in touch with the sensory dimension of myself whereas when speaking in Portuguese I was more engaged at a psychological level. (Mario's Journal)

Evidently, Mario, who is a trained clown and mask performer, processes his experience through the concepts and ideas that are deeply rooted in his practice and training. In a way, he verbalises his experience through the 'acting praxis' that underlies his training, hence his reference to the 'foreign mask' – something that does not appear in Yury's writing, which seems more concerned with authenticity or believability of actions and emotions. Yury's concern could perhaps be a result of Yury's own training – Stanislavskian realism, which is a dominant acting school in Russia. The Stanislavsky school of acting emerged as the ultimate actor training method in the early 20th century: through meticulous training, it teaches an actor to make the character's actions and words (verbal actions) the actor's own. Generally speaking, it is preoccupied with the sense of truth, i.e. believability or authenticity, on actions that actors do on stage. Consequently, because of the body-language-emotion split mentioned before, Yury questioned the very possibility to produce the same sense of truth (i.e. believable realist actions) in his L2 as the one he can produce in his L1.

In distinct ways it was clear that this divorce of body and language presented challenges for performing in a less dominant language for Mario, too. Nevertheless, for him, performing in his L2 and specifically in a new accent ('a thick British accent'), allowed him to be free from the 'memories' and 'feelings' that come with L1. Conversely, while Yury questioned the very possibility of a non-native speaker ever getting the 'right body' – which I interpreted above as a concern with authenticity or realism – Mario proposed a potentially unorthodox solution. He discovered the potential to reconnect the language and the body through the concept of the 'foreign mask'. In his interview, Mario provided more specifics on how both Portuguese and English feel in his body – he even specified a 'body location' for Portuguese:

> I do think that when I'm doing in Portuguese I feel more with my chest, I mean, literally, I feel more in my chest. [...] I seem to be in touch, in touch with ahhh body sensations in my chest. Uhh a warmth, like a warmth. Also a sensation of warmth, does this make sense? Um... doing it in English I, um, there was an effort, but there was also a detachment.
> (Mario's Interview)

Essentially, Mario, while confirming that there are differences between how he experiences performance in his English and his L2, challenges the idea of the lack of freedom that L2 brings. He points out that it is L2 that cancelled out the incessant 'self-evaluating noise' – something that makes acting particularly difficult as it essentially makes the actor be self-conscious instead of focusing on being organic in their acting. Unlike Yury, who was concerned with the authenticity and correctness of their non-dominant language, Mario asserts that the 'self-evaluation' is linked to the language that is full of 'personal history or conflict' (i.e. his L1, Portuguese). For Mario, English, a language he is fluent in, works in and is doing an advanced degree in, is associated with freedom, not with self-monitoring. It is Portuguese that brings the 'self-evaluating' noise along with evoking subtlety and associations. In his interview, Mario elaborated more on this point explaining where the self-evaluating noise was coming from:

A: Art (author)
M: Mario

A: Why do you think it didn't happen in Portuguese, the freedom? Or, the same level of freedom?

M: Uhh because I have a lot of subtext uhhh when I do speak in Portuguese, there's a lot of attachment, involvement. So, um... yeah. It's like the language, it's loaded with history and memories. So I can become a little more caught up on that, I can become more over involved and that will be a mistake or I can become involved and still have some detachment to be able to and yeah...

(Mario's Interview)

Mario's position on his performance in English and Portuguese is a radical departure from the orientating demonstrated by Yury (and, in fact, most other participants of my research). Mario's positionality is, perhaps, one of the most interesting discoveries of our PaR project. Without denying the deep connection with his first language, Mario perceives English not as a language of perpetual deficiency but a language of unexplored possibility for an actor. In other words, Mario's phenomenological experience shed light on a different way that people may orientate themselves towards their second language. To understand that shift of orientation towards one's L2, I introduce the concept of queer phenomenology and queer orientation proposed by Ahmed (2006).

Challenging the Monolingual Orientation

As Ahmed (2006) points out in *Queer Phenomenology*, 'orientation' is a result of a repeated direction, or repeated orientating towards an object in a specific way. Unlike Yury, Mario came to the project with a 'queer', i.e. unconventional, orientation towards his L2 (the object) already in place. In fact, he consistently encouraged us to explore the idea of liberty provided by a new language and, at some point, created an improvisation with two other participants: Amy, originally from the US (with English as dominant language), and Sepideh, originally from Iran (with Persian and English as dominant languages). In the improvisation, Mario and Sepideh performed two newcomers to Canada who do not speak English and who encounter a native speaker of English – the part performed by Amy, a participant with English as her first and dominant language. After both Mario's and Sepideh's characters demonstrate their inability to speak English, Amy's character immediately takes on the role of a diligent instructor and begins to teach English words to the 'newcomers': *It's a cup. Repeat! It's a cup.* Instead of taking this belittling experience as offensive, Mario accepted it as an invitation to play. Specifically, he adopted a 'baby mask' and began to 'learn' English by repeating words after Amy, but also by behaving like a little kid: impatiently throwing things around, happily laughing at most innocuous words, holding Amy's hand as if she were his mother, and copiously drooling onto the floor like a baby would. Aesthetically, Mario took the idea of liberty to the extreme, perhaps, inadvertently commenting on how some adult L2 learners may feel when they encounter a condescending attitude of English native speakers, including government officials or language teachers. He, nevertheless, made his point clear: performing a language learner likened him to 'a child' and allowed him to find a new mask and, consequently, do and say things that he would never be able to get away with as an adult native speaker of his first language.

In contrast, Yury's phenomenology remained deeply rooted in a more conventional monolingual framework, where his L2 could make him tired, while his L1 never did. To some extent, Yury agrees with Mario on how emotions are experienced in his second language:

> How do you sound when you are angry in English? What is your body doing when you are scared and talking at the same time. All those extreme emotions might be expressed and felt a bit plainer when speaking in non-dominant language. (Yury's Journal)

Nevertheless, he does not share Mario's challenging of the monolingual paradigm: Mario seems to have redirected himself towards his second language through discovering 'the sense of liberation' – that is, liberation from memory, and liberation from 'stronger psychological engagement' accompanied by an affordance to be playful in his L2.

As we transitioned to Phase Two, this clash of orientations coming from these two professional actors grew stronger. It turned out that the memories involved in that conflict were not only linguistic but also cultural: both Mario and Yury held a grudge against their respective home countries. Mario confessed that he had abhorred the violence that he observed in Portugal, which was typically related to football (soccer), a game with which he personally had a love-hate relationship. In turn, Yury revealed his tumultuous and yet loving relationship with Russia: a place where he knows most cultural codes, has a lot of connections, and yet where he was never fully accepted as a gay person. As we were devising our work, they also shared their attitude to Canada: while Mario enjoyed living in his new country and praised it for what it had to offer, Yury expressed mostly frustration. In his view, it was difficult for him to connect with his new compatriots on the same level he was able to connect with Russians. Furthermore, he had difficulty finding jobs as an actor – all because of his accent and perceived lack of pragmatic and cultural competences in English.

As Mario and Yury were devising their own material, I could not help noticing their diametrically opposed perspectives as well as striking similarities between their 'histories'. I eventually began to see some possibility for a strong dramatic conflict, and I encouraged them to work together. Their improvisation started with 'theatrical' cheek slaps – perhaps, a symbolic nod to clowning. Eventually, the slaps grew into words and then into a football (soccer) match. That double handler, performed in Russian and English by Yury and in Portuguese and English by Mario, was eventually entitled *Futebol* (the Portuguese word for *soccer/football*) and presented an emotional, artistic, athletic and philosophical duel between the two actors, where both expressed how they were orientating themselves to their old and new countries, cultures and languages.

It is evident that in Mario's and Yury's cases, memory is linked to emotion, specifically affection, or the lack of it. However, Yury's interview also showed that there was more to this metaphor of memory than simply affection. When I asked him to explain the difference between how performing in Russian and English felt to him, Yury once again confirmed what he had stated in his journal: Russian was natural and easy, English was not. However, he also reflected on memory as an embodied experience of living in his second language and acknowledged the possibility of gradually gaining that memory and becoming more at ease with one's less dominant language:

Y: Yury
A: Art (author)

Y: I'm less stressed when I'm speaking, performing in Russian because I don't have to keep so many things in mind like I do with English. And it doesn't sit yet as comfortable in me vocally wise, like its tiresome, speaking English so long, not anymore now like my first year in Canada it was so ridiculous like my jaws were like in pain like muscles are different and in Russian it's like I know where it sits. And there's no effort, in English there is.

A: But I'm speaking about this particular experience [participation in ISL]

Y: Same, yeah, same.

A: Still, English was still more work?

Y: English with an accent was more work.

A: Which accent?

Y: The one I don't have, the general American. No, but for the party scene or for the last piece when I mostly speak English I don't think the language was the problem because all the experience was from in that language, biking, auditioning, Bellwoods park, all that was my Canadian experience so the language naturally grew out of it. If it's like a magician, like I told before, like he have a text, and like it's so new I need time to get into it

(Yury's Interview)

In this interview, Yury recognises the very possibility of accumulating varied lived experiences in English or 'memories' – he also acknowledges that the variety of experiences he had had in English contributed to his ease with his L2, which, in his words, 'grew out' of these experiences 'naturally'. I would argue that this recognition may be the first sign of the 'direction' change, a possible re-orientation towards his less dominant language – English.

Conversely, this redirection may or may not be sustained in the long run in order to be turned into an orientation. Being a working actor, Yury is likely to continue auditioning for various productions and, within the context of the Canadian English-speaking entertainment industry, his accented English will (almost) always be perceived as deficient, jeopardising his employment prospects. The larger sociocultural context assigns power to certain accents, and Yury is fully aware of that: he mentions General American because it is the 'unmarked' accent that he knows he is expected to have when he comes to audition for film, television or theatre. In other words, due to the power relationships operating within a larger sociocultural context, Yury's potential re-orientation towards his L2 may quickly become obsolete. Overall, while it may be a really fruitful point for research, it lies largely outside of the focus of this chapter. Instead, below I will link Yury's idea of accumulating lived experiences with the linguistics concept of affective linguistic conditioning.

Discussion: Affective Conditioning and the Immigrant Actor

The idea of accumulated lived experiences in L2 being a potentially important tool for an immigrant actor or by extension any immigrant working, studying or simply living in their L2 brings us to a broader discussion of the language-body-emotion disconnect as well to a better understanding how emotions can be formed in L2. Here I would like to return to Pavlenko's writing on emotions and multilingualism.

Given my focus on the actors' perception, here, I will only address the level Pavlenko (2006) identifies as *neurophysiological*. This level is concerned with both the speaker's perception of emotions and the neurophysiological processes occurring in the speaker's brain when emotions are experienced in or through language. Pavlenko (2006: 153) argues that 'depending on their linguistic trajectories, bi- and multilinguals may have different neurophysiological responses to their respective languages, or at least to emotion-related words' (see also Ross & Rivers, 2018). Coincidentally, most studies that Pavlenko cites also concern late bilinguals, that is, people with similar L2 learning trajectories to Mario's and Yury's. Following neuroscientific research, Pavlenko specifies that, depending on the language learning environment, two very important language development processes – *conceptual development and affective linguistic conditioning* – may play out very differently. While conceptual development is concerned with lexical items acquiring 'denotative meanings' and links 'to each other through elaborate and conceptual networks' (Pavlenko, 2006: 154), to understand how those lexical items get emotional colouring one needs to take into account affective linguistic conditioning. Pavlenko (2006: 154–155) writes:

> In the parallel process of *affective linguistic conditioning*, words and phrases acquire affective connotations and personal meanings through association and integration with emotionally charged memories and experiences. Some words become linked to personal fears (clown, spider) or to positive memories (Citizen Kane's 'Rosebud' or Prouste's 'madeleine'), while taboo words, such as 'piss,' 'shit,' or 'cock,' become associated with experiences of prohibition, punishment, and social stigmatization. [...] Both processes contribute to the perception of *language embodiment*, whereby words invoke both sensory images and physiological reactions. Foreign languages learned in educational contexts are almost never perceived as embodied, because language learning in the classroom takes place without significant involvement of the limbic system or the majority of the sensory modalities.

The lack, or weakness, of emotional and bodily connection when speaking or performing in a dominant L2, reported by Mario and Yury (and a few other participants who were also late/sequential bilinguals) can indeed be explained by how each of them experienced affective linguistic conditioning while acquiring their languages. The concept of 'affective linguistic conditioning' also invokes the theme of body disconnect discussed earlier. The absence of affective linguistic conditioning can also affect the body-language relationship in various ways. It is not surprising, for instance, that Mario mentions his body disconnect in conjunction with his emotional disconnect from his L2. In very simplistic terms, a learner can learn a language without attaching it to emotions or to the body or by attaching only select emotions to select words. Such lack of affective conditioning may have serious consequence for actors attempting to perform in their L2.

My post-production interview with Yury showed that, being a working actor, Yury was very much aware of the 'emotion and body disconnect'. When asked to reflect on his process of embodying a character in English, Yury recognised that English occasionally fails him and blames it on his absence of certain emotional embodied experiences in English:

A: Art (author)
Y: Yury

A: So what you're saying is, and correct me if I'm wrong, is if you've experienced something as a human being in a particular language, right, it's easier to portray it on stage in that language rather than translate it in a different language.

Y: I'm not saying translating, when you're given the text, the cold reads, I haven't experienced that text I haven't seen it. There might be even a word I don't know or how to pronounce that word. It's rare but it happens. Like that audition piece I brought to the rehearsal like the, remember when three of us tried to do it, it's hard. So that takes time. What is this text, where is it coming from, what is the circumstances around it how can I embody it so it's mine. Possess? Присвоить?

A: (translates): Appropriate.

Y: Appropriate. Yeah, make it mine. So it's not text, so it's me. Yeah that's work

(Yury's Interview)

Essentially, in my reading, Yury voices very practical concerns about how to embody a character in English or in his words, how to 'appropriate' a character. In fact, Yury brought an audition monologue he was working on into rehearsal one day and said that he wanted to work on it. The monologue depicted an English-speaking character (an American) talking to another English character (also an American) and Yury was adamant to learn the General American accent for this monologue. As I pointed out earlier, Yury may be drawing from his training – the Stanislavskian school of acting that requires an actor to make a character their own – another possible translation of the Russian word «Присвоить».

In the interview, Yury indicates that an English text is difficult for him to 'make his own'. He first recognises that, occasionally, it may be his lack of linguistic competence (or lack of declarative knowledge) that causes difficulty: he admits that there may be occasional vocabulary or pronunciation problems he encounters. What seems more important to him is his lack of 'experience' of the text, by which, I would argue, he refers to his lack of experiential understanding of English. This lack of experiential, embodied understanding is very similar to the comment he made in regard to our very first improvisation – the 'shushing' improv I analysed earlier in this chapter. It is not necessarily the lack of semantic knowledge (or in Pavlenko's terms, 'conceptual development') that jeopardises his attempts of 'appropriation', it is the lack of a very specific 'embodied memory' that resonates with the text and/or the language. From Yury's LEDs and reflections, I can extrapolate that he feels that his 'embodied memory' in English is often insufficient when he has to concern himself with the authenticity of English-speaking characters he has to portray as an actor.

At the other end of the spectrum were Mario's and, to some extent, Sepideh's orientations (the latter omitted from this chapter). As their LEDs showed, Mario and Sepideh are not pre-occupied with making the character their own. Instead, they reoriented themselves towards their L2s and explored what it feels like to be different. For instance, Sepideh talked about the liberty of not being herself in English and the opportunity to imitate anyone, which is close to the idea of a 'mask', used by Mario. An L2 'mask' allows them to liberate themselves from the emotionality (and memory) of their L1.

This re-orientation resembles the position of translingual writers that Pavlenko discusses in her book. She brings up multiple examples of internationally recognised authors who made a writing career in their second or third language. In addition, she quotes a number of prominent writers whose sentiments about their L2 – their main writing instrument – resemble what Mario said about his relationship to Portuguese. Here is, for instance, a quote from a Canadian-born Anglophone – the famous French novelist Nancy Huston – where she describes her feelings towards French:

> Elle était froide, et je l'abordais froidement. Elle m'était égale. C'était une substance lisse et homogène, autant dire neutre. Au début, je m'en rends compte maintenant, cela me conférait une immense liberté dans l'écriture – car je ne savais pas par rapport à quoi, sur fond de quoi, j'écrivais. (Huston, 1999: 63)
>
> [It was cold and I approached it with coldness. I didn't care much for it. It was a smooth and homogenous substance—let us call it neutral. I now realise that at the beginning, it entrusted me with immense liberty in writing for I didn't know in relation to what I and against which backdrop I was writing.] (Author's translation)

The liberty of the second language, which Huston describes here, is partly based on the emotional detachment from it. It is this emotional detachment that can allow L2 speaking immigrants (in my case, actors) to orientate themselves towards that language as a language of possibility, liberty (including creative liberty) and even, in some cases, healing. For instance, recent research in linguistics shows that the same absence of affective conditioning can also give L2 speakers certain liberty from the weight of the negative or traumatic emotions and experiences associated with living in L1 (Cook & Deawale, 2022). This approach to L2 can have major implications not only for immigrant actors performing in their L2 but for all L2 speaking immigrants in general.

A new language may give one a space of exploration and potential liberatory practice – an allowance to try a new 'mask', even a mask that does not seem appropriate or fitting age- or gender-wise (for example, Mario tried a 'baby mask'). For instance, recent research (Jończyk *et al.*, 2019) confirms reduced affective sensitivity to L2 vocabulary words as opposed to lexical items in L1, which opens possibilities for acting improvisations in L2 that may have more freedom for L2 speaking actors in terms of lexical choices. Having said that, earlier research pointed out that the opposite is possible as well: Dewaele's (2004) work showed that those who switched to a dominant language different from their L1 rated words in L1 as less emotional than those in their dominant language. This opens a different set of possibilities for those who switched to a different language earlier in their lives (unlike Mario and Yury). It is perhaps not surprising that my other participants whose dominant language was also different from their L1 did not document any observations in relation to the stronger emotionality of their L1. Their orientating towards their languages was different from Mario's and Yury's.

Sadly, this radical diversity of orientations towards L2 is not yet approached by theatre scholars. In theatre studies, research on multilingual immigrant actors is currently very limited and often based on the assumption of a clear dichotomy: performing in L1 is easy and natural, while performing in L2 is exactly the opposite. For example, such positionality permeates the 2015 special issue of *Theatre Research in Canada/ Les Recherches théâtrales au Canada* entitled *Theatre and Immigration*, where a number of articles deal, both directly and tangentially, with the issue of multilingual actors. For instance, Manole (2015) presents a case study that primarily looks at the experience of Nada Humsi, an Arab Canadian actor. Humsi, in her phone interview with Manole, expresses a very strong monolingual positionality towards her L2 accent:

> I am an actress—I can play a tree, a bird, an old woman. I didn't care at all about my accent. Never wanted to learn the Canadian accent because I am above that. I know that you can't make an American speak Arabic like an Arab: you can't make a Russian speak English like an Englishman; you can't ask a tulip to become a jasmine. (Manole, 2015: 270)

Humsi seems to embrace the mother tongue valorising ideal: for her, L2 is always L2 – the language of the Other that one cannot fully master; hence, 'you can't make an American speak Arabic like an Arab'. I wrote someplace else that it is exactly the same, rather conventional, positionality that allows mainstream Anglophone and predominantly white Canadian theatres to only see her as an 'Arab' and, hence, not hire her and many other L2 speaking actors for roles that require an 'unmarked accent' (Babayants, 2019). Following Humsi's logic: just as an American cannot be Russian, an Arab cannot be Canadian. The issue of identity (*I am above that* [the Canadian accent]) seems central here.

In response to Humsi's statement, it is worth noting that Arabic possesses an inherently 'multilingual' nature as it exists within the situation of diglossia – a perpetual state of two recognised varieties functioning simultaneously: Classical/Quranic Arabic (the language of schooling in Arabic speaking countries) and local Arabic, or more precisely *Arabics* (the language of communication for most Arab-speaking people). Diglossia – arguably, a weaker form of heteroglossia – is essential to anyone who was educated in an Arabic-speaking place. Moreover, as some research shows, the literary variety of Arabic is processed by native speakers of Arabic similarly to how L2 is usually processed by L2 learners (Nevat *et al.*, 2014); thus, in a way, any educated native speaker of Arabic is simultaneously an L2 speaker of the same language due to the diglossia. In other words, one's L1 can also be one's L2, at least to some extent and in certain contexts. Unaware of this complexity of their own L1, L2 speaking immigrant performers might subscribe to the conventional monolingual paradigm (somewhat similar to Yury's), where only L1 feels 'authentic' or 'correct', while L2 will generally be felt as the language of deficiency or struggle.

Switching gears to theatre studies research, I can state that while linguistic research is beginning to embrace emotions and memory as inherent to L2 language speaking and learning, theatre research remains generally behind that trend. Lutterbie (2011), who was first to propose a general theory of acting without reducing acting to one particular school, suggested a set of six tools that all actors use in order to create their craft and he speaks of language as one of those tools. Lutterbie (2011: 118) does subscribe to an embodied model of language, rooted in neuroscience – he writes: 'The fundamental tenet of the neural theory of language is that abstract thought, long considered an autonomous function of the mind, is based on embodied experience'. Lutterbie, however, is only concerned with monolingual actors. The bilingual, let alone the multilingual actor, remains completely outside of his scope. At the same time, more and more multilingual artistic work is being created by immigrant performers in theatres located in larger multicultural urban centres, such as Berlin, Dublin, Hong Kong, Melbourne or Toronto (Meerzon, 2020; Meerzon & Pewny, 2020) and while the aesthetics and the politics of such performances gets a significant amount of scholarly attention, multilingual performers' process and labour do not receive the same treatment.

Going back to affective linguistic conditioning and its potential role in the immigrant actor's attempt to 'appropriate a character' [Присвоить Персонаж], in Yury's terms, the following has transpired in my study given its limited focus on two professional actors: immigrant actors performing in the L2 may experience a language-body-emotion disconnect that could have been prompted by the lack of affective linguistic conditioning in relation to their L2. L2 speaking actors can experience and approach that disconnect in diverse ways: it can be both perceived as an impediment to portraying a character in a realist way or an opportunity to create a 'foreign mask' that could potentially provide more creative freedom than performing in one's L1. It is also probably safe to assume that acknowledging the very necessity of affective linguistic conditioning might be a useful starting point for immigrant actors learning or practising performing in their L2, although this point would require further investigation both through PaR means and other research methods.

In conclusion, I would like to return to the quote I provided at the beginning of this chapter on Pavlenko's relationship with her L1 and L2. Pavlenko's (2006) position sheds light on the complexity of bilingual perception and her own struggle with the concept of 'self' that is deeply associated with her native language. Interestingly, her position still grounds itself in the monolingual paradigm, as it comes from a position of one single mother tongue – in her case, Russian. One can only imagine the levels of complexity if this grounding is different, for instance if a person forgets their mother tongue and switches to a different dominant language, or if a person grows up with two or three first languages simultaneously – and all of this while living in a multicultural and multilingual place where languages other than their own first (or second) might (or might not) be dominant. While it might seem like a hypothetical fantasy, it is in fact a given reality for many inhabitants of large urban centres of the modern world and it is relevant to immigrant actors. It is thus necessary to reframe the theoretical lens through which we see multilinguals in general, and multilingual actors specifically.

From a theoretical standpoint, one potential reframing can be done through the concept of *plurilingualism*. Applied linguists Grommes and Hu (2014: 2) write:

> The concept of plurilingualism puts the individual at centre stage. It focuses on the individual's ability to make use of two or more languages in speaking, reading and writing at varying levels of competence and in varying contexts. It is assumed that these languages do not coexist in separate silos in a person's mind, but that they form a composite competence.

Perhaps, taking the plurilingualism stance along with an interdisciplinary approach that includes both linguistics and theatre research (see, for instance, Babayants, 2019; French, 2021), could eventually lead to a more profound understanding of how multilingual immigrant actors experience working in different languages, how that affects their working life, and ultimately how it shapes and reshapes their identity. As Angouri and Piekkari (2017: 22) point out, true engagement with interdisciplinarity could undo disciplinary orthodoxies, challenge existing categories and, most importantly, allow researchers from different disciplines not to reinvent the wheel when talking about the same issues studied from different perspectives. In the case of studying immigrant multilingual actors, it appears that sociolinguistics, applied linguistics, immigration studies and theatre research would need to start a more profound interdisciplinary conversation.

Notes

(1) This research project was approved by the University of Toronto's Ethics Board: the performers' names here represent their actual names as the artistic project was open to public – there was no anonymity involved. For the research purposes, the actors were not doing anything that would be different from their regular work in theatre and no specific precautions were necessary to protect their identity.

(2) Here and throughout the chapter I have kept the original orthography and grammar of the journals.

References

Angouri, J. and Piekkari, R. (2017) Organising multilingually: setting an agenda for studying language at work. *European Journal of International Management* 12 (1–2), 8–27.

Ahmed, S. (2006) *Queer Phenomenology. Orientations, Objects, Others*. Durham, NC: Duke University Press.

Babayants, A. (2019) Resisting the monolingual lens: Queer phenomenology and multilingual dramaturgy. In Y. Meerzon and K. Pewny (eds) *Dramaturgy of Migration: Staging Multilingual Encounters in Contemporary Theatre*. New York: Routledge.

Cook, S.R. and Dewaele J.-M. (2022) 'The English language enables me to visit my pain'. Exploring experiences of using a later-learned language in the healing journey of survivors of sexuality persecution. *International Journal of Bilingualism* 26 (2), 125–139.

Dewaele, J.-M. (2004) Perceived language dominance and language preference for emotional speech: The implications for attrition research. In M. Schmid, B. Köpke, M. Kejser and L. Weilemar (eds) *First Language Attrition: Interdisciplinary Perspectives on Methodological Issues* (pp. 81–104). Amsterdam: John Benjamins.

Dewaele, J.-M. and Li, C. (2020) Emotions in second language acquisition: A critical review and research agenda. *Foreign Language World* 196 (1), 34–49.

Dong, Z.R., Han, C., Hestvik, A. and Hermon, G. (2022) L2 processing of filled gaps: Non-native brain activity not modulated by proficiency and working memory. *Linguistic Approaches to Bilingualism* 12.

French, C. (2021) Facilitating departures from monolingual discourses. *Applied Theatre Research* 9 (1), 7–23.

Grommes, P. and Hu, A. (2014) Introduction. In P. Grommes and H. Adelheid (eds) *Plurilingual Education: Policies – Practices – Language Development* (pp. 1–14). Amsterdam: John Benjamins.

Huston, N. (1999) *Nord perdu*. [The Lost North]. Arles: Actes Sud.

Imai, Y. (2010) Emotions in SLA: New insights from collaborative learning for an EFL classroom. *The Modern Language Journal* 94 (2), 278–292.

Jończyk, R., Korolczuk, I., Balatsou, E. and Thierry, G. (2019) Keep calm and carry on: Electrophysiological evaluation of emotional anticipation in the second language. *Social Cognitive and Affective Neuroscience* 14 (8), 885–898.

Kyd, T. (2007) *The Spanish Tragedy*. http://darkwing.uoregon.edu/%7Ebear/kyd1.html (accessed 25 June 2022).

Lutterbie, J. (2011) *Toward a General Theory of Acting: Cognitive Science and Performance*. New York: Palgrave.

Manole, D. (2015) Accented actors; From stage to stages via a convenience store. *Theatre Research in Canada* 36 (2), 255–273.

Meerzon, Y. (2020) *Performance, Subjectivity, Cosmopolitanism*. Cham: Palgrave.

Meerzon, Y. and Pewny, K. (eds) (2020) *Dramaturgy of Migration. Staging Multilingual Encounters in Contemporary Theatre*. New York: Routledge.

Nelson, R. (2013) *Practice as Research in the Arts: Principles, Protocols, Pedagogies, Resistances*. Houndmills: Palgrave.

Nevat, M., Khateb, A. and Prior, A. (2014) When first language is not first: A functional magnetic resonance imaging investigation of the neural basis of diglossia in Arabic. *European Journal of Neuroscience* 40 (9), 3387–3395.

Pavlenko, A. (2006) *Emotions and Multilingualism*. Cambridge: Cambridge University Press.

Ross, A.S. and Rivers, D.J. (2008) Emotional experiences beyond the classroom: Interactions with the social world. *Studies in Second Language Learning and Teaching* 8 (1), 103–126.

Stanislavski, K. (2008) *An Actor's Work. A Student's Diary*. New York: Routledge.

Swain, M. (2012) The inseparability of cognition and emotion in second language learning. *Language Teaching* 46 (2), 1–13.

Van Manen, M. (2014) *Phenomenology of Practice*. Walnut Creek, CA: Left Coast Press.

10 '[They] thought I didn't know how to be a chef because I didn't speak Finnish': Gatekeeping and Professional Role Enactment in a Multilingual Kitchen Context

Kristina Humonen and Jo Angouri

Introduction

Language plays a significant role in migrants' access to work and career progression. Limited proficiency in a local language can often place migrant employees in precarious positions and has been associated with difficulties in settling in the new societal context. In contrast, those who are perceived to meet the language expectations are usually seen as being more professionally competent, which may result in upward visibility and faster career progression (e.g. Kraft, 2020). This is particularly relevant to low-paid jobs, which are the focus of our chapter.

This chapter is concerned with the dynamic process of claiming and negotiating professional roles in a multilingual professional context. While sociolinguistic research has addressed exclusion and marginalisation through gatekeeping as enacted by the majority at the expense of the minority, we look into the complexity of claiming professional roles and show how employees use 'linguistic competence' to claim situated positions of power vertically (management) and horizontally (peers). We illustrate our core arguments through data from a multilingual restaurant. Even though kitchens are typically highly hierarchical work environments, our data shows that professional roles are negotiated in situ, and that the management of language repertoires allows some employees to bypass formal hierarchical constraints whilst other voices get silenced.

We draw on a corpus of 42 hours of ethnographic observations, 18 hours of interactional data as well as interviews collected from a Finnish restaurant. The staff at this site consists of an international workforce originating from six different countries. We place special focus on one employee, 'Ibou', and show how the strategic utilisation of linguistic resources and gatekeeping allows him to claim positions of power and how, at times, his self-claimed roles are contested by his peers. Ibou's case serves as an interesting example of a migrant worker who goes against the conventional expectations of his role as a language-learner, newcomer and lower-in-the-hierarchy employee. We illustrate how he expresses agency and navigates through social structures in order to (re)position himself higher in his workplace.

Our chapter provides an insight into the highly visible, yet underexplored, multilingual kitchen context. Although scarce, there are a few studies in the fields of socio- and applied linguistics focusing on this professional environment. For example, Pennycook and Otsuji (2014) drew on the data from Japanese and Australian restaurants to show how kitchen workers perform multiple daily tasks and routines using the linguistic resources available to them, *metrolingual multitasking.* Barrett (2006) examined the impact of language ideologies and racial inequality for Spanish speaking employees at an Anglo-owned Mexican restaurant in the US. Karrebæk and Maegaard's (2017) and Toback's (2017) studies show how restaurants discursively construct and perform 'authenticity' with semiotic effects as a means to show distinction and a way to gain competitive advantage.

Given that the hospitality sector – i.e. food and accommodation services – serves as the first opportunity for employment for migrants in many parts of the world (OECD, 2020), and the restaurant industry specifically is one of the main employers for many migrants living in Finland (Forsander, 2002; Ollus, 2016), we consider the professional kitchen as an ideal environment for studying the dynamic process of socialisation into a new context in and through language. However, as suggested by Roberts (2010: 211), 'the notion of the workplace as a site where language socialization takes place is becoming increasingly complex and contested'. We unpack this in the light of the data and in relation to power position claims/resistance by employees, and seek to provide an insight into the working lives of migrants in this setting.

The rest of the chapter is organised in six parts. We start by introducing the wider societal context. We then turn to issues of professional roles and (linguistic) gatekeeping in multilingual work settings. Following this, methodological considerations and research context are described before paving the way for the analysis. Finally, we close the chapter by proposing a model emerging from this study and suggest directions for future research.

Briefly on the Role of Language in the Finnish Labour Market

There is currently a paradox in relation to the global workplace: on the one hand, the labour market is becoming more globalised and therefore multilingual; on the other hand, access to workplaces and social participation are restricted by societal and organisational language policies (e.g. Duchêne & Heller, 2012) that promote monolingualism or draw on ideologies that perpetuate a value system whereby social prestige is associated with language.

Finland, where our data collection took place, is a Northern European welfare state which has a relatively short history of attracting migrants. Rapid inward migration began in the early 1990s as a consequence of the collapse of the Soviet Union, and since then migrant numbers have been steadily increasing from different countries (Statistics Finland, 2020). Notions of employment and good citizenship permeate discourses of societal inclusion and integration, and the current government emphasises the importance of language for those seeking to settle in the country (Ministry of Economic Affairs and Employment, 2021). However, having two national languages, Finnish and Swedish, which are not widely spoken elsewhere (e.g. see Vikør, 2010, on linguistic purism in Nordic countries) brings challenges to migrant employability. Despite the government providing some basic language training, statistics show that it is not enough, with the OECD's (2018: 14) report concluding that 'poor language skills leave migrants isolated' in Finland.

Although access to work is a multifactorial issue, there is a certain inclination in Finnish public discourse to associate migrants' lower success rates in gaining jobs with limited knowledge of the Finnish language (Ahmad, 2015), which in turn is interpreted as unwillingness to integrate and commit to Finnish society (Forsander, 2002). Such views are further supported by reports conducted by public authorities that classify language as a barrier to entering the job market (e.g. the Ministry of Employment and the Economy, 2012), irrespective of the language needs for work roles and whether the newcomers will interact with the public or not. These discourses also find their way into the media and are exploited in populist rhetoric.

The discourse and ideology of 'our' national language is used to appeal to the notion of (imagined) community (Anderson, 1991) that is distinct from others and, thus, should be valued by the 'Others'. Similarly, Ruuska (2019) argues that language is a fictitious sociocultural construct in the sense that multilingual repertoires, which may come more naturally for bi/multilingual speakers, can be restricted due to prevailing language ideologies and their sociolinguistic status within specific social settings. Such artificial ideology follows an evaluative stance (Ruuska, 2019) in which non-standard language variations are often devalued against the dominant ideologies (Kroskrity, 2004). These can be so pervasive that non-L1 (first language) speakers themselves might start to internalise 'standard' language ideologies by positioning non-L1 competence as inferior.

This pattern is typical across different contexts (Piller, 2016) and Finland is not an exception. Forsander (2002), for example, argues that language carries symbolic value for Finnish employers which is associated with migrants' commitment to Finland and, subsequently, to work. Substantial Finnish language skills are required to qualify even for positions which have no front stage interaction such as cleaning jobs (Ahmad, 2015). However, even though language sets limitations on migrants' access to employment – regardless of their educational backgrounds or professional experience – Ollus (2016) argues that many will nevertheless end-up in the second labour market, with the biggest employers being the restaurant and cleaning sectors.

Language and Professional Roles

Language and communication skills are seen to add value to employees' human capital, making them appear more flexible in the 'linguistic market' (Duchêne & Heller, 2012; Flubacher *et al.*, 2018). Such a view of language can be traced back to Bourdieu's (1986, 1992) classic work on *linguistic capital*. According to Bourdieu, the possession of the 'right' kind of linguistic capital (subject to context) contributes to *symbolic capital* which is a source of power and influence. Consequently, the accumulation of symbolic capital is closely related to Bourdieu's (1989: 16) conceptualisation of *habitus*, which refers to 'a "sense of one's place" but also a "sense of the place of the others"'. According to this perspective, language is commodified and reconfigured to meet the needs of market conditions; it is seen to be correlated with economic exchange value, increased social power and has an impact on how individuals are positioned in the workplace. Following from this position, it would make sense for migrants to invest in their language learning, and in this regard Norton Peirce (1995: 17–18) argues that:

> if learners invest in a second language, they do so with the understanding that they will acquire a wider range of symbolic and material resources, which will in turn increase the value of their cultural capital... an investment in the target language is also an investment in a learner's own social identity, an identity which is constantly changing across time and space.

Here the conception of *investment* represents the multifaceted relationship between language learners and their wish to use the target language across a variety of contexts to improve their positions (Darvin & Norton, 2015). The cause-and-effect relationship between language and (workplace) integration, however, has been widely criticised. For example, in a recent work Flubacher *et al.* (2018) raise three main issues with the notion of 'language investment' (see also Duchêne, 2016). First, language as a determinant for employment is too vague as it is equally a matter of class, gender and race; second, the value of language investment divides potential employees and further marginalises low-skilled migrants; and third, related to the second point, are the effects of decapitalisation of the resources of other job seekers: i.e. who can claim investment and become an in/excluded member of society? The authors raise relevant questions but conclude, in line with other sociolinguistic studies, that 'language – as elusive a concept it might be – is and remains a key both to inclusion as well as to exclusion' (Flubacher *et al.*, 2018: 110). Even if one learns the needed language, 'sounding different' could be still interpreted as a marker of 'Otherness'.

A number of workplace discourse studies, particularly on intercultural encounters, have concentrated on power relations between a linguistic majority or official language policy (often English in multinational organisations) and language minorities (e.g. Duchêne *et al.*, 2013; Lønsmann, 2014). Different language ideologies are often contrasted, with the dominant linguistic group seen as having power over the others. Recently though, language complexity at workplaces has been acknowledged; specifically, how employees organise their work drawing on a whole range of linguistic resources by 'mixing and matching' languages depending on the situation (e.g. Janssens & Steyaert, 2014; Otsuji & Pennycook, 2010). Our interest for this chapter lies in the nuances of employees' daily language use and agency, and how utilisation of linguistic resources contributes to power relationships in the negotiation of professional roles.

The notion of professional role is closely related to a work title, responsibilities and the ways employees navigate power structures in the workplace. Some roles may evolve more naturally over time through socialisation, whereas other roles may be imposed as a consequence of structural role positions (Sarangi & Roberts, 1999) in the form of promotions and improved organisational status, for instance. Professional role expectations and performance are typically associated with relevant work experience and social networks, although roles are never singular or fixed, nor do they come with any specific behaviours (Sveningsson & Alvesson, 2003). Individuals can have several distinct roles which may stabilise or be incompatible with their personal identities and/or other's expectations.

For the most part, professional roles are observable and can be examined through the subjective positioning of how they are embraced, negotiated or rejected (Angouri, 2018). Roles are constantly enacted in and through language in relation to (self-other) positioning within a specific context (e.g. Angouri & Mondada, 2017). Employees may use 'a range of linguistic features and discursive devices to negotiate positions of power, emphasise collegiality or camaraderie' (Rogerson-Revell, 2011: 64). In a multilingual work environment, language choice is particularly relevant for role negotiations, (non-)participation, and power asymmetries. Gumperz and Cook-Gumperz (2005: 14), for example, note that different communicative and linguistic backgrounds have an impact on daily interactions and that 'those less powerful are likely to be judged and evaluated by the bureaucratically dominant'. For the purposes of this chapter, we see work roles as being constructed through different interactional stances that speakers adopt in a particular context (Ochs, 1993). More specifically, special attention is given to describing how one 'does power' in order to reaffirm a senior role (e.g. Holmes & Stubbe, 2015; Holmes *et al.*, 1999; Locher, 2004) and how this is related to negotiating social boundaries.

(Linguistic) Gatekeeping

According to Holmes (2007: 2011) 'gatekeeping is a matter of monitoring boundaries' and is typically achieved through discourse, particularly in workplace contexts. Gatekeeping 'relates to the physical and social passage from *outside* to *inside*' (Kirilova & Angouri, 2017: 547), and we would add that it is specifically the *allowing* or *granting* of such passage. Currently, a number of gatekeeping studies in sociolinguistics tend to focus on institutional gatekeeping (e.g. Sarangi & Roberts, 1999) by analysing job interviews (Kirilova & Angouri, 2017; Roberts, 2013; Tranekjær, 2015). This critical body of research has provided valuable insights into how institutional gatekeepers (e.g. an interviewer) make evaluations of others (non-native language speakers) on the grounds of dominant discourses and ideologies (Tranekjær, 2015). The consequences of misaligning with dominant rules, e.g. by sounding and behaving differently from hegemonic norms and sociocultural conventions, may result in unfavourable evaluations, or 'linguistic penalty' as described by Roberts and Campbell (2006; also Roberts, 2013).

Those individuals who do pass the institutional gate are often at first dependent on their co-workers. In this regard Holmes (2007: 2012) expands the concept of gatekeeping 'to include the process of monitoring progress across boundaries *within* an institution, as well as providing access to institutional membership'. She identifies three types of gatekeeping encounters: (1) promotional gate (career progression), (2) facilitative role of gatekeeping (e.g. senior figure mentoring junior colleague) and (3) gatekeeping for monitoring team boundaries (e.g. subtle strategies for in/excluding a new colleague). Holmes's conceptualisation of gatekeeping includes both positive and negative encounters while negotiating 'fitting in' to a workplace. When it comes to multilingual work settings, employees with limited language proficiency in the dominant language manoeuvre at the interface of linguistic boundaries. Strömmer's (2016) research, for example, demonstrates how outsourced cleaning jobs in Finland provide only occasional opportunities for migrants to interact with their colleagues and clients. Consequently, these employees may become isolated within their work communities and must rely on intermediaries in communication between themselves and clients. Intermediaries in this context could also be labelled as linguistic gatekeepers in that they both have the power to facilitate information sharing and control memberships (see also Suni, 2017, on Finnish health care). This has wider implications as workplaces are typically places where social integration is negotiated.

In a parallel but useful line of scholarship, international business management research (e.g. Piekkari *et al.*, 2014; Vaara *et al.*, 2005) uses gatekeeping to refer to people who are proficient in the needed work language(s) and so have access to corporate information and knowledge. Employees with the right linguistic skills can become 'boundary spanners' (Barner-Rasmussen *et al.*, 2014) which places them in positions where they can exchange information, link groups, facilitate and intervene in workplace interactions. Being able to navigate across different language-based networks and having access to corporate information can thus be used as a source of power (Charles, 2007). Put differently, occupying a linguistic gatekeeping position can provide social recognition and the tools for enhancing one's power in the workplace, as shown in our own study.

Methodology and Data

The chosen data is drawn from the first author's multi-sited, ethnographically-informed PhD research conducted between 2017 and 2018 in a Finnish multinational food and catering service corporation, pseudonymised as 'Tasty Co'. The wider study sought to understand the relationship between language policy and practice, and the ways language influences the distribution of power and in/exclusion processes. The data collection took place at the corporation's headquarters and its seven restaurants. In this chapter, we focus on one restaurant context that we shall call 'Finlicious', and address the following research question: *How does access to language resources and gatekeeping enable employees to claim positions of power?* The excerpts discussed come from a corpus of 18 hours of audio-recorded workplace interactions and 42 hours of ethnographic observations. In addition, the interactional excerpts are supplemented with quotes from semi-structured interview data with eight Finlicious employees (3 hours 29 minutes) as a means of providing a more comprehensive analysis with further insights into how participants index various roles and stances (e.g. De Fina, 2011).

We draw on the interactional sociolinguistics (IS) framework as it enables us to bridge the gap between (macro) societal conditions and (micro) interactive processes (Gumperz, 1982, 2001; Jaspers, 2012). IS analyses interactions line-by-line and makes links with social aspects outside of that talk. At a theoretical level, IS postulates that interactions are influenced by social orders and pre-existing taken-for-granted frames which all have an impact on individuals' meaning-making processes (Gumperz, 2001). It provides a useful approach for analysing how various (language) ideologies may guide positions that employees take or reject in social interactions. Influenced by social constructionist (Berger & Luckmann, 1966) views of discourse, IS recognises the agency of speakers. For example, according to Jaspers (2012: 140) language is not only a 'reflection of pre-existing social structures, language use is seen as one of the primary resources for social actors to shape and reshape their social surroundings actively and creatively'. In the analysis we do not focus on any specific linguistic features *per se*; rather, we look into control acts (or lack thereof) and language choice as the employees negotiate their roles. This is reflected in the analysis where both data sets are drawn on throughout.

Research context

The case study restaurant, Finlicious, has a central location in one of the busiest business districts in Helsinki. It is a relatively large-sized establishment which serves buffet style lunches to approximately 700+ daily diners. The restaurant also provides pre-ordered catering services for corporate clients and events. The first author spent one week working side by side with the kitchen employees, mainly assisting with simple food items such as salads, pizzas, etc., while observing and conducting conversational interviews. At the time of the fieldwork, the kitchen staff consisted of 11 employees out of which nine were responsible for food preparations and two for dishwashing. Depending on the day, Finlicious also had 6–8 waiting staff members at the front of the house. The following excerpts involve six kitchen employees whose short profiles are presented in Table 10.1.

When discussing the data, we refer to the *front of house* (FoH) and *back of house* (BoH). The BoH refers to the workspaces 'behind the scenes' like the kitchen area, dishwashing stations, office(s), storage rooms, etc. The FoH, then, stands for spaces where customers and employees may interact such as food stations, the dining room, tills, etc. One might find resemblance with these terms and Goffman's (1959) classic notions of 'front stage', in which performance is visible to the public, and 'back stage' behaviour, in which agents act out their authentic selves in a protected space. We refrain from referring to Goffman's notions for two main reasons: first, we follow the standard kitchen terminology where BoH and FoH represent two different working spaces *and* teams; second, BoH does not necessarily represent a private area or safe space as kitchens are highly hierarchical spaces, where employees are under constant surveillance and pressure to enact their professional expertise.

In the course of the data collection, the first author had a central location at the BoH facing the entire kitchen. While this provided rich

Table 10.1 Finlicious's kitchen staff mentioned in the excerpts

Pseudonym	Position and work experience from Tasty Co's restaurants	Main responsibilities
Pekka	Executive/Group Chef • 25 years	Special orders; business clients; inventory; food orders and other administrative tasks. Spends most of the time in the office.
Heikki	Kitchen Duty Manager & Head Chef • +10 years	Managing the kitchen staff; going through the daily menus and ensuring the food 'goes out' smoothly; food supplies.
Ryan	Substitute Sous Chef • 8 years – rotating between Tasty Co's restaurants as a part-time employee	Warm dishes and oven-baked items. Also helps to heat the baked goods and desserts prepared by the pastry cook 'Nina'.
Akene	Pantry cook • 2 years	Cold buffet dishes.
Ibou	Trainee sauté/grill cook • Approx. 2 years (working on-off at various Tasty Co's locations) *	Warm dishes; sauces; grill station; helps with the inventory.
Mali	Trainee cook • 3 months + 3 months. *	Assists with the warm dishes; buffet fill-ups.

*The trainees, Ibou and Mali, are at the final stages of their culinary degrees. They study at different institutions in Helsinki; Ibou attends a Finnish taught programme and Mali an English one.

observational insights, the early period of the fieldwork was characterised by the challenge of obtaining interactional data. At first the recorders were placed on carefully chosen kitchen shelves; however, due to high noise levels and the constant movement of employees, the recorded material ended up being too scattered and unclear for analysis. At the same time while working with the line cooks, one of the trainees, 'Ibou', stood out and appeared to have a key role in the kitchen team as a linguistic gatekeeper. Guided by this insight, a new strategy was implemented that sought to understand and build on Ibou's central location in his workspace. The good rapport between the researcher and the participants, and Ibou's expressing his interest in the study, led to him agreeing to carry one of the recorders and a microphone. Even though it was made clear that he could withdraw from the study at any point and switch off the recorder, Ibou carried the device for three days and collected the interactional data discussed here (a reflexive account of doing ethnography is provided in Humonen & Angouri, 2023).

Ibou's (language) biography

During the fieldwork, Ibou was doing his second traineeship at Finlicious as part of his culinary degree (see Table 10.1). His official role

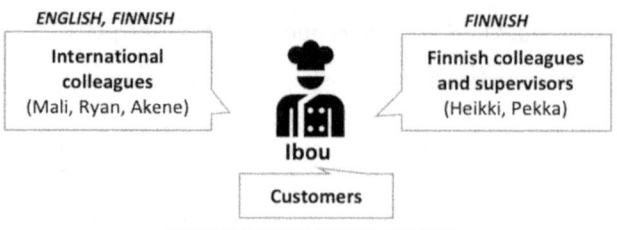

Figure 10.1 Illustration of Ibou's use of diverse linguistic resources at work (Note: The illustration includes *only* the employees mentioned in the upcoming excerpts.)

is a trainee cook but the data show a more complex picture in terms of his claimed and projected positioning. More specifically, he appeared to be in a position of influence that went beyond his official title. We identified two reasons for this: first, he bridged the language gap between different employees, and also between employees and customers; second, his workstations had central locations. These are further explained below.

As illustrated above, Ibou's language resources allow him to engage and respond to different language needs. He speaks five languages, but we did not include his native language in the figure as he did not use it at work. Although Finnish is (supposed to be) the official language at Tasty Co's restaurants, in reality Finlicious's BoH constitutes a multilingual environment with a representation of seven to eight different native languages, depending on the day. Ibou is mainly (but not always) speaking in English with other international employees, Finnish with his Finnish speaking colleagues, and he may occasionally use his second native language, French, and/or some Spanish with familiar customers. He learned the latter language while working in Spain prior to moving to Finland. The managers of Finlicious see Ibou as enriching and improving the customer experience (see also Duchêne, 2011) because of his diverse linguistic capital. They also trust his (language) ability of coordinating work tasks between L1 and non-L1 speaking employees.

In terms of Ibou's physical position in the material space, his workstations are centrally located (see Angouri & Humonen, 2022, on spatiolinguistic practices and in/visible boundaries) at both BoH and FoH. In fact, he is the only kitchen employee who moves to the front-of-house and has his own workspace – a grill and pizza station – for the duration of the lunch period. This makes him physically visible and approachable to *all* employees – managers and co-workers, waiting staff and kitchen staff – as well as customers.

In the light of the above, Ibou provides an interesting case for studying the relationship between gatekeeping and role positioning in a professional kitchen context. We show how he crafts agency and strategically mobilises language resources which allows him to claim a more senior position in the hierarchy.

Analysis

The following sections illustrate how the management of linguistic resources serves as a powerful tool for negotiating professional role boundaries. In the representation of the excerpts, we include descriptions of the context so the reader can place the interaction; kitchen interactions are short and, as is necessary for the cooking praxis, heavily depend on professionals' embodied behaviours which, however, go beyond the scope of the analysis here.

In the first excerpt, we show how Ibou is positioned by his co-workers in the role of controller and facilitator.

Gatekeeping and limited information sharing

Context: Mali (M) is preparing soup but is missing an ingredient. The following interaction starts when she approaches Ibou (I) on the matter.

Excerpt 1

		Spoken Data	English translation of Finnish utterances
1	M:	where is kermaviili?	*sour cream*
2	I:	u:m ask Heikki I think	
3	M:	[o:h here here here	
4	I:	I think you can do that u:m let me see (reads	
5		the recipe out loud:) ruohosipuli basilika chip chip	*chives basil*
6		(makes a chopping sound)	
7		it's really good really good if you have lime (.) (tastes the soup)	
8		hei ihan oikeesti suola (.) suola ja	*hey seriously salt (.) salt and*
9	M:	[mutta hän (Heikki) sanoo a:h!	*[but he (Heikki) says a:h!*
10	I:	toi kyl ihan <u>oikeesti</u> tarvii	*it really needs it*
		(Ibou takes vegetable stock powder from the shelf and is about to add it into the soup)	
11	M:	but if you put it they won't like it (.) if you put	
12		this one (the powder) it won't melt you know?	
13	I:	really?	
14	M:	yeah like a thick texture	
15	I:	this one? (points at the powder)	
16	M:	um but (.) but what he (Heikki) thinks?	
17	I:	I can I can let you know	
18	M:	I cannot do it (.) (whispers) ask after you (?)	
		(Ibou shouts across the kitchen:)	

19	I:	onks tähä ollenkaa kasvislientä?	*is there a vegetable stock for this?*
20	H:	häh?	*huh?*
21	I:	se ei maistu niinku um kasvikselle	*it doesn't taste of like um vegetables*
22	H:	ei se oikeen niin (.) tai sit maustat vielä	*not really yeah (.) or you can season it*
23		suolalla	*more with salt*
24	I:	joo okei se maistuu vähän niinku juures	*yeah okay it tastes a bit of like root*
25		niinku	*vegetables like*
26	H:	[niin maistuu juures mut sit taas siellä on	*[yeah tastes of root vegetables but it*
27		hentoja makuja (.) siellä on porkkanaa,	*has delicate flavours (.) it has carrots,*
28		palsternakkaa ja sit se mantelimaito (.)	*parsnip and that almond milk*
29		se ei voi olla semmonen	*it can't be like*
30	I:	[joo nii semmonen maukas	*[yeah like tasty*
31	H:	niin (.) normisuola vaan kohilleen ja sitte siihe	*yes (.) with the right amount of salt and*
32		niinku (.) toki jos vielä tuntuu et se tarvii viel	*then like (.) surely if it still feels that it's*
33		kasvisliemen niin voi sinne	*missing the veg stock you can add it a*
34		vähän laittaa	*little bit*
35	I:	joo se voi maistuu vähän paremmalle	*yeah it can make it taste a bit better*
36	H:	mut sitä ei kannata laittaa kokonaan sillee	*but it's better not to put it straight from*
37		suoraan pussista	*the bag*
38	I:	Joo	*yeah*
39	H:	koska sit se jää semmoseks kokkareiseks	*because then it will stay lumpy*
40	I:	mm kokkareiseks	*uhum lumpy*
41	H:	sen voi sekottaa pieneen määrään	*it can be mixed with a small amount of*
42		vettä ja laittaa sit sinne	*water and then added in*
43	I:	okei (.) Mali kuule (laughs and walks to Mali) he	*okay (.) Mali listen*
44		said you put a little bit of water first and then	
45		after that you throw it in	
46		not so much a little bit (4.0) o::h too much (laughs)	
47		yeah good work (.) a little bit of water (.) not so	
48		much (.) yeah it's very good (.) leave it (Mali starts stirring the soup without saying anything)	

Control of recipes, ingredients and preparation procedures indexes expertise and power in kitchen contexts. In this excerpt, when Mali asks for a missing ingredient from Ibou – that she immediately finds herself – Ibou stays next to her and takes control of the food preparation. Specifically, from line 4 onwards Ibou starts reading the recipe out loud, provides a recommendation (line 7) and then switches from English to Finnish to issue a directive (lines 8 and 10), i.e. the need for adding more salt. Code-switching is indicative of group membership which may reflect distancing and repositioning (De Fina, 2011), power asymmetry and inequality (Auer, 1998). Discourse-related code-switching indexes elements of a wider society, e.g. in terms of why certain language is used (Auer, 1998). Here Finnish is a marked code for authority underpinned by local language ideology and power. Namely, throughout our dataset Ibou code-switches to Finnish whenever he wants to make a point which appears to give him more legitimacy among non-Finnish speaking employees (see also Excerpt 4).

However, in this example Mali does not accept Ibou's directive unquestionably and contrasts his advice with that of the Head Chef's, Heikki's, possible reaction. Her expressive reply in line 9 (*but he says aaah!*) implies Heikki's disapproval of putting more salt. After adding an intensifier: 'it really needs it' to strengthen his statement, Ibou acts upon it by starting to search for the vegetable stock himself. Again, Mali questions him by making an assumption that '*they* won't like it' (line 11) which is followed by her telling Ibou that the product he chose is not appropriate on account of its texture (lines 11, 12 and 14). She then reiterates her concern in terms of getting Heikki's approval, but the hesitation in line 16, whispering and asking Ibou to approach Heikki on her behalf (line 18), reflects her diffidence in interacting with the Head Chef.

The discursive construction of 'them' (and 'us') indexes group identity and membership (non-)belonging. It is the most common category throughout our datasets. Consider the positioning of 'us' and 'them' in one of the interviews following the collection of the kitchen interaction data: 'we're maahanmuuttajat so we have to (help each other)' (Akene), and, 'they are ulkomaalainen, they are the same as me so it's easier to ask them' (Mali). Acceptance and perpetuation of labels such as 'maahanmuuttaja' (immigrant in Finnish) and 'ulkomaalainen' (foreigner) reflects dominant public discourses and reinforces perceived 'difference'. Under such conditions, the migrant employees at Finlicious (and other studied restaurants) have formed their own informal support networks. Hence, Mali's 'they' may refer to the Finnish employees and customers. Alternatively, Mali's Otherisation of Heikki could also be associated with the hierarchical remoteness. Specifically, Mali asking Ibou to approach Heikki carries meaning and, in this context, it shows the perceived power distance re-enacted through the ways in which the message is signalled: whispering and coded in the common language, English (line 18). Also, language on its own is a significant factor impacting power relations; here Mali's Finnish is at beginners' level while Heikki rarely uses English and prefers to use Finnish instead. This could have a negative influence on the interactional dynamics between the two employees.

Continuing the reading of the excerpt, in line 19 Ibou asks Heikki about an ingredient in a rather ostentatious way, compared to Mali's whispering in the previous turn, by shouting across the kitchen. This in itself is not uncommon in kitchen interactions (e.g. Fine, 1996); however, it represents an atypical behaviour in our data. Interestingly, as Ibou moves closer to the Head Chef his demeanour changes and he shows more deference. Specifically, in lines 21 and 24 he is lowering his voice, uses a hesitation marker (*um*) and softeners (*like, a bit*) prior to criticising the recipe.

Following this, Ibou gives affirmative answers by agreeing with the Head Chef, repeating his words and trying to guess what Heikki says next by finishing or interrupting his sentences (lines 30 and 40). By doing so he might be trying to prove his expertise (Sarangi & Roberts, 1999) to his superior, or perhaps by verbally repeating the words he is trying to learn and get accustomed with the kitchen terminology.

Given that employees are expected to speak in institutionally accepted ways in order to be credible, learning the correct terminology is important at any workplace. This learning happens through a gradual socialisation into the discourses of the professions (Sarangi & Roberts, 1999). Perceived professional competence is closely associated with language competence. The following extract exemplifies Ibou's initial struggles in proving his professionalism due to perceived language limitations and prejudice:

> when I started I had colleagues who thought that I didn't know how to be a chef because I didn't speak Finnish but when he (a senior chef) saw that I do speak um like Finnish and I do know the recipes and I can finish [...] he said to me it's nice to have you and it's good you speak Finnish. He would always comment if someone didn't speak Finnish. (Interview data)

Returning to the excerpt, from line 43 onwards Ibou's assertiveness returns as he walks back to Mali's workstation and gives directives again (*throw it in, not so much, leave it*) as well as compliments (*good work, it's very good*). The explicit statements of approval and instructions signify Ibou's move to take on a supervisor's role again (Holmes & Stubbe, 2015). This is, at least partly, successful as indexed by Mali finishing the work tasks as well as the pattern of Mali returning to Ibou. Mali's silence, however, does not necessarily mean agreement; on the contrary, it can signal several meanings out of which one could be perceived as workplace injustice, i.e. silence as a response to perceived ill treatment (Pinder & Harlos, 2001). Our data shows that in possible conflict situations Mali adopts a strategy of avoidance. This involves her walking away or finishing the tasks silently. As she later reflected in her interview: *if they don't understand what I mean I just walk away, so no more talking.*

Excerpt 1 provides a particularly interesting interaction because in the first half of the excerpt Mali takes agency and demonstrates her expertise; she stops Ibou in lines 11–12 and 14 from making a critical mistake that would have ruined the entire dish. Even though Heikki confirms that Mali was correct (line 39), Ibou does not give her any acknowledgement on the matter. This could potentially have a negative impact on Mali's confidence, and reinforces her reliance on Ibou.

The excerpt captures the situated negotiation of Ibou's authority; specifically, gatekeeping puts him in the position where he can decide what information to share and what to discard. Studies from corporate contexts have shown that gatekeeping can function as a resource for 'boundary spanning' (Barner-Rasmussen *et al.*, 2014) in that it gives control beyond official titles. Here, this is seen in Ibou ignoring his superior's advice of adding salt (lines 23 and 31) and, instead, he follows his initial plan of using the stock powder. Excerpt 1 is one of many recorded interactions where Ibou bypasses the Executive and Head Chefs' instructions and stays (informally) in control. His linguistic capital in particular allows him to access different centres of power and to re-enact boundaries locally. This is further illustrated in the next excerpt.

From a trainee to a 'co-leader': Why is Ibou's position accepted by the supervisors, and what challenges does it bring?

Context: The following interaction starts when Ryan (R) (Sous Chef) approaches Heikki (H) (Head Chef) to confirm food quantities, until Ibou (I) intervenes and offers his input.

Excerpt 2

1	R:	how many more (.) how many more will I make (.) everything o:r?
2	H:	u:m if you have time maybe everything
3	R:	okay
4	I:	how many do you have?
5	R:	two trays
6	I:	huh?
7	R:	two trays
8	I:	okay so put more

Heikki's response to Ryan's question and his use of hesitation markers (*um, if, maybe* in line 2) can be linked to uncertainty in professional talk (e.g. Sarangi & Clarke, 2002). Despite the vague answer, Ryan responds affirmatively. Ibou overhears the conversation and steps in; he asks questions (lines 4 and 6) and uses a directive to instruct Ryan to make more rice (line 8) – although the exact quantity remains unclear. Ibou's type of intervention, question and language style can be associated with authoritative power here, indexing someone who is in a higher organisational position and can control talk and action (Holmes *et al.*, 1999; Vine *et al.*, 2008).

Hierarchically and expertise-wise both Heikki and Ryan hold seniority over Ibou. Despite Ryan's extensive work experience, however, the data show that he is dependent on Ibou's translations because of his limited Finnish. This allows Ibou to be in a position of power in spite of his trainee status. Our corpus consists of a number of interactional events where Ibou instructs or answers Ryan's questions without confirming with his managers first. Once this resulted in a large quantity of food waste for which

Ryan received the blame. This raises a question: why does Ibou have so much power in a context that traditionally tends to be hierarchical?

Ibou's claimed position is supported by his supervisors within the limits of him instructing international employees. Heikki and Pekka (Executive/Group Chef) appear to have delegated managerial responsibilities to Ibou due to their limited capacity to manage their international subordinates. This is exemplified in the following interview extract:

Heikki:	You need to have eyes everywhere like if we agree that let's do something in a specific way, the most common answer is a nod with a 'yeah yeah' reply but then as soon as you turn your back they [=migrant employees] do everything in a completely opposite way
Researcher:	mhmm how do you handle it? Like if you feel you can't get your messages across?
Heikki:	(laughter) That's why I have the emotional translator [Ibou] next to me. He can translate things in a way they understand. The dude speaks French, Spanish, English, Finnish, Arabic so there are not many with whom he couldn't have a chat one way or another (laughter) (English translation)

In the first part, Heikki describes the challenge of needing to have 'eyes everywhere' because of the possible misunderstandings. He then refers to Ibou as an 'emotional translator' who is perceived to be a better communicator with the international employees. Hence, in addition to having access to the relevant linguistic resources (although to our knowledge he does not speak Arabic), Ibou is perceived to have the needed sociopragmatic competence (Gumperz, 2001), i.e. the appropriate language use and appeal to 'them' (the migrant employees). However, reliance on Ibou on the basis of his *perceived* language knowledge is not unproblematic. Our recordings captured his information distortion in Finnish on several occasions, which he then in turn 'translated' into English and forwarded to the international employees. A marked example of this was a misunderstanding in health and safety instructions issued in Finnish at a team meeting. Upon realising the seriousness of the misunderstanding in question, the first author felt obliged to intervene and clarify the safety regulations to Ibou and his non-Finnish speaking colleagues. One could assume that the managers would attempt to translate or at least confirm comprehension of such crucial information with their staff, but this appeared to be hampered by their own reported language limitations.

Namely, the Restaurant Manager, Executive Manager and Duty Manager all described their English language skills as limited. Heikki, for example, says that he 'survives' on a daily basis but perceives his English to be 'very bad or maybe passable', and notes that: 'when we applied for jobs, English wasn't required […] now it's unavoidable'. The Executive

Chef, Pekka, also points out that: 'it's difficult when you think about it like hey you should really get the work done and the other one doesn't understand what you're saying'. For this exact reason, Ibou is legitimised by his superiors to intervene and instruct English speaking employees. However, this does not mean that the other employees automatically accept Ibou's role, as will be shown in the next and final section of our analysis.

Ibou rejecting identity claims imposed by his colleagues

The following two excerpts demonstrate how humorous comments are used as a strategy to soften criticism regarding Ibou's role and behaviour at Finlicious. Ibou's different response strategies illustrate situated role negotiations within different power relationships.

Context: Kitchens have clear regulations in regard to tidiness and equipment placement. Mali, however, had misplaced an item, which had been removed and put back to its correct place by Ibou (I). Prior to the interaction below, she had asked Ibou about the missing item. After telling Mali where to find it, Ibou stays in the kitchen and starts talking to Ryan (R).

Excerpt 3

1	I:	she put this (the tray) here (points at it) and now it's not there (laughs)
2	R:	oh (.) did you say it to her?
3	I:	yeah but I'm tired to say it you know what I mean?
4		I'm tired to say it (.) every time I feel there is something
5	R:	huh?
6	I:	I think all the time I say something
7	R:	yeah
8	I:	I don't want to get in trouble (.) usually see I'm not doing this (laughs)
9	R:	um I don't think so (.) you have to
10	I:	usually I'm not good in saying like <u>do this do this</u> (laughs)
11	R:	just tell her (.) you don't have to be angry
12	I:	yeah maybe (.) there's no reason to be
13	P:	joo-o like yesterday (all start laughing)
		(Pekka and Ryan start sarcastically imitating Ibou:)
14		hurry hurry!
15	R:	we need to have this <u>now</u>!

In this interaction, Ibou appears to position himself in a non-authoritarian role: that of a supportive team member. This role positioning, however, is not supported by his senior colleagues.

Here Ibou provides an account of his attempts to speak to Mali while at the same time signalling team identity to Ryan. The tag question 'you know what I mean?' (line 3) has a well-known function of initiating alignment by opening the interactional floor, and Ibou also uses the marker to allow Ryan to provide an opinion on the matter. Ryan, however, seems to either ignore the cue or fails to hear him, hence Ibou continues talking in line 4, which finally leads to a short 'yeah' answer (line 7). Despite Ibou's probing, Ryan offers minimal involvement in the interaction.

The reference to trouble in line 8 is ambiguous. It may refer to getting in trouble in terms of always instructing Mali. This account, however, is offered by someone who has been granted informal legitimatisation by management within the remit of supervising non-Finnish employees. Trouble, thus, in this context *could* also mean not adequately overseeing the finishing of tasks and consequently facing reprimand, which again assumes a position of power and role beyond Ibou's job description. This reading of 'trouble' would provide justification for why he 'has to' be in control.

Ryan finally gives an affirmative answer in line 9, after a hesitation particle (*um*), which leads to Ibou explaining how he is not used to telling people what to do (line 10). This indexes another attempt to build common ground with Ryan. Ryan, however, does not respond or join Ibou in laughter; rather, he advises Ibou to talk to Mali instead of getting angry (line 11) which Ibou appears to agree with. Suddenly Pekka, the Executive Chef, steps into the conversation in line 13 and starts it with a Finnish expression: 'joo-o'. *Joo* on its own means *yes* in English, but the prolongation/break between the o-letters and rising intonation at the end of the word changes the meaning. 'Joo-o' could be freely translated as 'yeah right'. Hence even though 'yes' usually signals agreement, in this particular context the word stands for the opposite. This is further emphasised by the sarcastic remark: 'like yesterday' followed by laughter. After this, Pekka starts imitating Ibou and says in a demanding voice: 'hurry, hurry!', which is followed by Ryan's imitation: 'we need to have this now!'. Humour can be used as a strategy to soften disagreement or to mitigate the effects of criticism (Holmes & Stubbe, 2015; Marra, 2012). In this interaction, Pekka and Ryan challenge Ibou's role claim and the uptake shows that they are successful as he does not join the laughter. It might be difficult for Ibou to challenge the sarcastic assertions about himself due to the hierarchical status differences, hence he leaves the conversation by walking away.

Even though similar in tone, in the next excerpt Ibou does not accept a critical comment provided by a more equal colleague.

Context: The first author (Res) is speaking with Mali at the grill station when Ibou (I) and Akene (A) approach them. Ibou opens the interaction by reflecting on the day.

Excerpt 4

		Spoken data	English translation of Finnish utterances
		(Ibou says to the researcher:)	
1	I:	I think we're under too much stress (.)	
2		when you're stressed it's easy to get tired	
3	A:	you get mad (Mali and Akene laugh)	
4	I:	I'm not mad (.) you're mad	
5	A:	no I'm always smiling	
6	I:	well you can smile and still be mad	
7	A:	yeah inside but you can't see it (Mali and Akene laugh)	
8	I:	okei sä peität ni mä en nää	*okay you hide it so I can't see*
		(Akene looks at the researcher and says:)	
9	A:	se on ihan totta kyllä (.) ei ehdi tekee	*it's true though (.) there's no time to do*
10		mitään samaan aikaan	*anything at the same time*
11	I:	[samaan aikaan niin	*[at the same time yeah*
12	Res:	mhmm	
13	I:	Akene jos haluat ni mene syömään	*Akene if you want then go eat*

As in Excerpt 3, Akene uses a humorous comment to challenge Ibou. However, unlike with the previous excerpt in which Ibou did not question his superiors' jocular remarks, this interaction takes a different form. Here Ibou is trying to raise his concern about stress and tiredness the employees are under at Finlicious when Akene adds in line 3 that Ibou also gets 'mad'. Mad here could indicate an extreme form of anger and unreasonable behaviour; however, the laughter at the end suggests that this was supposed to be a jocular comment. In this specific example we can see how humour can function as a critical discourse device (Holmes, 2000) where one can express a 'socially risky' opinion (Winick, 1976: 177, cited in Holmes, 2000) to challenge someone. Mali responds positively to Akene's comment but Ibou disaffiliates himself from the claim by rejecting it in line 4. In the next three lines, we can see how the two are quibbling. When Akene makes another comment in line 7 that results in laughter, Ibou code-switches into Finnish.

Those working with Ibou have learned that his code-switching often carries a meaning of him being serious. This can be seen in Akene's response to this, i.e. she stops joking, follows the code-switching and gives an agreeable answer in lines 9–10. Her reply can be seen as a discourse strategy aiming to rebuild and restore their relationship. This can be interpreted as a successful move because Ibou then rewards Akene by letting her have lunch. Ibou giving permission for a break could also be interpreted as a demonstration of power by sending her off (after being laughed at). Explicit control of the development and direction of an interaction is one way of 'doing power' as it signifies authority status (Holmes *et al.*, 1999). However, Ibou's use of power could be seen as being wielded with a certain benevolence. More specifically, usually the line cooks are expected to clean the FoH workstations together but, knowing Akene was tired, Ibou *allows* her to leave early and finishes the final physical task himself.

The last two excerpts provided nice examples of Ibou's fluid role positioning and different response strategies to criticism. Together the interactional excerpts have illustrated how Ibou's access to the kitchen's linguistic ecosystem is part of him doing his professional role and claiming power in this context. This is not to say that Ibou attained his current position *only* because of his language skills, but it is certainly a significant resource for professionals claiming their positions at work.[1]

Discussion and Conclusion

The aim of this empirical chapter was to explore the relationship between gatekeeping and professional role enactment. Despite the conventional expectations of our main research participant's role as a language learner, newcomer and lower-in-the-hierarchy employee, our excerpts show how Ibou was able to discursively claim positions of power. Traditionally, people get to positions of power through formal organisational structures, work experience or specialised expert knowledge (e.g. Sarangi & Roberts, 1999). In our case here, Ibou demonstrated authority beyond his formal position both vertically (e.g. by intervening in his superiors decisions) and horizontally (instructing those ostensibly equal to him). In line with Holmes's and colleagues' (e.g. 1999) criteria of how managers 'do power', we showed how he often controlled the development of interaction through explicit directives, appraisals, advice, warnings, silence and (strategic) information sharing. This position, however, was not fixed and was challenged by others (Excerpts 3 and 4).

In addition, our chapter provides insights into the complicated relationship between the agency of an individual, dominant language ideologies and social structures. Our study suggests that dominant ideologies are perpetuated by migrant employees in the ways they position themselves and/or each other. If we return to Excerpts 1 and 4, Ibou's code-switching practices present useful examples of this: by code-switching from English to Finnish when claiming a higher position against his migrant co-workers, Ibou perpetuated the dominant language ideology and contributed to discourses of Othering. This reinforced superiority-inferiority relationships between Finnish and non-Finnish speakers. Interactional membership dis/affiliations based on language skills, however, are dependent on the social context. For example, when surrounded by Finnish only speakers, Ibou's knowledge of the local language affords him less power. More precisely, he might be re-positioned from being the 'expert' in the local language to a language learner.

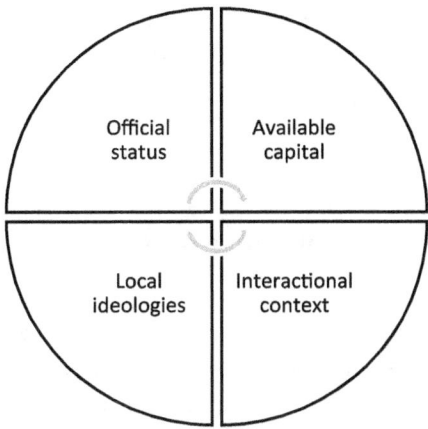

Figure 10.2 Factors influencing power negotiations and role enactment in multilingual work settings

Looking into backstage encounters in professional spaces where newcomers and established professionals interact provides a window into the dynamics of negotiating access to the social structure. Building on the discussion, we provide a framework (Figure 10.2) that summarises our reading of our data but also an approach that can offer a starting point for studies interested in multilingualism at work and professional role negotiation.

The dynamic relationship between factors pre-existing an encounter (such as official roles and status in the company, ideologies and capital) are mobilised in a particular moment depending on the local agendas of the core protagonists.

The workplace is a highly politicised site. Legitimised authorities make discretionary decisions and create regulatory systems of what is un/accepted language use based on local ideologies (e.g. Duchêne *et al.*, 2013). Such ideologies are rooted in specific sociocultural frames and are always evaluative. Local language ideologies do not only apply to the host language, but they are also relevant to the role of global language, such as English in a workplace. The discursive reproduction and perpetuation of language ideologies constructs modes of in/exclusion in which non-native speakers might be positioned in numerous ways. Difference, hence, becomes political (Angouri, 2018) and is closely tied with power. However, as shown in our study, power is not exclusive to majority-minority relations only as minority groups may also create their own informal hierarchies drawing on local language ideologies.

To conclude, our study shows that not one single factor can determine the access prospect and career progression of professionals. 'Language' represents and encapsulates a range of ideologies that are mobilised in work settings as professionals carry out their roles/responsibilities. In line with the stance of this volume, we argue that a holistic and multi-layered perspective is necessary in order to understand how professionals claim and grant professional roles in multilingual encounters. This applies to our particular context but also more broadly to any modern workplace. Moving beyond gatekeeping, research needs to consider new theoretical and methodological frameworks for capturing the nature of migratory re/settlement in relation to accessing work. Our work seeks to contribute to this agenda and pave the way for more studies in the field.

Acknowledgements

Kristina Humonen would like to thank the following foundations for the financial support of her PhD research: Economic and Social Research Council (UK), the Foundation for Economic Education (Liikesivistysrahasto) and Eino Jutikkala Fund of the Finnish Academy of Science and Letters.

Appendix: Transcription Conventions

____	Underline indicate emphatic stress, e.g. 'do it now'
[	Left square indicate an interruption
(.)	Pause
( )	Researcher's notes or clarifications
(?)	Researcher's best guess of an utterance
?	Rising/questioning intonation
…	Section of transcript omitted

All names are pseudonyms.

Note

(1) In the post-fieldwork phase, we were informed that Ibou's work and interactional efforts were rewarded and he was offered a permanent position.

References

Ahmad, A. (2015) 'Since many of my friends were working in the restaurant': The dual role of immigrants' social networks in occupational attainment in the Finnish labour market. *Journal of International Migration and Integration* 16, 965–985.

Anderson, B. (1991) *Imagined Communities: Reflections on the Origin and Spread of Nationalism*. London: Verso.

Angouri, J. (2018) *Culture, Discourse, and the Workplace*. London: Routledge.

Angouri, J. and Mondada, L. (2017) Meetings. In R. Wodak and B. Forchtner (eds) *The Routledge Handbook of Language and Politics* (pp. 468–484). London: Routledge.

Angouri, J. and Humonen, K. (2022) 'I just sit, drink and go back to work'. Topographies of language practice at work. *Multilingua* 42 (1), 55–82.

Auer, P. (1998) *Code-Switching in Conversation: Language, Interaction and Identity*. London: Routledge.

Barner-Rasmussen, W., Ehrnrooth, M., Koveshnikov, A. and Mäkelä, K. (2014) Cultural and language skills as resources for boundary spanning within the MNC. *Journal of International Business Studies* 45 (7), 886–905.
Barrett, R. (2006) Language ideology and racial inequality: Competing functions of Spanish in an Anglo-owned Mexican restaurant. *Language in Society* 35, 163–204.
Berger, P.L. and Luckmann, T. (1966) *The Social Construction of Reality: A Treatise in the Sociology of Knowledge*. London: Penguin Books Ltd.
Bourdieu, P. (1986) The forms of capital. In J. Richardson (ed.) *Handbook of Theory and Research for the Sociology of Education* (pp. 241–261). Westport, CT: Greenwood.
Bourdieu, P. (1989) Social space and symbolic power. *Sociological Theory* 7 (1), 14–25.
Bourdieu, P. (1992) *Language and Symbolic Power*. Cambridge: Polity Press.
Charles, M. (2007) Language matters in global communication. *Journal of Business Communication* 44 (3), 260–282.
Darvin, R. and Norton, B. (2015) Identity and a model of investment in applied linguistics. *Annual Review of Applied Linguistics* 35, 36–56.
De Fina, A. (2011) Discourse and identity. In T.A. van Dijk (ed.) *Discourse Studies: A Multidisciplinary Introduction* (pp. 263–282). London: Sage.
Duchêne, A. (2016) Language investment and political economy. *Langage et société* 157 (3), 73–96.
Duchêne, A. and Heller, M. (2012) *Language in Late Capitalism: Pride and Profit*. New York: Routledge.
Duchêne, A., Moyer, M. and Roberts, C. (2013) *Language, Migration and Social Inequalities: A Critical Sociolinguistic Perspective on Institutions and Work*. Bristol: Multilingual Matters.
Fine, G.A. (1996) *Kitchens: The Culture of Restaurant Work*. Berkeley, CA: University of California Press.
Flubacher, M.C., Duchêne, A. and Coray, R. (2018) *Language Investment and Employability: The Uneven Distribution of Resources in the Public Employment Service*. Basingstoke: Palgrave Macmillan.
Forsander, A. (2002) Luottamuksen ehdot: Maahanmuuttajat 1990-luvun suomalaisilla työmarkkinoilla. *Väestöntutkimuslaitoksen julkaisusarja D 39/2002*. Helsinki: Väestöliitto.
Goffman, E. (1959) *The Presentation of Self in Everyday Life*. New York: Doubleday Anchor.
Gumperz, J. (1982) *Discourse Strategies*. Cambridge: Cambridge University Press.
Gumperz, J. (2001) Interactional sociolinguistics: A personal perspective. In D. Schriffin, D. Tannen and H. Hamilton (eds) *The Handbook of Discourse Analysis* (pp. 215–228). Malden, MA: Blackwell Publishers Ltd.
Gumperz, J. and Cook-Gumperz, J. (2005) Language, culture and miscommunication. *Kroeber Anthropological Society Papers* 91, 6–24.
Holmes, J. (2000) Politeness, power and provocation: How humour functions in the workplace. *Discourse Studies* 2 (2), 159–185.
Holmes, J. (2007) Monitoring organisational boundaries: Diverse discourse strategies used in gatekeeping. *Journal of Pragmatics* 39 (11), 1993–2016.
Holmes, J. and Stubbe, M. (2015) *Power and Politeness in the Workplace: A Sociolinguistic Analysis of Talk at Work* (2nd edn). London: Routledge.
Holmes, J., Stubbe, M. and Vine, B. (1999) Constructing professional identity: 'Doing power' in policy units. In S. Sarangi and C. Roberts (eds) *Talk, Work and Institutional Order: Discourse in Medical, Mediation and Management Settings* (pp. 351–389). Berlin: Mouton de Gruyter.
Humonen, K. and Angouri, J. (2023) Revisiting ethnography and reflexivity for language-sensitive workplace research. In P. Lecomte, M. Vigier, C. Gaibrois and B. Beeler (eds) *Understanding the Dynamics of Language and Multilingualism in Professional Contexts: Advances in Language-sensitive Management*. London: Edward Elgar.

Janssens, M. and Steyaert, C. (2014) Re-considering language within a cosmopolitan understanding: Toward a multilingual franca approach in international business studies. *Journal of International Business Studies* 45 (5), 623–639.

Jaspers, J. (2012) Interactional sociolinguistics and discourse analysis. In J.P. Gee and M. Handford (eds) *The Routledge Handbook of Discourse Analysis* (pp. 135–145). New York: Routledge.

Karrebæk, M.S. and Maegaard, M. (2017) Pigs, herring, and Bornholm on a table: A high-end restaurant's construction of authenticity. *Semiotic Review* 5.

Kirilova, M. and Angouri, J. (2017) Workplace communication practices and policies. In S. Canagarajah (ed.) *The Routledge Handbook of Migration and Language* (pp. 540–557). New York: Routledge.

Kraft, K. (2020) Trajectory of a language broker: Between privilege and precarity. *International Journal of Multilingualism* 17 (1), 80–96.

Kroskrity, P.V. (2004) Language ideologies. In A. Duranti (ed.) *A Companion to Linguistic Anthropology* (pp. 496–517). Malden, MA: Blackwell Publishing Ltd.

Locher, M. (2004) *Power and Politeness in Action: Disagreements in Oral Communication*. Berlin: Mouton de Gruyter.

Lønsmann, D. (2014) Linguistic diversity in international workplace: Language ideologies and processes of exclusion. *Multilingua* 33 (1–2), 89–116.

Marra, M. (2012) Disagreeing without being disagreeable: Negotiating workplace communities as an outsider. *Journal of Pragmatics* 44 (12), 1580–1590.

Ministry of Economic Affairs and Employment (2021) Government report proposes extensive programme to speed up integration of immigrants. https://valtioneuvosto.fi/en/-/1410877/government-report-proposes-extensive-programme-to-speed-up-integration-of-immigrants (accessed May 2021).

Ministry of Employment and the Economy (2012) Valtion kotouttamisohjelma. Hallituksen painopisteet vuosille 2012–2015. https://tem.fi/documents/1410877/3342347/Valtion+kotuttamisohjelma+21092012.pdf (accessed May 2021).

Norton Peirce, B. (1995) Social identity, investment, and language learning. *TESOL Quarterly* 29 (1), 9–31.

Ochs, E. (1993) Constructing social identity: A language socialization perspective. *Research on Language and Social Interaction* 26 (3), 287–306.

OECD (2018) Working together: Skills and labour market integration of immigrants and their children in Finland. https://doi.org/10.1787/9789264305250-en (accessed May 2021).

OECD (2020) International migration outlook 2020. https://doi.org/10.1787/ec98f531-en (accessed May 2021).

Ollus, N. (2016) From forced flexibility to forced labour: The exploitation of migrant workers in Finland. *European Institute for Crime Prevention and Control, affiliated with the United Nations (HEUNI), Publication Series* No 84.

Otsuji, E. and Pennycook, A. (2010) Metrolingualism: Fixity, fluidity and language in flux. *International Journal of Multilingualism* 7 (3), 240–254.

Pennycook, A. and Otsuji, E. (2014) Metrolingual multitasking and spatial repertoires: 'Pizza mo two minutes coming'. *Journal of Sociolinguistics* 18 (2), 161–184.

Piekkari, R., Welch, D.E. and Welch, L.S. (2014) *Language in International Business: The Multilingual Reality of Global Business Expansion*. Cheltenham: Edward Elgar Publishing Limited.

Piller, I. (2016) *Linguistic Diversity and Social Justice: An Introduction to Applied Sociolinguistics*. Oxford: Oxford University Press.

Pinder, C. and Harlos, K.P. (2001) Employee silence: Quiescence and acquiescence as responses to perceived injustice. *Research in Personnel and Human Resources Management* 20, 331–369.

Roberts, C. (2010) Language socialization in the workplace. *Annual Review of Applied Linguistics* 30, 211–227.

Roberts, C. (2013) The gatekeeping of Babel: Job interviews and the linguistic penalty. In A. Duchêne, M. Moyer and C. Roberts (eds) *Language, Migration and Social Inequalities: A Critical Sociolinguistic Perspective on Institutions and Work* (pp. 81–94). Bristol: Multilingual Matters.

Roberts, C. and Campbell, S. (2006) Talk on trial: Job interviews, language and ethnicity. *Department of Work and Pensions, Research Report* No 344.

Rogerson-Revell, P. (2011) Chairing international business meetings: Investigating humour and leadership style in the workplace. In J. Angouri and M. Marra (eds) *Constructing Identities at Work* (pp. 61–84). Basingstoke: Palgrave Macmillan.

Ruuska, K. (2019) Languagised repertoires: How fictional languages have real effects. In J. Jaspers and L.M. Madsen (eds) *Critical Perspectives on Linguistic Fixity and Fluidity: Languagised Lives* (pp. 53–75). New York: Routledge.

Sarangi, S. and Roberts, C. (1999) *Talk, Work and Institutional Order: Discourse in Medical, Mediation and Management Settings*. Berlin: Walter de Gruyter.

Sarangi, S. and Clarke, A. (2002) Zones of expertise and the management of uncertainty in genetics risk communication. *Research on Language and Social Interaction* 35 (2), 139–171.

Statistics Finland (2020) https://www.stat.fi/til/muutl/2019/muutl_2019_2020-05-14_kuv_001_en.html (accessed May 2021).

Strömmer, M. (2016) Affordances and constraints: Second language learning in cleaning work. *Multilingua* 35 (6), 697–721.

Suni, M. (2017) Working and learning in a new niche: Ecological interpretations of work-related migration. In J. Angouri, M. Marra and J. Holmes (eds) *Negotiating Boundaries at Work: Talking and Transitions* (pp. 197–215). Edinburgh: Edinburgh University Press.

Sveningsson, S. and Alvesson, M. (2003) Managing managerial identities: Organizational fragmentation, discourse and identity struggle. *Human Relations* 56 (10), 1163–1193.

Toback, E. (2017) Cross-modal iconism at Tully's Coffee Japan: Authenticity and egalitarian sociability as projections of distinction. *Semiotic Review* 5.

Tranekjær, L. (2015) *Interactional Categorization and Gatekeeping: Institutional Encounters with Otherness*. Bristol: Multilingual Matters.

Vaara, E., Tienari, J., Piekkari, R. and Säntti, R. (2005) Language and the circuits of power in a merging multinational corporation. *Journal of Management Studies* 42 (3), 595-623.

Vikør, L.S. (2010) Language purism in the Nordic countries. *International Journal of the Sociology of Language* 204, 9–30.

Vine, B., Holmes, J., Marra, M., Pfeifer, D. and Jackson, B. (2008) Exploring co-leadership talk through interactional sociolinguistics. *Leadership* 4 (3), 339–360.

Winick, C. (1976) The social contexts of humour. *Journal of communication* 26, 124–128.

Index

Affiliation 76, 83, 86, 89, 210
Agency 3–4, 150–1, 155–6, 192, 195, 198, 200, 210
Agenda-setting 32, 34–5
Alignment 83, 85, 118, 208
Authenticity 100, 104, 114, 117, 160, 178, 184, 192

Belonging 3, 7–8, 18, 28, 53, 61, 79–80, 82, 203; *see also membership*
Bourdieu 3, 53–4, 60, 69, 128, 194; *see also capital, habitus*, and *symbolic power*

Capital
  cultural 7, 53, 80, 139, 194
  language 1, 4
  linguistic 53, 194, 205
  symbolic 128, 194
Citizenship 79, 125, 134, 193
Competence
  intercultural 54, 66
  linguistic 8
  pragmatic 8, 87, 122–3, 133
  sociopragmatic 206
Contextualisation
  contemporary 14–5, 22, 26, 28
  cues 63, 80
  discursive 16
  historical 15
  recontextualisation 22, 28
  sociolinguistic 18
  temporal 27, 29
Conversation analysis (CA) 82–3

Discourse
  analysis 10, 32, 35–6
  mediatised 32, 34, 48
  multimodal 32, 35
Diversity
  cultural 18, 22–3, 28, 52, 54, 61, 68
  linguistic 13–4, 18–9, 22, 27–8, 61
  temporal 14–6

Employability 7, 96, 116, 193
English as a Second Language (ESL) 100, 125, 127, 132–3, 136
Ethnicity 5, 39, 48
Ethnography 83, 156, 167–8

Framing 32, 34–5

Gatekeeping 3, 9, 53, 68, 75–6, 78–9, 81, 88–9, 196–7, 204; *see also job interview*
Goffman 35, 59, 82, 149, 154–5, 167–8, 198
Gumperz 4, 63, 79–80, 82, 196–8, 206

Habitus 4, 54, 194

Identity
  cultural 80, 89, 126–7, 163
  migrant 5, 47
  professional 9, 53, 83, 116
Impression management 149–150, 153–5, 157–9, 166–8
In/exclusion 4, 6, 75, 79–80, 88, 193, 195
Indexicality 57, 76, 82–3, 88
Indirectness 102, 104, 109–10, 122, 166
Integration 1, 37, 74–5, 79, 128, 195, 197
Interactional Sociolinguistics (IS) 78, 82, 197
Interculturality 52, 54, 67
Intersectionality 5–6, 35

Job interview 3, 75–7, 82–3, 88–9, 124, 141, 196

Language
  assessment 2, 96, 99–100, 102, 107, 110–11, 113–7

dominant 52, 54, 174, 177–9, 185–6, 188, 196, 210
first (L1) 5, 8, 79, 82, 89, 176–8, 185–7, 188, 194, 200
ideology 19, 75–6, 192, 194–5, 203, 210–11
professional 96, 98, 101–2, 104, 107, 113–5, 117
proficiency 2–4, 58, 95–7, 106–7, 114, 122, 196
policy 2, 14, 96–9, 116, 127, 193, 195, 197
second (L2) 5, 32, 76, 79, 81, 88, 97, 115, 144, 172
skill 5, 95, 98–99, 102–3, 106, 118, 125–6, 153, 193–4, 210
structure 76, 80
Linguistic conditioning 173, 182–3, 185, 187
Linguistic penalty 4, 53, 77, 196

Marginalisation 53, 64, 68, 191
Mutlimodal analysis 32, 35–6
Membership 64, 75, 78–80, 196–7, 202–3, 210
  ascription 75, 78–80
  co-membership 81–3, 88–9
  negotiation 79
Migrant
  economic 37–8, 42, 45
  multilingual 53–6, 58, 61, 64
  worker 5, 19, 48, 127, 192
Migration
  emigration 39–40, 44, 46, 151
  immigration 26, 33, 45, 125–6, 144, 152–3, 175
  labour 2, 96, 103
  work 13–4, 17, 26, 28
Mobile worker 152, 155, 167
Mobility 13, 20, 28, 53–4, 96–7, 116, 152, 167–8
Monolingualism 52, 58, 193
Mother tongue 125, 145, 174, 186, 188
  see also first language
Multilingualism 2, 6–7, 9–10, 17, 19–20, 52, 59, 61, 172–3, 211

Narrative 4, 23, 28, 36, 45–6, 53, 55–6, 59, 64, 69
  network analysis 35–6

Newcomer 3–4, 9, 74–5, 77, 125–6, 130, 144, 179, 192, 210–11
Norm 4, 10, 64, 79, 81, 88, 126, 196
  cultural 135, 143, 135, 143
  group 81–2, 87
  linguistic 19, 54, 65, 127
  native speaker 8, 77

Performance
  oral/written 103, 108
  test 96, 101–2, 113–4, 117
Phenomenology 173–4, 179–80
Plurilingualism 188
Power
  asymmetry 3, 5–6, 196, 202
  relation 109, 182, 195, 203, 207
  symbolic 3, 53–4
Practice
  as research (PaR) 173–4
  language 2, 54, 100
  multilingual 8, 20, 25, 60, 65, 78, 117
Pragmatic competence 8, 87, 122–3, 133, 206
Professional settings
  Call centre Chapter 8
  Company Chapter 2
  Health care Chapter 6
  Kitchen Chapter 10
  Theatre Chapter 9
  Vocational training Chapter 7

Reflexivity 53, 66, 68–9
Refugee 1, 37, 74–5

Securitisation 32–3, 43, 46–7, 79
Shibboleth 74–5, 79–80, 82, 88–9
Skills
  communication 2, 108, 124, 136, 141, 194
  interpersonal 124
  language 5, 8, 95, 88–9, 102–3, 106, 125–6, 153, 193–4, 210
  soft 10, 123–6, 129, 132–4, 141, 144
Subjectivity 48, 54, 69

Workplace
  culture 125, 129, 135
  communication 64, 123, 136
  discourse 10, 195
  interaction 7, 53, 56, 61, 64, 68, 131, 197

For Product Safety Concerns and Information please contact our EU Authorised Representative:

Easy Access System Europe

Mustamäe tee 50

10621 Tallinn

Estonia

gpsr.requests@easproject.com